Ninth Edition

Music Skills for Classroom Teachers

Robert W. Winslow

Leon Dallin

Shelley B. Wiest

Boston   Burr Ridge, IL   Dubuque, IA   Madison, WI   New York   San Francisco
St. Louis   Bangkok   Bogotá   Caracas   Lisbon   London   Madrid   Mexico City
Milan   New Delhi   Seoul   Singapore   Sydney   Taipei   Toronto

McGraw-Hill Higher Education

A Division of The **McGraw-Hill** *Companies*

MUSIC SKILLS FOR CLASSROOM TEACHERS

Published by McGraw-Hill, an imprint of The McGraw-Hill Companies, Inc., 1221 Avenue of the Americas, New York, NY 10020. Copyright © 2001, 1992, 1987, 1979, 1975, 1970, 1964, 1958, by The McGraw-Hill Companies, Inc. All rights reserved. No part of this publication may be reproduced or distributed in any form or by any means, or stored in a database or retrieval system, without the prior written consent of The McGraw-Hill Companies, Inc., including, but not limited to, in any network or other electronic storage or transmission, or broadcast for distance learning.

Some ancillaries, including electronic and print components, may not be available to customers outside the United States.

This book is printed on acid-free paper.

1 2 3 4 5 6 7 8 9 0 QPD/QPD 0 9 8 7 6 5 4 3 2 1 0

ISBN 0-07-232465-1

Editorial director: *Phillip A. Butcher*
Senior sponsoring editor: *Christopher Freitag*
Editorial assistant: *Nadia Bidwell*
Marketing manager: *David Patterson*
Senior project manager: *Gladys True*
Production supervisor: *Debra Sylvester*
Senior designer: *Jennifer Hollingsworth*
Photo research coordinator: *Keri Johnson*
Media technology producer: *Kimberly Stark*
Cover illustrator: *Tim Hughes*
Interior design: *Karen LaFond*
Compositor: *A-R Editions, Inc.*
Typeface: *11/13 Times Roman*
Printer: *Quebecor Printing Book Group/Dubuque*

Library of Congress Cataloging-in-Publication Data

Winslow, Robert W.
 Music skills for classroom teachers / Robert W. Winslow, Leon Dallin, Shelley B. Wiest.--9th ed.
  p. cm.
 Includes indexes.
 ISBN 0-07-232465-1 (softcover : alk. paper)
 1. Music--Handbooks, manuals, etc. 2. School music--Instruction and study--United States. I. Dallin, Leon. II. Wiest, Shelley B. III. Title.

MT10.W743 M8 2000
372.87'044--dc21   00-042714

www.mhhe.com

Preface

Music Skills for Classroom Teachers is designed as a college textbook for courses that prepare teachers for teaching music in the classroom and for introductory music courses that combine the study of fundamentals with performance activities. The book can also be used as a reference tool for those already teaching and for in-service workshops. *Music Skills* targets the learning of both concepts and skills—music reading, analysis, singing, playing classroom and social instruments, and listening. The book also provides guidelines, exercises, and song suggestions needed by teachers to conduct an effective music program in the primary and intermediate grades. Materials are presented systematically at the level of the adult beginner with no previous musical training. Examples are drawn from music that is appealing to children and appropriate for use in the elementary classroom.

This edition retains the basic approach that has proven successful in the previous editions, but with significant updates and additions. The ninth edition includes:

- A compact disc with selected performance examples.
- An entire chapter devoted to the use of the Omnichord in the classroom.
- An updated chapter on the use of the guitar in the classroom.
- A new section on current keyboard trends and music technology.
- Expanded pitch and rhythm chapters.
- More exercises and songs for those who have had no prior musical experience.
- More emphasis on the importance of singing in the classroom and the addition of many more updated and multicultural songs.
- More explanation on the approaches of Kodály and Orff.
- More readable graphics for finger positions.
- An expanded section on the effects of music education on a child's ability to learn, an overview of the National Standards for Music Education, and the need for the integration of music with other subjects.

Suggestions for the Use of This Book

The ninth edition has been reorganized as to the presentation of chapters. Whereas the teacher of the course is allowed complete freedom in the order of presentation, the basic elements of music are presented first: rhythm, melody, harmony, form, and expression. Then, each of the performance areas is presented in chapter form with musical examples, exercises, and songs: singing, keyboard instruments, percussion instruments, mallet instruments, the recorder, the Omnichord/Autoharp, and the guitar. The final portion of the book covers the application of acquired musical skills.

Musical activities, performance techniques, pedagogical and theoretical information are presented in a manner appropriate for individual practice and study, as well as group preparation outside of class.

Song materials are cross-referenced extensively and can be used with multiple functions. Songs in the instrumental and theoretical chapters that are not in a comfortable vocal range can be transposed to an appropriate key for singing.

Materials recommended for the use of this book include a CD system; a keyboard(s); soprano recorders; Omnichords; bell, mallet, or Orff instruments; percussion instruments; guitars; and state and local series of school songbooks with accompanying recordings. The keyboard chart in the endleaf pocket inside the back cover can be placed upright behind the piano keys as an aid when practicing at the keyboard or it can be placed flat on a desk as a substitute for a keyboard when none is available.

Acknowledgments

I wish to recognize Robert W. Winslow and the life of Leon Dallin, who co-authored the first eight editions of *Music Skills for Classroom Teachers,* both who presented me with the opportunity to continue their life's work. I wish to thank the students in my elementary music education classes at both Emporia State University (Kansas) and Midwestern State University (Texas) who tested and verified the effectiveness of these materials. I am grateful to my colleagues Ruth Morrow (piano), Bruce Canafax (guitar), and Linda Jones (voice and music education), who graciously supported me with specific help in many chapters. I wish to thank Avery and Brady Archambo, Colt and Amber Canava, and Josh and Lindsay Thornton for their help with the photographs.

I am indebted to the music publishers who have generously granted permission for the use of copyrighted songs. Appropriate notice is given with each example. A conscientious effort has been made to acknowledge all copyrights, but many of the songs are so much a part of our musical heritage that it is not always possible to determine the original source. For these songs we are indebted to the singers who have remembered and sung them and to the teachers who have taught them to generations of children.

I would also like to thank Nadia Bidwell, Chris Freitag, editors, and Gladys True, project manager, at McGraw-Hill, for their constant support, and the following reviewers for their contributions to this revised edition:

Carolyn Bryan
Georgia Southern University

Patricia Hoover
Arkansas Tech

J. Bryan Burton
West Chester University

Susan Kane
Murray State University

Emily Butterfield
Morehead State University

Wendy Sims
University of Missouri

Carolyn Copeland
Bethune-Cookman College

Lelouda Stamou
University of Nevada, Las Vegas

Jana Fallin
Kansas State University

Janice Wiberg
Montana State University, Northern Havre

Shelley Batt Archambo Wiest

Contents

CHAPTER 1

Teaching Music in the Elementary Classroom

Early man was a musician.
Every man could beat the drums, ring the bells,
  blow the flutes and sing.
Music belonged to everyone and men came
  together with music and dance,
Chanting and singing the humanity
Which was so basically theirs.

Kent Kieth

More than a century and a half ago, Lowell Mason, a musician and teacher who believed that every child had a right to study music during school hours, influenced an education committee in Boston to include music as a regular classroom subject. This movement spread across the country rapidly and provided a strong beginning for music education.

Early in the twentieth century, John Dewey, one of the founders of modern education as we know it today, fortified the work of Lowell Mason by emphasizing music as an *integral* part of educating the *whole* child. In his philosophy of education he strongly recommended music in the developmental process of the human personality, citizenship, and self-discipline. He envisioned musical groups performing accurate rhythm and harmony as a very worthy cooperative activity. Throughout the twentieth century, music has been used in virtually every venue of the educational process in our public and private schools. But, as educators, we are perpetually called upon to defend our programs in the musical arts.

Why Continue to Teach Music in the Classroom of the Twenty-First Century?

From long experience we know that the arts are inseparable from the very meaning of the term "education." No one can claim to be truly educated who lacks basic knowledge and skills in the arts. As art, music is deeply embedded in our daily lives—responding to, performing, and creating music are fundamental processes in which nearly every human engages on a daily basis.

> *Education in music is most sovereign, because more than anything else, rhythm and harmony find their way into the secret places of the soul.*
>
> *Plato*

"Educational standards" has been a topic of great interest in the 1990s. Four agencies banded together in 1992 to study and determine what the nation's school children should know and be able to do in the arts: the Consortium of National Arts Education Associations, the U.S. Department of Education, the National Endowment for the Arts, and the National Endowment for the Humanities. The process involved a review of state-level arts education programs, standards from other nations, and a consensus of national forum comments and testimonies. The result is the passage of the *Goals 2000: Educate America Act,* where the arts are now actually written into federal law.

The law acknowledges that the arts are a core subject, as important to education as English, math, history, science, and geography. The act establishes specific objectives of what students should know and be able to do in each specific art (music, dance, theatre, and the visual arts) at each specific grade level K–12. These unilateral objectives are now published in "scope and sequence" format and broken down into groups of grade levels (K–4, 5–8, 9–12) in the resulting book *National Standards for Arts Education.* For more information on the national standards for music, visit the website at <www.menc.org>.

The Value of Music in the Classroom

1. Music is first and foremost a valuable content area in its own right, a unique form of *human expression.* Spencer and Miguel Kagan have stated (*Multiple Intelligences: the Complete MI Book*):

   We like to think we make music for the same reasons we paint, and sculpt, and dance—not as a way of surviving but as a way of expressing our joy and wonder in the miracle of life. We make music because we are human.

2. Students can learn music in many different ways—*by performing, by listening, and by creating music in the classroom.*

   The Suzuki Talent Education program believes and demonstrates that musical skills can be taught and developed to a high degree in most people. The success of their programs in the areas of string instruments and keyboard playing have been evidenced worldwide for nearly one hundred years.

3. Statistics show (Howard Gardner, *Multiple Intelligences: The Theory in Practice*) that music students are often *better all-around students.* Gardner points out that music overwhelmingly passes the test as one of the "Seven Intelligences" (Spencer and Miguel Kagan, "Eight Intelligences") because certain parts of the brain play important roles in perception and production of music. Students celebrate their musical conquests through recitals, concerts, and programs, as well as through various recorded examples.

4. The development of problem-solving and higher-order thinking skills necessary for success in life and work are also proven to be *a part of the eight theories of multiple intelligences,* of which music is one component part (Gardner; Kagan). This proof is offered in the example of the many composers throughout history who were also professionals, such as lawyers and physicians.

5. By learning about music, children can discover both the beauty of music and the personal satisfaction that musical activities offer. They will continue this discovery into adulthood: lifelong *music appreciation.*

6. Music education can open the doors to a child's *worthy use of leisure time*. Music can "be made" alone or in large or small groups, solidifying evidence as to the educational and personal value of music as a lifetime sport or activity.

   Many *avocational* objectives stem from music education. Listening and understanding good music in the schools, at home, in the concert hall, and joining school and community vocal and instrumental performance groups can, indeed, start in the classroom.

7. Today's classroom is inclusive, and *musical activities can be modified* for children with special needs and those with specific types of learning incapacities. Many students find successes in music whereas they may not in other areas.

8. *Music correlates naturally* and readily with most of the elementary school curriculum, especially all of the fine arts—poetry, drawing, painting, dance, drama, and the social studies. Indeed, it is not a "frill" to be added to the daily schedule "if time permits" but a regular educational process in the child's physical, emotional, and intellectual development.

9. The transformation of technology is a force found not only in the economy of today but also in the arts. Music technology has become a multibillion dollar business, and students are fascinated to learn how *music technology* can be used in their daily lives.

10. The *unifying power of music* in today's mixed-ethnic classroom is realized when children sing, dance, and play folk music from many cultures. Understanding of and appreciation for their classmates and the world in which they all live can be developed naturally through the message of the music itself. Research studies have shown the importance of music education in developing these attitudes before the child reaches the age of nine years.

The Classroom Teacher's Role in Music Education

Willing, equipped teachers who provide many musical avenues for their students continue to be needed greatly as time continues. Some school districts will provide music specialists for regularly scheduled instruction with suggested follow-up activities by the classroom teacher. Numerous school programs, however, do not include specialists for various reasons—lack of funds, smaller enrollments, and lack of interest in the arts by school administrators. This is especially true in the primary grades, where the musical foundations *should* be built for positive attitudes toward music and basic musical skills. In some schools, classroom teachers may be the only providers of music education to children.

Whether or not the school district provides specialized instruction in music, the classroom teacher has a unique and important role in the child's musical development.

1. The classroom teacher *knows* each individual child, his or her interests, needs, and abilities. Therefore the teacher can assess the total program of studies and decide where music "fits" in his or her classroom. Classroom teachers need to provide music instruction: For some children, music may be the only area in which the student feels talented and successful, changing the whole perception of self and self-esteem.

2. Music can be *offered any time* throughout the school day, whenever it satisfies the students' needs best—for relaxation, for pleasurable emotional release, PTA programs, or just "music for music's sake."
3. The teacher *can integrate* music with other subjects into the total curriculum whenever it is appropriate and meaningful.

The musical arts will continue to live. We must be skillful in our presentation of music so that it will flow through us and speak to others. Music is inside each of us, and the quality of our lives gives rise to the quality of our music. *Music Skills for Classroom Teachers* is designed specifically to provide the elementary teacher with techniques and materials for achieving the aims and objectives set forth in this chapter's pages.

CHAPTER 2

Reading Rhythm

The years, the seasons, the phases of the moon, and the rising and setting of the sun are all evidence of a cosmic system, a regular and orderly sequence of events in extended time. Shorter but equally significant units of time are defined by the beating of the heart, breathing, and such physical activities as walking, running, and skipping. Quite naturally, time units organized systematically constitute an essential feature of music. The element of music that encompasses all aspects of sound organized in time is *rhythm*.

Beats and Notes

The pulse of music, which is one aspect of rhythm, can be felt by everyone, including those who have had no musical training and claim to have no musical talent. This fact is easily demonstrated. Play a recording of a John Philip Sousa march, such as *Stars and Stripes Forever*. As soon as you feel the pulse, tap your toes in time with the music. Everyone will tap at the same time because everyone has the innate ability to sense the underlying pulse of music. The rhythmic pulses to which you are responding are *beats*. One way of notating beats is with the following symbols.

The symbols used to notate the rhythm and pitch of musical sounds are *notes*. The symbols shown are *quarter notes*. The term *note* is also used to denote a musical sound, though *tone* is a more appropriate term.

Measures and Bar Lines

With the march music still playing, stand up, pat your thighs (*patschen*) with your left and right hands. Marking time in place with your feet will also serve the purpose. Now, you are not only keeping time with the beats in the music, but you are also grouping the beats into pairs by using the left hand with the strong beat or by stepping first with one foot and then with the other.

left　　right　　left　　right　　left　　right　　left　　right

Listen carefully to the music, and you will discover that one beat is stronger than the other. The stronger beat, which comes with the left foot in marching, marks the beginning of the group. It is stressed, or *accented*. The weaker beat that follows is unstressed, or *unaccented*. Accented and unaccented beats can be indicated by poetic scansion signs.

Groups of accented and unaccented beats form metric units called *measures*. Measures of music are divided by vertical lines called *bar lines*. The beat just before a bar line is unaccented, and the beat right after a bar line is accented. Two bar lines together, called a *double bar,* indicate the end of an exercise or a composition.

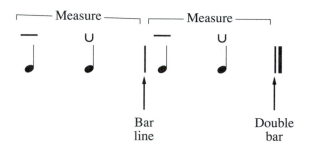

The beats in a measure are numbered consecutively, and one way of expressing musical rhythm is by counting. Continue patting your thighs to the music and count with the beats: *one, two, one, two*.

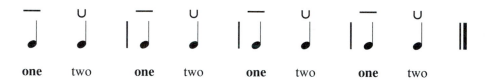

To illustrate a different kind of rhythm, play a recording of a waltz, such as the *Waltz of the Flowers*[1] from Tchaikovsky's *Nutcracker Suite*. The beat can be felt and the toes tapped in time to it, but the rhythm will not be appropriate for marching. Instead, you will want to waltz to the music.

The rhythmic group consists of one accented beat and two unaccented beats. While doing a waltz step to the music, count *one, two, three, one, two, three*.

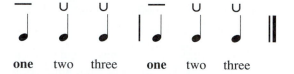

[1] The waltz rhythm is clearer after the introduction.

Some music has a two-beat, or *duple,* rhythm; some has a three-beat, or *triple,* rhythm. Marches and waltzes illustrate the two basic patterns. Repetitions of these patterns produce the larger rhythmic and structural units of music.

Exercise 1

When recordings are played, clap with the beat. Determine whether the rhythm is basically marchlike (duple) or waltzlike (triple). Locate the accents, which will occur regularly every second or third beat. Clap on the accented beats and snap on the unaccented ones. Count **one**, two, **one**, two when the rhythm is duple; count **one**, two, three, **one**, two, three when it is triple.

Exercise 2

Sing familiar songs, and decide which ones have two-beat patterns and which have three-beat patterns. They need not be marches or waltzes. These were used first only because their rhythms are most obvious. With practice you will be able to determine the underlying rhythm of any song.

2/4 Time Signature and Conductor's Beat

At the beginning of each piece of music there are two numbers, one above the other. This is the *time signature,* or *meter signature.* The lower number represents a kind of note, ordinarily the one used to express the beat. The upper number indicates the number of such beats in a measure. A 2/4 time signature, which is one used for marches, indicates that in each measure the total duration will equal two quarter-note beats.

Two
Quarter notes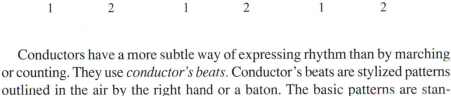

Conductors have a more subtle way of expressing rhythm than by marching or counting. They use *conductor's beats.* Conductor's beats are stylized patterns outlined in the air by the right hand or a baton. The basic patterns are standardized, but each conductor makes personal variations and adds embellishments. The ability to conduct is an essential skill for classroom teachers.

The first beat of a measure, referred to as the *downbeat,* is marked in conducting patterns by a downward stroke directly in front of the conductor. The lowest point is reached precisely with the accent. From this point in 2/4 time, the hand bounces to the conductor's right and up slightly. For the second beat, the *upbeat,* the motion is reversed, and the hand returns to the starting point. All conducting diagrams show the pattern for the right hand from the conductor's viewpoint, so the right hand motions of students doing the conducting exercises duplicate the pattern of the diagrams. For the left hand and from the viewer's perspective, the patterns are reversed, or mirrored.

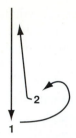

Perform the conductor's beat for 2/4 time while counting *one, two, **one**, two* until coordinating the hand motions with the numbers and the quarter-note beats comes naturally.

A note with double the rhythmic value of a quarter note is a half note, as the fractional name implies. Two quarter notes equal one half note. The symbol for a half note is like the symbol for a quarter note except that at the end of the *stem* (the vertical line) the oval-shaped *heads* are different, as shown.

Two quarter notes ♩ ♩ = ♩ one half note

A note with half the rhythmic value of a quarter note is an eighth note, again as the fractional name implies. One quarter note equals two eighth notes. Two note symbols like quarter notes but with their stems connected by a *beam,* as shown, are eighth notes.

One quarter note ♩ = ♫ two eighth notes

Hot Cross Buns is a familiar song in 2/4 time using half, quarter, and eighth notes.

HOT CROSS BUNS

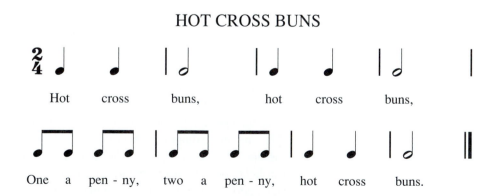

Exercise 4

Sing *Hot Cross Buns* while doing the conductor's beat. Next, recite the words with the rhythm of the song but without the tune. Then, count the beats and clap the rhythm, associating the rhythm with the notation.

The complete notation for many of the songs in this chapter, including *Hot Cross Buns,* is given elsewhere in the book. Consult the Alphabetical Song Index for page numbers.

Counting Eighth Notes

When learning to read rhythmic notation, it is helpful to have a system for counting and tapping eighth notes. One method, *traditional* counting, is to say the number of the beat on the first eighth note and to say *"and,"* written *"&,"* on the second eighth note. The tapping of the toe, heel, or fingers coincides with the beats, and the high point of the upward motion coincides with the half beats.

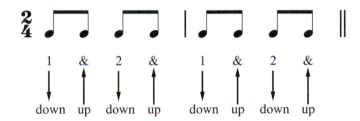

Zoltán Kodály (1882–1967) was a Hungarian music educator who lived and worked in the first half and middle of the twentieth century. He developed an alternative system to traditional counting that has been proven to be successful in the past and today.

In the Kodály approach, the initial rhythm exercises are notated with just the stems and beams of the note symbols. Note heads are introduced later to notate the longer durations. Rhythms are chanted with syllables similar to those used in French solfège, though many variants are found in books written in English. Rhythm syllables adapted from Kodály are given for quarter and eighth notes. In the syllables the vowel *a* is pronounced "ah" and the vowel *i* is pronounced "ee."

The Kodály method of reading rhythm is quickly becoming one of the most popular counting systems in elementary schools today, due largely to the good articulation and forward vocal placement it encourages. As well, the ease with which rhythm skills can be learned *without* another numerical system is really appreciated by teachers and new learners alike.

Tapping, counting, and chanting with rhythm syllables provide ways of relating the varied durations in a melody to the constant pulse of the beat. While tapping the beat, recite the rhythm of *Hot Cross Buns,* using first the beat counts and then the rhythm syllables. Numbers enclosed in parentheses are not pronounced in reciting the rhythm of the melody. When using the rhythm syllables, repeat the vowel sound on the second beat of half notes.

HOT CROSS BUNS

1	2	1	(2)	1	2	1	(2)
ta	ta	ta	- a	ta	ta	ta	- a

1	&	2	&	1	&	2	&	1	2	1	(2)
ti	ti	ti	ti	ti	ti	ti	ti	ta	ta	ta	- a

Exercise 5

Establish a steady background beat, and then perform the following rhythm patterns by counting, clapping, and/or chanting the rhythm syllables. Do each line twice without any break in the rhythm. Write the numbers and/or the rhythm syllables under the notes as an aid to accurate performance wherever difficulties are encountered in the rhythm exercises. This and all subsequent rhythm exercises can also be performed on rhythm instruments (see chapter 8).

Repeat Signs

You were directed to do each line of the previous exercise twice because at the end of each line there are two dots on the left side of the double bar. This is a *repeat sign*. It indicates that all or part of an exercise or composition is to be repeated. If the piece is to be repeated from the beginning, no other sign is necessary. If only part is to be repeated, that part is enclosed between a double bar with dots on the right and a double bar with dots on the left.

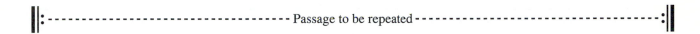

If the ending is different the second time, a *first ending* and a *second ending* are provided, each numbered and bracketed as shown. The first ending is performed the first time only; in the repetition the second ending is substituted.

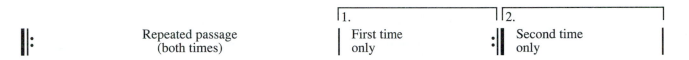

	1.	2.
Repeated passage (both times)	First time only	Second time only

Oh, Dear! What Can the Matter Be? (p. 13) has a repeat sign indicating a repetition of the first part of the song from the beginning. *Ring, Ring the Banjo* (p. 185) has facing repeat signs indicating a repetition of the passage between them. The repeat signs in both songs have first and second endings.

The abbreviation *D.C.*, for the Italian words *da capo*, is also used to indicate repetitions. *Da capo* means "repeat from the beginning." *D.C.* can be used to direct an additional repetition of a passage already marked for one repetition by a double bar with dots. Dot-double-bar repeat signs are ignored when making *D.C.* repeats. After a repetition indicated by *D.C.* or *D.C. al Fine*, the place to end is marked *Fine. Joshua Fit the Battle of Jericho* (p. 245) has repetitions indicated by *D.C. al Fine. D.S.* is the abbreviation for *dal segno*, which indicates that repetition goes back to the sign 𝄋.

Exercise 6

Practice reading the following songs that have first and second endings: *D.C.* and *D.S.*

OVER THERE

George M. Cohan

George M. Cohan

O - ver there, _____ o - ver there, _____ send the word, send the word o - ver
pare, _____ say a pray'r, _____ Send the word, send the word to be -

1. F₇ B♭ E♭ E♭m F₇   B♭ Cdim Gm B♭m₆ F Cdim

there, _____ That the Yanks are com-ing, the Yanks are com-ing, The drums rum -
ware. _____

C₇   F₇ Cm A♭₇ F₇   2. F₇   B♭

tum-ming ev-'ry - where _____ So pre - _____ We'll be o - ver, we're com-ing

F₇   B♭ B♭₇ E♭ G♭₇ F₇   B♭

o - ver, And we won't come back till it's o - ver o - ver there.

OH! SUSANNA

Stephen C. Foster

Stephen C. Foster

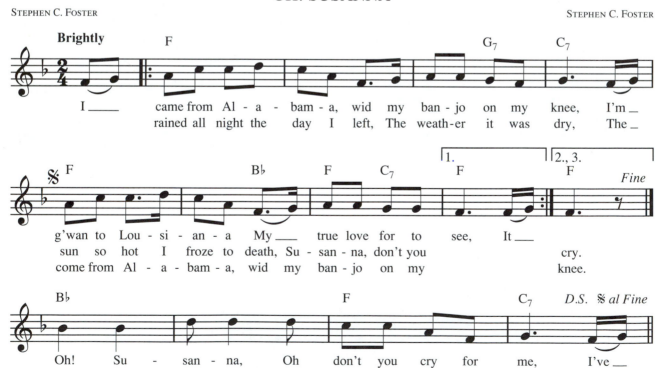

Brightly F   G₇ C₇

I _____ came from Al - a - bam - a, wid my ban - jo on my knee, I'm _
rained all night the day I left, The weath-er it was dry, The _

F   B♭ F C₇   1. F   2., 3. F   *Fine*

g'wan to Lou - si - an - a My _____ true love for to see, It _____
sun so hot I froze to death, Su - san - na, don't you cry.
come from Al - a - bam - a, wid my ban - jo on my knee.

B♭   F   C₇ *D.S. al Fine*

Oh! Su - san - na, Oh don't you cry for me, I've _

OH, DEAR! WHAT CAN THE MATTER BE?

TRADITIONAL

Oh, dear! What can the mat-ter be? Dear, dear, what can the mat-ter be?
Oh, dear! What can the mat-ter be?

John-ny's so long at the fair. ___ He prom-ised to buy me a trin-ket to please me, And
prom-ised to buy me a bunch of blue rib-bons to

then for a smile, Oh he vowed he would tease me, He tie up my bon-nie brown hair. ___

MICKEY MOUSE MARCH

From Walt Disney's T.V. Series *THE MICKEY MOUSE CLUB*

JIMMIE DODD   JIMMIE DODD

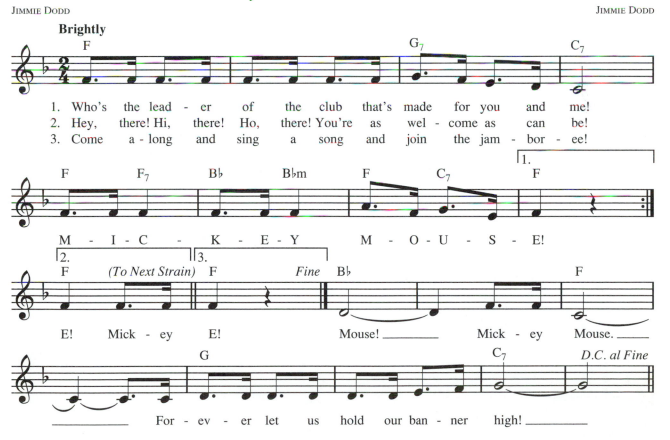

1. Who's the lead - er of the club that's made for you and me!
2. Hey, there! Hi, there! Ho, there! You're as wel - come as can be!
3. Come a - long and sing a song and join the jam - bor - ee!

M - I - C - K - E - Y   M - O - U - S - E!

E! Mick - ey E! Mouse! _____ Mick - ey Mouse. ____

_____ For - ev - er let us hold our ban - ner high! _____

3/4 Time Signature and Conductor's Beat

Measures of three quarter-note beats, such as the measures in waltzes, are indicated by a 3/4 time signature.

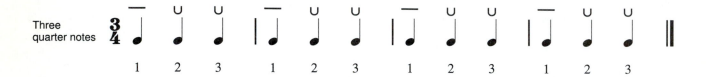

The conductor's beat for 3/4 time approximates the outline of a triangle, with a slight bounce for each beat. As always, the first beat of the measure comes with the downbeat of the pattern.

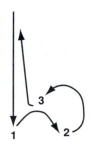

Exercise 7

Perform the conductor's beat for 3/4 time while counting *one, two, three, one, two, three* until coordinating the hand motions with the numbers comes naturally.

A full measure in 3/4 time contains the rhythmic equivalent of three quarter notes. The note symbol with a rhythmic value equal to three quarter notes is a dotted half note, that is, a half note with a dot by the head, as shown.

Three quarter notes ♩ ♩ ♩ = ♩. one dotted half note

Lavender's Blue is a folk song in 3/4 time using quarter, eighth, and dotted half notes.

LAVENDER'S BLUE

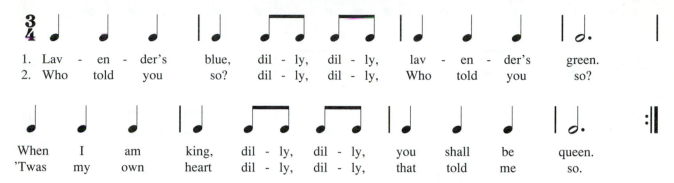

1. Lav - en - der's   blue,   dil - ly,   dil - ly,   lav - en - der's   green.
2. Who   told   you   so?   dil - ly,   dil - ly,   Who   told   you   so?

When   I   am   king,   dil - ly,   dil - ly,   you   shall   be   queen.
'Twas my   own   heart   dil - ly,   dil - ly,   that   told   me   so.

Exercise 8

Sing *Lavender's Blue* while doing the conductor's beat. Next, recite the words with the rhythm of the song but without the tune. Then, count the beats and clap the rhythm, associating the rhythm with the notation.

The counting and rhythm syllables are the same in 2/4 time and 3/4 time, except that in 3/4 time there are three beats in a measure. The vowel sound of *ta* is repeated on the second and third beats of measures filled by a dotted half note.

LAVENDER'S BLUE

1   2   3   1   2   &   3   &   1   2   3   1   (2)   (3)
ta   ta   ta   ta   ti   ti   ti   ti   ta   ta   ta   ta - a - a

1   2   3   1   2   &   3   &   1   2   3   1   (2)   (3)
ta   ta   ta   ta   ti   ti   ti   ti   ta   ta   ta   ta - a - a

---

Exercise 9

Establish a steady background beat, and then perform the following rhythm patterns by counting, clapping, and/or chanting the rhythm syllables. Observe the repeat signs. Write the numbers and/or the rhythm syllables under the notes as an aid to accurate performance whenever difficulties are encountered.

4/4 Time Signature and Conductor's Beat

Thus far, only simple duple and triple meters like those found in marches and waltzes have been considered. Although units of two or three beats are the basis of most rhythms, measures may contain more than one such unit. Two pairs of quarter-note beats constitute a measure in 4/4 time which, like 2/4 time, is also used for marches.

A measure of 4/4 time is not the same as two measures of 2/4 time. Each measure has only one *primary accent,* and it falls on the first beat of the measure. The third beat in 4/4 time is accented, but it is a lesser *secondary accent.* The second and fourth beats of 4/4 measures are unaccented. The metric pattern of 4/4 measures can be shown with scansion signs. Accented beats are marked by dashes—primary accents by a long dash and secondary accents by a short dash. This explanation of accents is valid for the folk and familiar songs in this book and for most of the standard concert literature. It does not apply to many jazz, rock, and avant-garde styles of music.

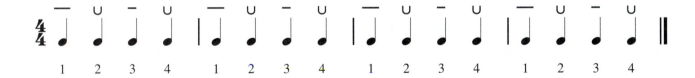

The following diagram shows the conductor's beat for 4/4 time.

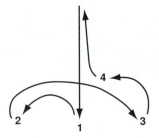

Exercise 10

Perform the conductor's beat for 4/4 time while counting the beats until coordinating the hand motions with the numbers comes naturally.

Sing *Are You Sleeping*, or recite the words with the correct rhythm, while doing the conductor's beat. Pay special attention to the correlation between the accented syllables in the poem and the accented beats in the music.

ARE YOU SLEEPING

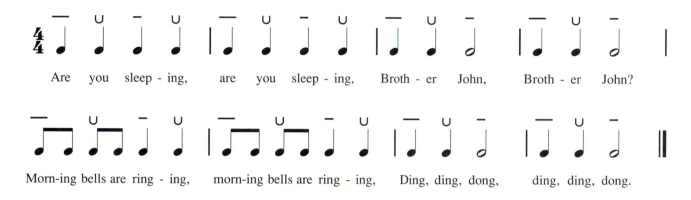

Are you sleep - ing, are you sleep - ing, Broth - er John, Broth - er John?

Morn-ing bells are ring - ing, morn-ing bells are ring - ing, Ding, ding, dong, ding, ding, dong.

Exercise 11

The rhythmic notation of *Are You Sleeping* is given. Write the numbers of the beats under the notes occurring on a beat and an ampersand (&) under the eighth notes not on a beat. Below the numbers, write the rhythm syllables. Refer to the rhythmic notation of *Hot Cross Buns* and *Lavender's Blue* as models. Recite the rhythm with the numbers and syllables.

ARE YOU SLEEPING

The note symbol for a full measure in 4/4 time is a *whole note*. A whole note has no stem, and its head is open like a half note but is somewhat larger and different in shape, as shown. A whole note has the same rhythmic value as four quarter notes.

Four quarter notes ♩ ♩ ♩ ♩ = 𝅝 one whole note

In 4/4 time, whole notes most often occur at the ends of phrases and songs. *The Woodchuck* is a song that ends with a whole note.

THE WOODCHUCK

While doing the conductor's beat, sing *The Woodchuck* with the words, and then recite the rhythm with the numbers. Be sure to sustain the vowel sound with the whole note in the last measure for four full beats.

Instead of a 4/4 time signature, a symbol that looks like a large C is sometimes used to indicate measures of four quarter-note beats, or *common time*. In the past, 4/4 and **C** time signatures were used interchangeably, but numerical time signatures are recommended in recent manuals on notation.

Exercise 12

Go through the chapters "Developing the Singing Voice" (chapter 5) and "Singing for Fun Is Learning" (chapter 6) and identify songs in duple or triple time. Specify the accents of the beats by clapping, chanting the words, etc.

Exercise 13

Have a student lead the class in a series of rhythmic movements in duple or triple time to solidify steady beat. Each movement or action should be done two, three, or four times before going on to the next. Samples include:

- Clap
- Snap
- Patschen
- Wings
- Pat head
- Pat shoulders
- Twist
- "bounce ball"
- "he-man"
- mark time
- hammer
- arms in circle
- etc.

Ties, Dots, and Flags

A curved line connecting two notes with the same pitch is a *tie*.

A tie has the effect of joining the two notes. The tone is sustained without interruption for their combined value. In vocal music, tied notes have only one syllable. Ties may be used with all note values any place in the measure and across bar lines, but most often they connect fractions of beats or notes in different measures.

A *dot* after a note increases its value one half. A dotted half note equals a half note plus a quarter note. A dotted quarter note equals a quarter note plus an eighth note. A single eighth note is written like a quarter note with a *flag* (as shown) in place of the beam that connects pairs of eighth notes.

Some rhythms can be written with a tie or a dot, and some eighth notes can be written with a beam or a flag.

1	(2)	&
ta	- i	ti

1	(2)	&
ta	- i	ti

1	(2)	&	3
ta	- i	ti	ta

1	(2)	&	3
ta	- i	ti	ta

1	(2)	(3)	4	&
ta	- a	- a	ti	ti

1	(2)	(3)	4	&
ta	- a	- a	ti	ti

In notating rhythm it is customary to use a dot rather than a tie when both are possible, though exceptions occur when the tie connects to an eighth note written with a beam. Across a bar line a tie must be used, and some rhythms can be notated only with a tie.

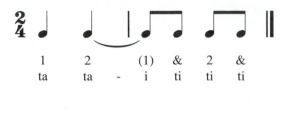

1   2   (1)   &   2   &
ta   ta - i   ti   ti   ti

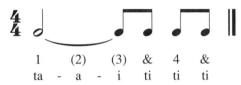

1   (2) - (3) &   4   &
ta - a   - i   ti   ti   ti

All through the Night is a song that makes extensive use of dotted rhythms. The first, second, and fourth lines of the song have the same rhythm and melody, so they could be notated with a repeat sign and a *da capo* (see p. 11).

ALL THROUGH THE NIGHT

Sleep, my child, and peace at-tend thee all through the night.

Guard - ian an - gels God will send thee all through the night.

Soft the drow - sy hours are creep - ing, hill and vale in slum - ber steep - ing,

I my lov - ing vig - il keep - ing all through the night.

Sing *All through the Night* while doing the conductor's beat. Then, count the beats and clap the rhythm. Finally, recite the rhythm with the rhythm syllables.

Exercise 14

Ties and dots are used in the notation of the following rhythms. Write the numbers and rhythm syllables under the notes in the manner of the illustrative examples. Then, perform the rhythms in the ways suggested in previous rhythm exercises.

2/2 Time Signature

In all of the preceding exercises the beats have been represented by quarter notes, but beats can also be represented by half notes. When the beat is represented by a half note, the lower number of the time signature is 2. Half-note beats most often occur in measures of two beats for which the numerical time signature is 2/2. The pattern of accents and the rhythm numbers and syllables are the same as for 2/4 time.

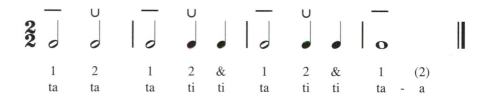

1	2	1	2	&	1	2	&	1	(2)
ta	ta	ta	ti	ti	ta	ti	ti	ta	- a

Measures of two half-note beats can be indicated by a 2/2 time signature or by a symbol like that for common time with a vertical line through it (¢) denoting *cut time,* or *alla breve* (by half notes). The symbols equivalent to 4/4 and 2/2 time signatures are common in the music of the past. Though rare in recent concert music, the symbols persist in other types of music, particularly in marches and popular music. Cut time is used for relatively fast tempos.

The conductor's beat for 2/2 and ¢ is the same as for 2/4. The appearance of the notation is changed, but not the sound, when a half note is used for the beat. When the time signature is 2/2 or ¢, a half note receives one beat, a quarter note receives a half beat, and so on.

It's a Small World in the original version and as reproduced on page 111 is written in cut time. As notated below, *Jacob's Ladder* is in 2/2 time, but it could have been written in 4/4 time as well.

Exercise 15

Do the conductor's beat (the same as for 2/4 time), and sing *Jacob's Ladder,* or recite the words rhythmically, paying particular attention to the relationship between the beat and the note values.

JACOB'S LADDER

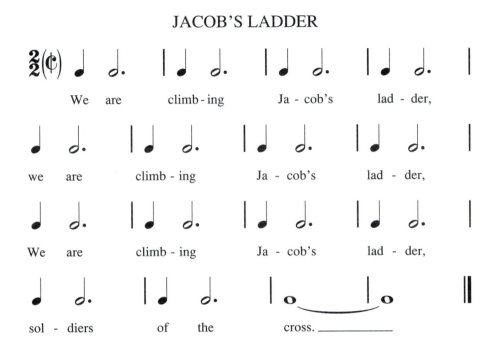

Exercise 16

Practice the following 2/2 (¢) rhythms in all of the ways suggested for previous rhythm exercises.

22   Reading Rhythm

3/8 Time Signature

In addition to quarter notes and half notes, eighth notes can also be used to represent beats. When the beat is represented by an eighth note, the lower number of the time signature is 8. The time signature for measures of three eighth notes is 3/8. Measures in 3/8 time contain the rhythmic equivalent of three eighth notes or a dotted quarter note. Consecutive eighth notes within a measure are beamed together, as shown. The pattern of accents and the conductor's beat for 3/8 time are the same as for 3/4 time, but the rhythm syllables are different. The following example shows the same rhythmic relationships notated first in 3/4 time and then in 3/8 time for comparison.

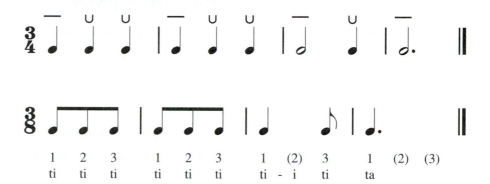

Since the same rhythmic relationships can be notated in both 3/4 and 3/8 time, it is apparent that note symbols represent only relative values, not precise durations that can be measured in seconds and fractions of seconds. The 3/8 time signature is rare in children's music.

6/8 Time Signature and Conductor's Beat

A more usual time signature with eighth-note beats is 6/8. Measures in 6/8 time contain the rhythmic equivalent of six eighth notes. Consecutive eighth notes are beamed in groups of three, as in 3/8 time. The note symbol for a full measure in 6/8 time is a dotted half note, and the note symbol for a half measure is a dotted quarter note. The pattern of accents, the beat numbers, and the rhythm syllables for 6/8 time are shown in the following example.

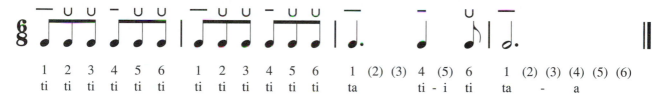

The following diagram shows the conductor's beat for 6/8 time.

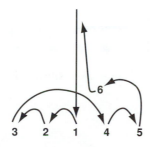

Perform the conductor's beat for 6/8 time while counting the beats and reciting the rhythm syllables of the preceding example until coordinating the hand motions with the numbers and syllables comes naturally.

Rockabye Baby is a lullaby in 6/8 time. Sing the song while doing the conductor's beat if the melody is familiar. Recite the rhythm with numbers and syllables even if the melody is not familiar.

ROCKABYE, BABY

Rock - a - bye, ba - by,   on the tree - top,   When the wind blows, the   cra - dle will rock,

When the bough breaks, the   cra - dle will fall, And   down will come ba - by,   cra - dle and all.

Since *Rockabye Baby* is a lullaby, it is sung slowly, or, to use the musical terminology, at a slow *tempo* (rate of speed). The 6/8 time signature is also used for songs that are sung at a fast tempo. *Three Blind Mice* requires a fast tempo. Sing it in the usual way, and clap or tap the pulses. There are only two pulses in a measure. The beat is represented by a dotted quarter note, the equivalent of three eighth notes.

THREE BLIND MICE

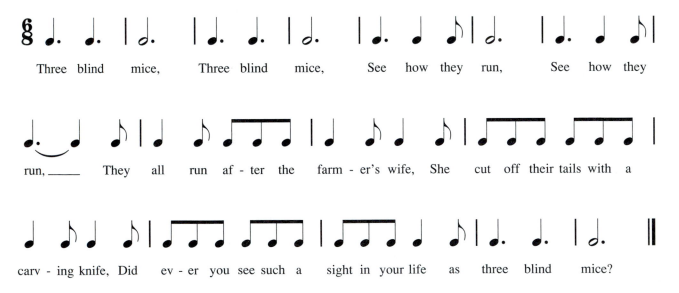

Three blind   mice,   Three blind   mice,   See how they   run,   See how they

run, _____ They   all   run af - ter the   farm - er's wife, She   cut off their tails with a

carv - ing knife, Did   ev - er you see such a   sight in your life   as   three blind   mice?

Fast 6/8 time with two pulses per measure is conducted in two, like 2/4 and 2/2 time. Many marches are written in 6/8 time, and these are always conducted in two. Moderate 6/8 tempos (between fast and slow) may be counted and conducted either way, in two or in six, at the discretion of the conductor or performer.

A different method of counting is required for fast 6/8 rhythms because the dotted-quarter beats divide in thirds. The number of the beat can be used for notes occurring on the beat, with the syllables *la* (pronounced "lah") and *li* (pronounced "lee") for the divisions of the beat. In the Kodály method the same syllables are used for the beats and divisions as in 2/4—*ta* for the beats and *ti* for the divisions.

Exercise 18

Write the numbers over the notes using the eighth note as the beat and the numbers and syllables under the notes using the dotted quarter note as the beat, as in the model. Recite the rhythms with the numbers and syllables, first slowly in six and working up to a fast tempo in two. Then, tap or clap the rhythms or perform them on percussion instruments.

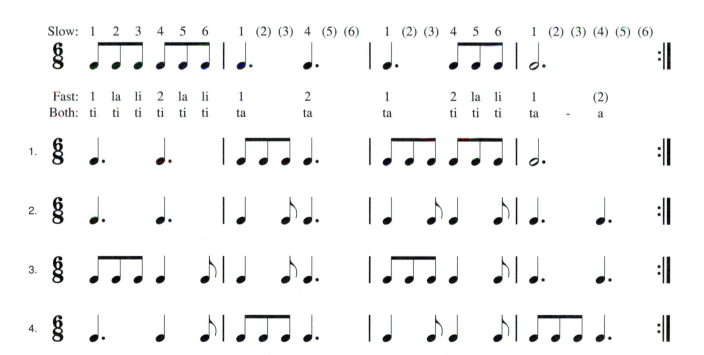

Reading Rhythm

25

A new system of time signatures that offers certain advantages is gaining acceptance. In this system the lower number of the conventional signature is replaced by the appropriate note symbol. The system is not completely standardized, but even with minor variations the meaning is evident. The new equivalents for all of the time signatures studied thus far are shown.

$\frac{2}{4}$ = $\frac{2}{\text{♩}}$ $\frac{3}{4}$ = $\frac{3}{\text{♩}}$ $\frac{4}{4}$ = $\frac{4}{\text{♩}}$ C = $\frac{4}{\text{♩}}$

$\frac{3}{8}$ = $\frac{3}{\text{♪}}$ $\frac{6}{8}$ = $\frac{6}{\text{♪}}$ or $\frac{2}{\text{♩.}}$ $\frac{2}{2}$ = $\frac{2}{\text{♩}}$ ¢ = $\frac{2}{\text{♩}}$

Time signatures like 3/2, 9/8, and 12/8 are routinely included in theoretical studies, but they are rare in school music.

Rests

Durations of silence as well as durations of sound must be notated in music. The symbols used to notate silence are *rests*. The rest equivalents for the note values studied thus far are shown. Whole and half rests are distinguishable only in relation to a line (of the staff). Whole rests are below the line; half rests are above the line. Whole rests are used to notate complete measures of silence in all meters.

Memorize the rest equivalents for all of the note values in the following table.

Notes:						
	Whole	Dotted half	Half	Dotted quarter	Quarter	Eighth
Rests:		or		or		

Exercise 19

Write the numbers for the beats under the notes and rests. Then, while counting aloud, perform the rhythms on a rhythm instrument or by clapping or tapping.

1.

2.

Slow:
Fast:

Kodály Equivalency Chart

In the following chart, remember that *ta* stays constant as the unit of beat in 2/4, 3/4, and 4/4. Compare the following syllables and how they stay the same or change from time signature to time signature:

	2/4	3/4	4/4	2/2	6/8
ta-a-a-a	—	—	𝅝	—	—
ta-a-a	—	𝅗𝅥.	𝅗𝅥.	—	—
ta-a	𝅗𝅥	𝅗𝅥	𝅗𝅥	𝅝	𝅘𝅥.
ta	𝅘𝅥	𝅘𝅥	𝅘𝅥	𝅗𝅥	𝅘𝅥.
ti-i	𝅘𝅥𝅘𝅥	𝅘𝅥𝅘𝅥	𝅘𝅥𝅘𝅥	𝅘𝅥𝅘𝅥	𝅘𝅥
ti	𝅘𝅥𝅮	𝅘𝅥𝅮	𝅘𝅥𝅮	𝅘𝅥	𝅘𝅥𝅮
ti-ri	𝅘𝅥𝅯𝅘𝅥𝅯	𝅘𝅥𝅯𝅘𝅥𝅯	𝅘𝅥𝅯𝅘𝅥𝅯	𝅘𝅥𝅯𝅘𝅥𝅯	𝅘𝅥𝅯𝅘𝅥𝅯

Upbeats

When the words of a song begin with an unaccented syllable, the music begins with an *upbeat,* pick-up, or *anacrusis.*[2] An upbeat is one or more notes, but less than a measure, preceding the first primary accent in either vocal or instrumental music. When a piece begins with an upbeat and consequently an incomplete measure, it ends with a complementary incomplete measure, and the two incomplete measures combined are equal to one full

[2]All three terms have the same meaning.

measure, as in the following song. This song begins with a quarter-note upbeat and ends with a half note, for a correct total of three beats in 3/4 time.

OH WHERE, OH WHERE HAS MY LITTLE DOG GONE?

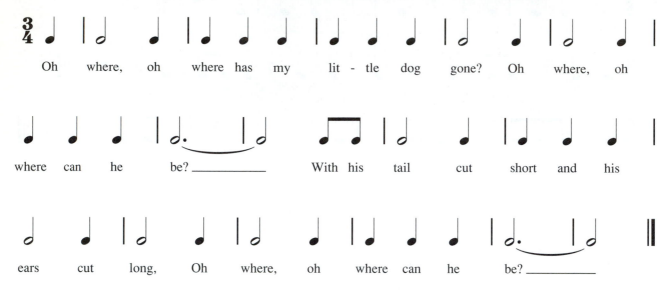

Oh where, oh where has my lit - tle dog gone? Oh where, oh

where can he be? _____ With his tail cut short and his

ears cut long, Oh where, oh where can he be? _____

Exercise 20

Perform the rhythm of *Oh Where, Oh Where Has My Little Dog Gone*, using patschen. The right hand should be used for the upbeat and all unaccented beats and the left hand for the accented beats. The notes for each hand are placed on the appropriate line in the following notation. (Patschen skills transfer readily to percussion instruments.)

OH WHERE, OH WHERE HAS MY LITTLE DOG GONE?

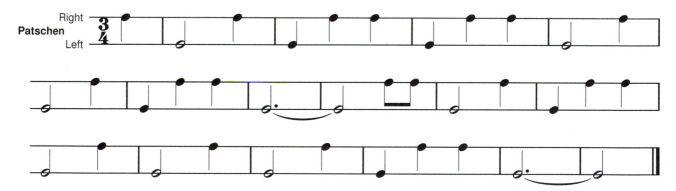

Reading Rhythm

Exercise 21

For this exercise the teacher or one member of the class serves as the leader, and the other members of the class are followers. The leader, seated facing the class, establishes a meter and tempo by counting the beats with patschen. The followers imitate the leader immediately without breaking the rhythm, producing an echo effect. The leader then improvises a series of one-measure rhythm patterns, each of which is echoed by the followers. Sample 4/4 and fast 6/8 patterns are given. Members of the class can take turns serving as the leader and improvising rhythms in various meters. As facility improves, longer and more complex patterns can be used. (These exercises can also be performed on percussion instruments.)

Transcribing Rhythm

Transcribing rhythm, that is, notating rhythms that you hear or create is a useful extension of the skills required to read rhythmic notation and to translate it into sound. One way to approach rhythmic transcription is to recite names rhythmically while tapping a steady beat. Multiple versions are possible. Determine the relative duration of the syllables in the names, and then notate the rhythm in an appropriate meter with the stressed syllables coinciding with the beats and/or accents in the music. The following examples are possible rhythms for some celebrated names.

George Wash-ing - ton, Sen - a - tor Glenn.

Ab - ra - ham Lin - coln, An - drew Lloyd Web - ber.

Mi - chael Jor - dan, Sam - my So - sa.

Exercise 22

Write appropriate rhythms for your own name and for the names of your classmates.

The ability to notate rhythms invented and performed by children, an invaluable asset for classroom teachers, can be developed by taking rhythmic dictation in the following manner. The teacher announces the meter and establishes the tempo by counting two measures and then claps (or performs in some other way) a four-measure rhythm pattern, which is repeated immediately. Here is a model exercise.

On the repetition the class joins the teacher in clapping the rhythm while counting the beats. Each student then writes the rhythm from memory, including the time signature and bar lines as well as the proper note values. As a sort of rhythmic shorthand, durations of a quarter note or less can be written without note heads in the manner of Kodály (see p. 9). Students then perform the rhythm, reading from the notation to check its accuracy.

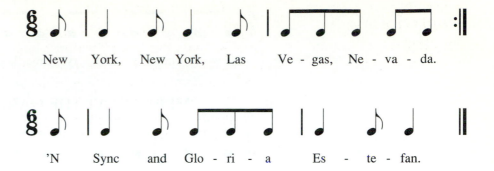

New   York,   New York,   Las   Ve - gas,   Ne - va - da.

'N   Sync   and   Glo - ri - a   Es - te - fan.

Exercise 23

Here are some sample rhythms in various meters for rhythmic dictation following the procedures outlined.

Exercise 24

Make up additional exercises and dictate them to your classmates. The difficulty and length of the exercises can be increased as proficiency in taking rhythmic dictation improves.

Exercise 25

"Cheers" for ballgames, rap, and speech chants are words repeated in a specific rhythmic pattern. Try the following exercises, adding movement and/or percussion instruments. For enhancement, form a circle and bounce a ball to this chant, getting faster or slower each time:

1. Chew - y chunk - y cher - ry choc-'late cheese - cake.

MEET ME AT THE GARDEN GATE

2. Two, four, six, eight. Meet me at the gar - den gate.

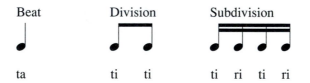

If I'm late, please wait. Two, four, six, eight.

Subdivisions of the Beat

Beats can be divided and subdivided. Divisions of quarter-note beats are written as eighth notes (introduced early in this chapter). Equal subdivisions of quarter-note beats are written as *sixteenth notes*. The symbols for sixteenth notes are like those for eighth notes but with a second beam or flag. The symbol for a sixteenth rest is like that for an eighth rest but with a second appendage.

Sixteenth notes and rests:

One quarter note equals two eighth notes or four sixteenth notes. The Kodály rhythm syllables are shown for quarter-note beats, eighth-note divisions, and sixteenth-note equal subdivisions.

Beat	Division	Subdivision
ta	ti ti	ti ri ti ri

Rhythm Equivalency Chart

In the following table the relative durations of equally-divided undotted notes are shown graphically. Observe that the longer durations are represented by the simpler symbols and the shorter values by the more elaborate symbols.

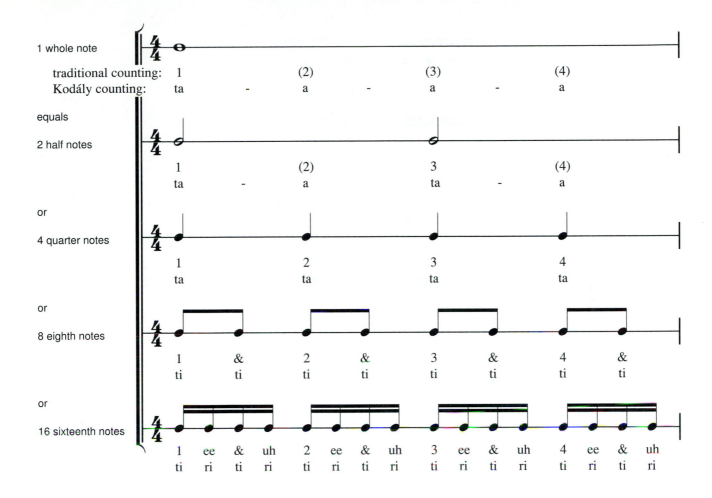

1 whole note

traditional counting: 1   (2)   (3)   (4)
Kodály counting: ta   -   a   -   a   -   a

equals

2 half notes

1   (2)   3   (4)
ta   -   a   ta   -   a

or

4 quarter notes

1   2   3   4
ta   ta   ta   ta

or

8 eighth notes

1   &   2   &   3   &   4   &
ti   ti   ti   ti   ti   ti   ti   ti

or

16 sixteenth notes

1 ee & uh   2 ee & uh   3 ee & uh   4 ee & uh
ti ri ti ri   ti ri ti ri   ti ri ti ri   ti ri ti ri

Beats can be divided into unequal subdivisions. The unequal subdivisions of quarter-note beats are shown. The notation on the left with ties is for illustrative purposes only. The normal notation of these rhythms is on the right. (The rhythm syllables *ti* and *ri* are pronounced "tee" and "ree"; *tim* and *rim*, like the name and the word.)

1	&	uh
ti	ti	ri

1	ee	&
ti	ri	ti

1	ee (&)	uh
ti	ri	ri

1	(ee) (&)	uh
ti	- i	ri
(or) tim		ri

1	ee (&)	(uh)
ti	ri - i	
(or) ti	rim	

Equivalent unequal subdivisions of half-note beats are notated thus:

Exercise 26

The following rhythm patterns exploit characteristic unequal subdivisions of beats in 2/4 and 2/2 time. Practice these patterns until you can perform them accurately and recognize them instantly.

1. (2/4 rhythm pattern)

2. (2/4 rhythm pattern)

3. (2/2 rhythm pattern)

4. (2/2 rhythm pattern)

Dotted notes require a different table of relative durations. Observe that the dotted quarter notes in this context divide in thirds, unlike the other note values, which divide in halves. Dotted whole notes and groups of six sixteenth notes occur rarely, if at all, in familiar music but are included to parallel the preceding table.

1 dotted whole note

equals

2 dotted half notes

or

4 dotted quarter notes

or

12 eighth notes

or

24 sixteenth notes

There are many possibilities for unequal subdivisions when the beat is represented by a dotted quarter note, but only the following are usual in familiar songs.

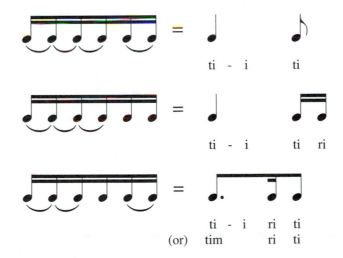

Exercise 27

Practice the following rhythm patterns, beginning slowly with the eighth value as the beat. Increase the speed in successive repetitions until the dotted quarter value is perceived as the beat.

Exercise 28

The following rhythms from familiar songs contain equal and unequal divisions of the beat and involve most of the common rhythmic problems. Recite the rhythms with syllables and/or numbers. See if you can recognize the songs from the rhythm alone before looking at the titles listed at the end of the exercise. This material can also be used for supplementary drill in all of the response modes suggested previously.

4.

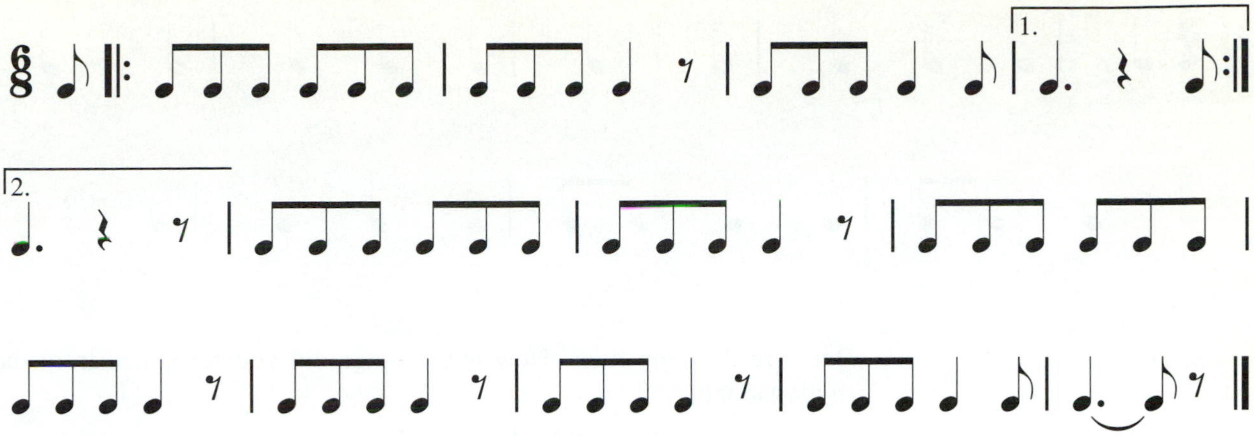

5.

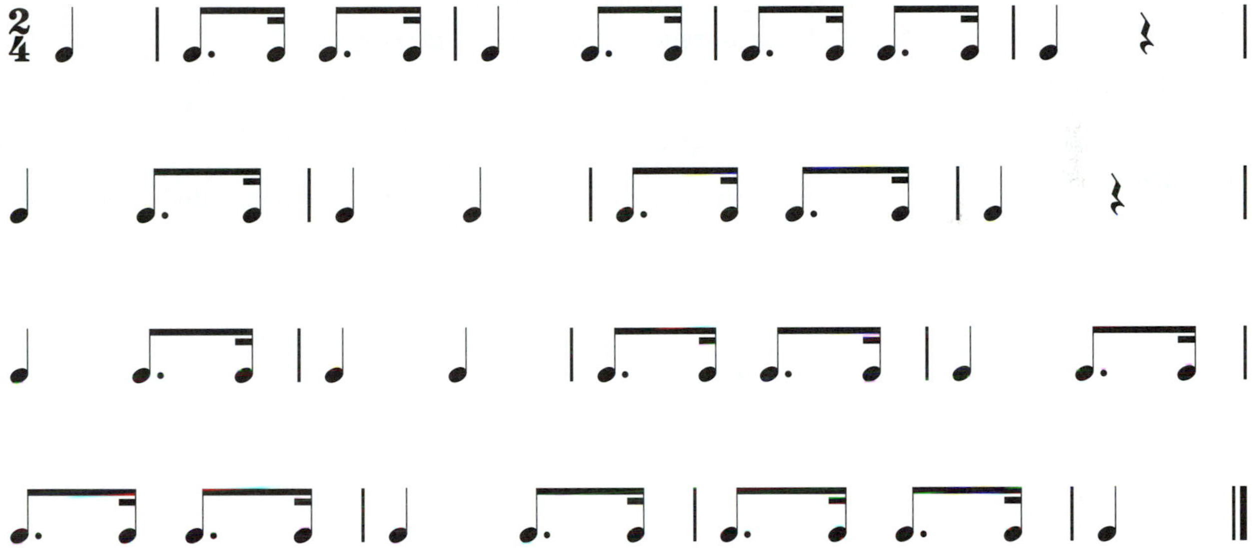

6.

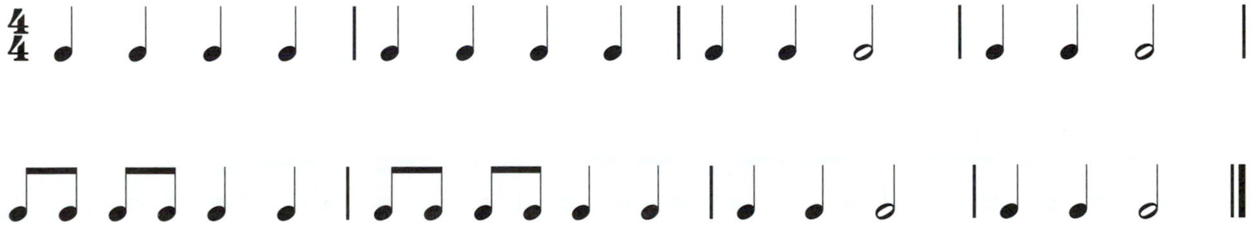

Here are the song titles. How many songs did you recognize from the rhythm alone?

1. *Auld Lang Syne,* Scottish folk song
2. *The First Noel,* carol
3. *Joy to the World,* Mason
4. *Vive l'Amour,* college song
5. *Eency, Weency Spider*
6. *Where is Thumbkin (Frère Jacques)*
7. *Good Morning to You (Happy Birthday)*

Triplets

Three notes of equal value within a beat that normally divides in halves and fourths are *triplets*. Triplets are indicated by a 3 in the middle of the beam that joins the notes of the group.

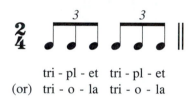

tri - pl - et   tri - pl - et
(or) tri - o - la   tri - o - la

The song *Row, Row, Row Your Boat* contains triplets.

ROW, ROW, ROW YOUR BOAT

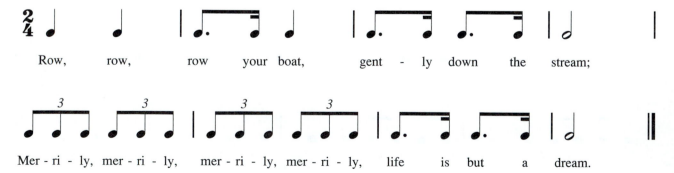

Syncopation

When the rhythmic flow momentarily fails to coincide with the beat, the effect is *syncopation*. Tying a weak beat or portion of a beat to a strong one produces syncopation. A short rest occurring where an accent is expected, a common rhythmic device in jazz, produces a similar effect.

TOM DOOLEY

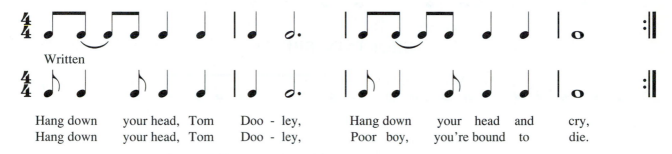

Written

Hang down   your head, Tom   Doo - ley,   Hang down   your   head   and   cry,
Hang down   your head, Tom   Doo - ley,   Poor   boy,   you're bound to   die.

Suggested Assignments

1. Place bar lines in the proper places in the following songs, and write the beat numbers and/or the rhythm syllables under the notes.

AMERICA

DECK THE HALLS

SWEET AND LOW

SHORTNIN' BREAD

2. Complete the measures with notes and/or rests.

Reading Rhythm

3. Transcribe the following measures, substituting notes for the rests and rests for the notes.

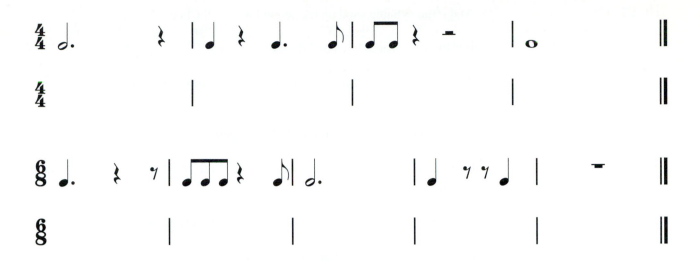

Exercise 29

This is a partner game that stresses the beat and the pulse of the song. On the first two notes the partners take hands and move them side to side in a sweeping motion. Clap partner's hands on the double *x* and clap own hands on the single *x*. Show the motions for "long-legged" and other descriptions— jumping up on no-legged. Salute on the word sailor and place your hand over your heart on the word wife. Speed up the song after the students know it.

LONG-LEGGED SAILOR

X = clap your own hands
XX = clap your partner's hands

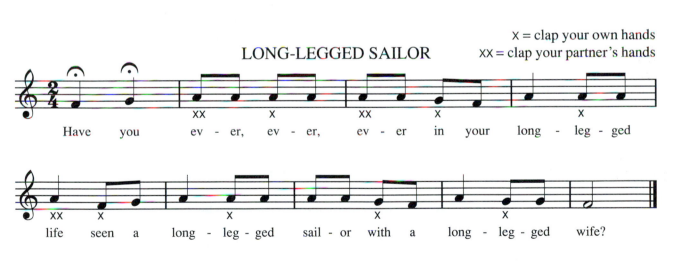

Always answer each verse with "No, I've never, never, never in my. . . ."
Additional verses should include:
Short-legged
Cross-legged
Bow-legged
One-legged
No-legged

Rhythm Terminology Glossary

Accented beat – a beat with a stress placed on it

And – the syllable used on the second half of the beat

Bar lines – vertical lines that divide measures (|)

Beam or ligature – the horizontal bar connecting eighth or sixteenth notes (♩♩ ; ♫)

Beats – rhythmic pulses often grouped together

Conductor's beats – patterns used by the director to express different beat patterns

Counting – expressing musical rhythm by numbering the beats in a measure

Da Capo (D.C.) – the Italian words meaning return to the beginning of the piece or section of music

Dal Segno (D.S.) – the Italian words that indicate to return to the indicated sign in the music (𝄋)

Double bar – two bar lines together, indicating the end of an exercise or composition (‖)

Downbeat – the first beat of the measure

Duple – music with a two-beat rhythm (marches)

First ending – a passage that is performed only the first time through

Flag – single eighth notes and sixteenth notes are distinguished by the addition of flags to their stems

Marking time – marching in place

Measures – groups of accented and unaccented beats

Notehead – the round portion of the note, either open or closed (• ∘ o)

Notes – the symbols used to show rhythm and pitch of musical sounds

Patschen – patting the thighs in rhythm

Repeat sign – a double bar and two dots that indicates to repeat a passage (:‖)

Rhythm – organized or organizing sounds in time

Second ending – a passage that is performed only the second time through

Reading Rhythm

Stem – the vertical line on the notehead

Syncopation – weak beats that are accented

Time signature (meter signature) – two numbers, one above the other, placed at the beginning of a piece of music. The top number tells how many beats in a measure; the lower number tells what type of note receives one beat. ($\frac{3}{4}$, $\frac{2}{4}$, etc.)

Triple – music with a three-beat rhythm (waltzes)

Triplet – three notes of equal value within a beat (♪♪♪)

Tone – the term used to denote a musical sound

Unaccented beat – a beat that is not stressed

Upbeat (pick-up, or anacrusis) – the unaccented beat that comes before the first strong beat of a section or piece of music (♪ | ♪♪ ♪ |)

CHAPTER 3

Reading Pitch

When musical rhythms are combined with systematically organized pitches, melody results. Since melodic elements are present in virtually all music, the ability to read pitch notation is an essential musical skill. Although the note symbols already studied are used to notate both rhythm and pitch in conventional notation, rhythms and pitches can be represented by simple graphic *line notation*.

Line Notation

In line notation, relative duration is represented by the length of the lines and relative pitch by the placement of the lines higher or lower on a page or blackboard. The line notation for *Under the Spreading Chestnut Tree* is given above the words.

Establish a regular beat by tapping at a moderate pace, or *tempo*. Then, while continuing the beat, recite rhythmically the words of *Under the Spreading Chestnut Tree*. Lines the length of that above the first syllable represent durations equal to one beat. Lines half as long represent durations equal to half a beat, and lines twice as long represent durations equal to two beats.

Exercise 1

While the teacher plays or sings the melody of *Under the Spreading Chestnut Tree*, follow the line notation and act out the pitches with the right hand. Move the hand up when the pitch goes higher and down when the pitch goes lower. Whenever the same pitch recurs, represent it by the same hand position. Keep your hands about chest level, as in regular conducting. This process is called *conducting the pitch* and is very useful as a visual aid.

Exercise 2

Sing *Under the Spreading Chestnut Tree*, using the line notation to aid your memory of the teacher's performance. The relative height of the lines above the syllables accurately represents the relative pitch of the tones in the melody.

Line notation and conducting the pitch provide a simple musical shorthand useful for writing creative melodic ideas and as an easy process for teaching songs to young children. Acting out the pitches with the hand serves as a preliminary exercise for more precise hand signals.

UNDER THE SPREADING CHESTNUT TREE

―	―	―	―	―	―	―		―	―

Un - der the spread - ing chest - nut tree,

When I held you on my knee,

We were hap - py as can be,

Un - der the spread - ing chest - nut tree.

The Staff and Ledger Lines

K–4, 6c

Line notation shows only the general contour of a melody. Melodic contours are represented more precisely in conventional music notation on a *staff* consisting of five equidistant lines. The five lines enclose four spaces. The lines and spaces of the staff are numbered separately from bottom to top.

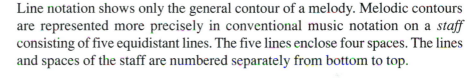

Note symbols are placed on the lines, in the spaces, and above and below the staff. The stems of notes below the middle line of the staff extend up from the right side of the head. The stems of notes on and above the middle line of the staff extend down from the left side of the head. The direction of all the stems in beamed groups is dictated by the note farthest from the center of the staff. Other factors being equal, stems go down. Chords are stemmed like beamed groups.

Short, discontinuous lines called *ledger* (also spelled *leger*) *lines* are used to notate pitches beyond the range of the staff.

The Treble Clef

The location of notes on a staff shows relative pitch relationships like hand positions and line notation. With the addition of a *clef sign,* each line and space indicates a specific pitch. The clef sign most often used for vocal music, the right-hand part in piano music, and in music for guitar and most melody instruments is a *treble clef.* This clef circles around the note G.

The staff notation for *Under the Spreading Chestnut Tree* follows. The treble clef sign is on the staff at the beginning of each line. The time signature appears only once, following the first clef sign. The rhythmic functions of the note symbols were introduced in chapter 2, *Reading Rhythm.*

UNDER THE SPREADING CHESTNUT TREE

ENGLISH FOLK SONG

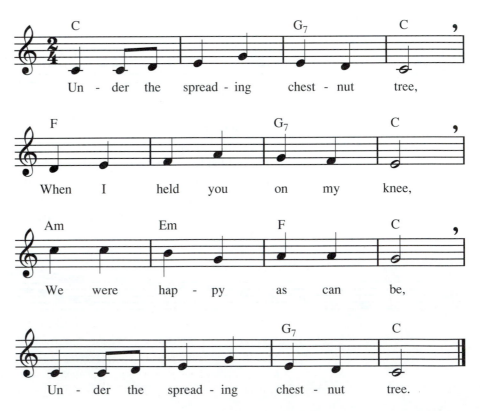

Note Names

Notes are identified by names. Every note has three—a letter, a number, and a syllable. The letter names indicate specific pitches. The number and syllable names indicate note positions in relation to a keynote and scale. The number and syllable names function in the same way, but the syllable sounds are more pleasing.

Exercise 3

The letter, number, and syllable names for the notes of *Under the Spreading Chestnut Tree* are given. Sing the melody, substituting, in turn, each set of note names for the words.

UNDER THE SPREADING CHESTNUT TREE

ENGLISH FOLK SONG

*Also spelled *sol*.

There are seven basic note names in each set, all of which are used in naming the notes of *Under the Spreading Chestnut Tree*. The note names occur in order when naming the notes written consecutively in ascending order on every line and in every space of the staff. After the seventh note, the sequence of letter and syllable names is repeated, starting again with the first. In this context, however, the number designation for the next note is 8 (or again, 1).

Reading Pitch

C	D	E	F	G	A	B	C	D	E	F	G	A	B	C
1	2	3	4	5	6	7	8(1)	2	3	4	5	6	7	8(1)
do	*re*	*mi*	*fa*	*so*	*la*	*ti*	*do*	*re*	*mi*	*fa*	*so*	*la*	*ti*	*do*
(Kodály) *d*	*r*	*m*	*f*	*s*	*l*	*t*	*d'*	*r'*	*m'*	*f'*	*s'*	*l'*	*t'*	*d''*

From any note up or down to the next note with the same name is an *octave,* meaning "eight." The numbers 1 and 8 are interchangeable. The letter names are the first seven letters of the alphabet, though the preceding example starts on C. In Kodály notation, pitches are sometimes represented by the initial letter of their syllable names, as shown. A prime sign (´) by a letter indicates the higher octave.

The C Major Scale

A series of notes arranged consecutively in ascending or descending order forms a *scale*.

Exercise 4

Sing the following scale both up and down with all three names. It probably has a familiar sound, because *Under the Spreading Chestnut Tree* and many of the songs you know are based on a scale pattern like this. It is a *major scale*. Each scale takes its letter name from the note on which it begins and ends. This scale begins and ends on C, so it is a *C major scale*.

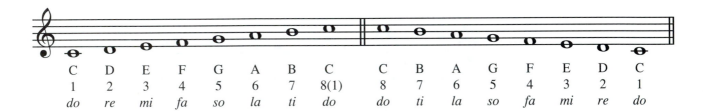

C	D	E	F	G	A	B	C	C	B	A	G	F	E	D	C
1	2	3	4	5	6	7	8(1)	8	7	6	5	4	3	2	1
do	*re*	*mi*	*fa*	*so*	*la*	*ti*	*do*	*do*	*ti*	*la*	*so*	*fa*	*mi*	*re*	*do*

You may have been unaware of it when you were singing, but the pitch differences between notes of a major scale are not all the same. This is easy to see if the notes are located on a piano keyboard.

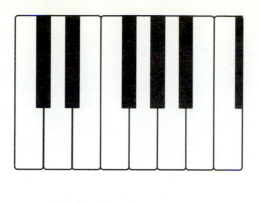

There is a black key between C and D and between D and E, but not between E and F. There is a black key between each pair of white keys from F to B, but not between B and C. The *interval* (difference in pitch) between white keys with a black key between them and between all alternate keys, whether white or black, is a *whole step,* or *whole tone.* The interval between white keys without a black key between them and between all adjacent keys, whether white or black, is a *half step,* or *semitone.* Two half steps equal one whole step.

Major scales are made up of whole steps and half steps. In the C major scale the half steps come between E and F and between B and C. Using the other names, the half steps come between 3 and 4 (*mi* and *fa*) and between 7 and 8 (*ti* and *do*). The pattern of whole steps and half steps is the same in all major scales.

Hand Signals

Hand signals have been used for centuries as an aid in learning music. The first system of hand signals is attributed to Guido d'Arezzo (c. 990–1050), who is also credited with being the first to use syllable names for notes. John Curwen's system of hand signals, adopted and popularized by Zoltán Kodály, associates each scale degree with a hand shape and position. The shape of the hand suggests the tendency of the tones in the scale: closed for *do,* which is most stable; open and level for *mi* and *so,* which are relatively stable; and pointing for active tones, which have a tendency to move in a particular direction. The relative pitch of each tone is represented by the position of the hand: waist level for low *do* and proportionately higher for each pitch up to high *do* above the head.

The hand signals for *Scale Song,* placed above the staff to reflect the relative pitch of the notes, are associated with corresponding number, syllable, and letter names in the words of the song. Sing the song while doing the hand signals until you instinctively associate the shape and position of the hand and the various names for the notes with the degrees of the C major scale.

SCALE SONG

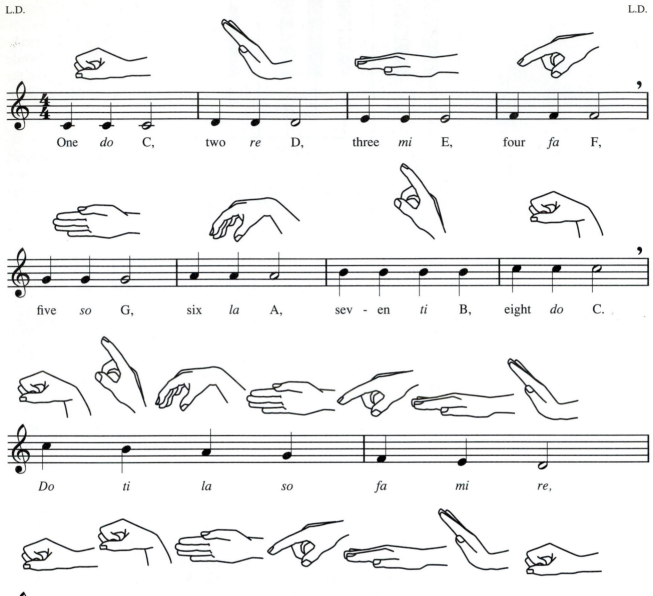

One *do* C, two *re* D, three *mi* E, four *fa* F,

five *so* G, six *la* A, sev - en *ti* B, eight *do* C.

Do ti la so fa mi re,

now I've sung my scale to - day.

Some teachers prefer the following hand signal for *fa*.

fa

To gain facility in forming and placing the hand signals, use them to represent the pitches in familiar songs as they are sung. Select songs that are simple and not too fast for these activities.

After the association between the hand signals and the pitches has been established, the hand signals can be used as an aid in teaching new songs. While learning songs in this manner, students should imitate the hand signals of the instructor. (See Suggested Assignments 2–4 at the end of this chapter for additional hand signal exercises.)

Sharps, Flats, and Naturals

5–8, 5c

Within an octave there are only seven staff positions and seven basic letter names for notes, but there are twelve different pitches. To notate the other five pitches, sharps and flats are used. A sharp (♯) to the left of a note indicates that the next higher pitch is to be sung or played. A flat (♭) to the left of a note indicates that the next lower pitch is to be sung or played. A natural (♮) cancels the effect of a sharp or a flat.

The illustration below shows where the sharp, flat, and natural notes are found in each octave of the piano keyboard. A full-sized, four-octave keyboard is enclosed in the endleaf pocket at the back of this book. The natural notes are played on the white keys; the commonly used sharp and flat notes, on the black keys. Observe that each black key serves for two notes, the sharp inflection of the note below and the flat inflection of the note above. The less usual sharp and flat notes, played on the white keys, are shown in parentheses. Two notes, such as C-sharp and D-flat, that are played on the same key and have the same pitch but are written differently are *enharmonic notes*.

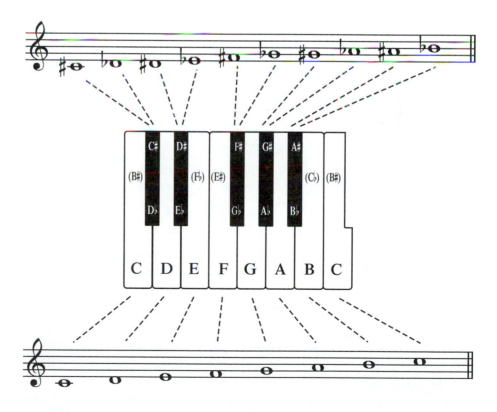

The sequence of notes that includes every pitch consecutively is a *chromatic scale*. The pitches of chromatic scales can be written with either sharps or flats, but it is customary to use sharps for notes that go up and flats for notes that go down. The C major syllable names are given above the letter names for both the ascending and descending chromatic scales. In the syllables, *O* is pronounced "oh," *i* like "ee," *e* like "ay," and *a* like "ah." Observe that the only natural notes not separated by a sharp or a flat note are E–F and B–C.

	do	di	re	ri	mi	fa	fi	so	si	la	li	ti	do
	C	C♯	D	D♯	E	F	F♯	G	G♯	A	A♯	B	C

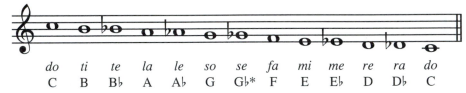

	do	ti	te	la	le	so	se	fa	mi	me	re	ra	do
	C	B	B♭	A	A♭	G	G♭*	F	E	E♭	D	D♭	C

*The G-flat notation is rare. The pitch is usually written as F-sharp, even descending.

All of the musical examples should be sung and/or played. Even students with no prior keyboard experience can play scales on the piano with one finger. Songs that are introduced before music reading skills are sufficiently developed should be learned partially by rote with the assistance of the teacher.

Exercise 5

Play the ascending and descending chromatic scales on the piano, and sing them with syllable and letter names. In this way you will become familiar with the sound, notation, and names of all the notes. The all-inclusive chromatic scale is introduced for this purpose. Only in the more complex works of the twentieth century is it used as a basis for composition. Most of our music is based on selective scales containing from five to seven of the twelve pitches available in an octave.

Pentatonic Music and Scales

Music in which only five tones are used is *pentatonic*, and the notes of such music arranged in order form *pentatonic scales*. Although numerous five-tone scale patterns are possible, the most prevalent ones contain no semitones and two gaps. *Barnyard Song* is based on a pentatonic scale of this type.

Exercise 6

Sing *Barnyard Song* according to these directions: Omit the 3/4 measure in the first verse and sing it only once in the second verse. Starting with the third verse, sing all of the animal names and sounds from the preceding verses in reverse order before going on to "Bird goes fiddle-aye-fee."

BARNYARD SONG

AMERICAN FOLK SONG

1. I had a bird, and the bird pleased me, I fed my bird by yon-der tree;
2. I had a hen, and the hen pleased me, I fed my hen by yon-der tree;

Bird goes fid-dle-aye-fee.   Hen goes chim-my chuck, chim-my chuck,   Bird goes fid-dle-aye-fee.

3. Duck: quack, quack
4. Goose: swishy, swashy
5. Sheep: baa, baa

6. Pig: griffy, gruffy
7. Cow: moo, moo
8. Horse: neigh, neigh

The pentatonic scale from which the notes of *Barnyard Song* are derived is shown below. It is like a C major scale with the fourth and seventh notes omitted: C D E __ G A __ C. The gaps between E–G and A–C are equal to a half step (H) plus a whole step (W), or vice versa. *Li'l Liza Jane* (p. 279) is another song based on the same pentatonic scale as *Barnyard Song*.

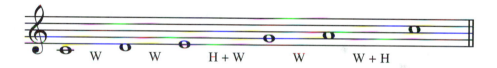

W   W   H + W   W   W + H

A pentatonic scale pattern identical with that of *Barnyard Song* and *Li'l Liza Jane* is produced by the black keys of the piano, which can be notated with either sharps or flats.

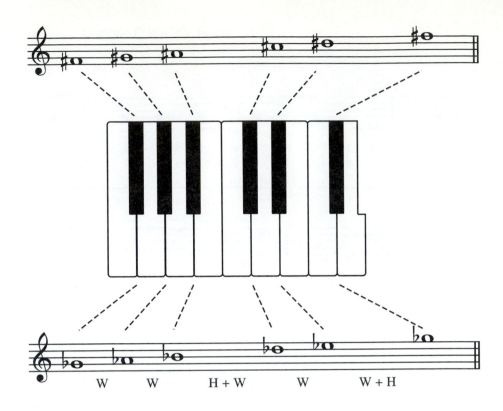

W W H + W W W + H

Going on a Picnic, like *Barnyard Song,* is based on a pentatonic scale that has no semitones and two gaps. The melody revolves around F, and the notes of its scale are F G A __ C D __ F.

GOING ON A PICNIC

Lynn Freeman Olson

Lynn Freeman Olson

Go-ing on   a pic - nic   in the park to-day.   If   it does-n't rain there's time to   play.

bas - ket?   bas - ket!   Read-y for a pic - nic,   here we   go!

1.–3. Did you bring the so - das?   Yes, I brought the so - das!
blan - ket?   blan - ket!

Pentatonic scales like those illustrated contain no sharp dissonances or tendency tones. Their pitches, played in almost any melodic succession or harmonic combination, consistently produce a pleasant sound. These attributes make pentatonic scales an ideal point of departure for group improvisation and spontaneous musical activities.

The melodies of many songs contain six or fewer different notes. Except for pentatonic melodies, however, they are generally regarded as being based on one of the seven-tone scales, of which the major scale is the most common.

Major Scales, Keys, and Signatures

The C major scale has been introduced (p. 48). Songs based on the C major scale are said to be in the key of C major. *Under the Spreading Chestnut Tree* (pp. 46–47) and *Scale Song* (p. 50) are in the key of C major. Starting on C, the major scale pattern is produced by the natural notes played on the white keys of the piano. The C major scale serves as the model for the other major scales. It has half steps (marked ⌃) between 3–4 and 7–8, whole steps elsewhere. Viewed another way, it consists of two identical whole–whole–half (W W H) patterns with a whole step between them, as shown.

G Major

To construct a major scale starting on any note but C, one or more sharps or flats are required. For example, F-sharp is necessary to produce the correct pattern of whole and half steps in the major scale starting on G. This is a G major scale. (Use the Scale Builder in the endleaf pocket at the back of this book to determine the notes in any major scale.)

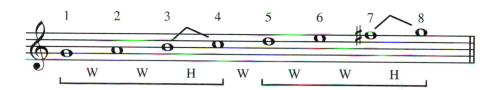

It is not customary to write the sharp by every F in the key of G major. Instead, a sharp is placed on the staff at the beginning of each line of music. This means that every F in the piece is sharp unless the sharp is canceled by a natural sign. Sharps or flats placed at the beginning of each line to indicate the key are called *key signatures*. The key signature for G major is one sharp. In the treble clef it is placed on the top line.

Are You Sleeping is in the key of G major, and it is customary to notate it with an F-sharp key signature even though the melody has only six different notes and no F or F-sharp.

ARE YOU SLEEPING

ROUND

FRANCE

Are you sleep - ing, are you sleep - ing, Broth - er John, Broth - er John?

Morn-ing bells are ring - ing, morn-ing bells are ring - ing, Ding, ding, dong, ding, ding, dong.

K–4, 5b

Letter names are associated with specific pitches and are the same regardless of the key. Syllable and number names reflect pitch relationships within a key, and they change, in relation to the letter names, as the key changes. The note from which a key takes its name is the *keynote*. In major keys the keynote is always *do* (1). The syllable and number names of the other notes are in a fixed relationship to the keynote and to each other. Observe these facts as you sing *Are You Sleeping* with syllable, number, and letter names. Each system is used in our schools—some more predominantly than the other(s).

ARE YOU SLEEPING

ROUND

FRANCE

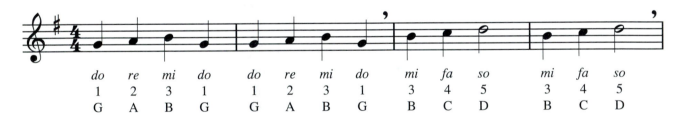

do	re	mi	do	do	re	mi	do	mi	fa	so	mi	fa	so
1	2	3	1	1	2	3	1	3	4	5	3	4	5
G	A	B	G	G	A	B	G	B	C	D	B	C	D

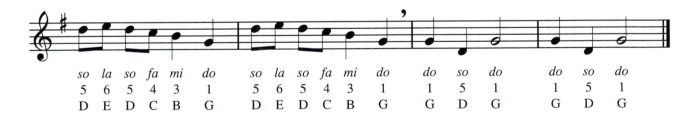

so	la	so	fa	mi	do	so	la	so	fa	mi	do	do	so	do	do	so	do
5	6	5	4	3	1	5	6	5	4	3	1	1	5	1	1	5	1
D	E	D	C	B	G	D	E	D	C	B	G	G	D	G	G	D	G

Exercise 7

Another common song in the key of G major (that includes F-sharps) is *Jingle Bells*. Sing it first with the words, and then with the syllable, number, and letter names.

JINGLE BELLS

JAMES PIERPONT

JAMES PIERPONT

Verse
Dash-ing through the snow, In a one-horse o-pen sleigh, O'er the fields we go, Laugh-ing all the way; Bells on bob-tail ring, Mak-ing spir-its bright, What fun it is to ride and sing a sleigh-ing song to - night!

Refrain
Jing - le bells, jing - le bells, jing - le all the way! Oh, what fun it is to ride in a one-horse o - pen sleigh! ___ one-horse o - pen sleigh!

F Major

The major scale starting on F requires a B-flat.

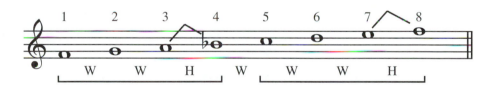

The flat in the key signature for F major, B-flat, goes on the third line in the treble clef.

Exercise 8

Oh, My Darling Clementine is in the key of F major. The keynote and first note of this song, F, is *do* (1). The note C is *so* (5). Sing the song in unison several times (everyone singing together) using the syllable, number, and letter names, and then as a round using the words.

OH, MY DARLING, CLEMENTINE

AMERICAN TRADITIONAL SONG

1. In a cav - ern in a can - yon, Ex - ca - vat - ing for a mine,
2. Light she was, so light and air - y, and her shoes were num - ber nine,
3. Drove she duck - lings to the wa - ter, Ev - 'ry morn - ing just at nine,
4. Ru - by lips a - bove the wa - ter, Blow - ing bub - bles soft and fine,

do do do so, mi mi mi do, do mi so so fa mi re,

Dwelt a min - er, for - ty - nin - er, And his daugh - ter, Clem - en - tine.
Her - ring box - es with - out top - ses, San - dals were for Clem - en - tine.
Hit her foot a - gainst a splin - ter, Fell in - to the foam - ing brine.
But, a - las, I was no swim - mer, So I lost my Clem - en - tine.

re mi fa fa, mi re mi do, do mi re so, ti re do

Refrain

Oh, my dar - ling, oh, my dar - ling, Oh, my dar - ling Clem - en - tine,

do do do so, mi mi mi do, do mi so so fa mi re,

You are lost and gone for - ev - er, Dread - ful sor - ry, Clem - en - tine.

re mi fa fa, mi re mi do, do mi re so, ti re do

D Major

Using the C, G, and F scales as models, it is not difficult to prepare the D major scale.

Exercise 9

Add the necessary sharps or flats to the notes to make a major scale starting on D. Mark the whole and half steps and the four-note patterns.

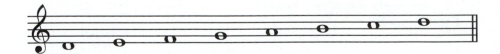

There should be sharps on F and C.

Reading Pitch

The key signature for D major appears in the following folk song, *Sweet Betsy from Pike*.

SWEET BETSY FROM PIKE

AMERICAN FOLK SONG

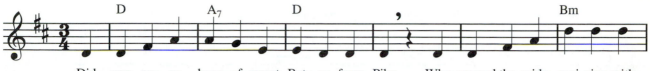

Did you ev-er hear of sweet Bet-sy from Pike, Who crossed the wide prai-ries with

her hus-band Ike, With two yoke of ox-en, a big yel-low dog, A — tall Shang-hai

roost-er, and one spot-ted hog? Sing-ing too-ra-li too-ra-li too-ra-li-ay.

2. The alkali desert was burning and bare,
   And Ike cried in fear, "We are lost, I declare!
   My dear old Pike County, I'll come back to you!"
   Said Betsy, "You'll go by yourself if you do." *(Refrain)*

3. They swam the wide rivers and crossed the high peaks.
   They camped on the prairie for weeks upon weeks;
   They fought with the Indians with musket and ball;
   And they reached California in spite of it all. *(Refrain)*

B-Flat Major

Scales may begin on black keys as well as on white keys. The B-flat major scale begins on a black key.

Exercise 10

Add the necessary flats to make a major scale starting on B-flat. Mark the whole and half steps, and show the four-note patterns, as before.

Besides the B-flats at the beginning and the end of the scale, a flat is required on E.

Exercise 11

Sing *Skinnamarink* in the key of B-flat major.

SKINNAMARINK

Tin Pan Alley Song

Skin-na-ma-rink a-dink a-dink, skin-na-ma-rink a-doo, I love

you; Skin-na-ma-rink a-dink a-dink, skin-na-ma-rink a-doo,

Yes, I do. I love you in the morn - ing and

in the af - ter-noon, I love you in the eve - ning, 'neath the sil - v'ry moon.

Skin-na-ma-rink a-dink a-dink, skin-na-ma-rink a-doo, I love you.

Finding the Keynote

A scale may begin on any note, and each one requires a particular key signature to produce the major scale pattern. Up to seven sharps or flats may appear in the key signature, but children's songs rarely have more than three or four. You must remember that the major key with no sharps or flats is C. The keynote, *do* (1), can be located for any other signature by a simple formula.

The keynote of a sharp key is always a half step above the last sharp, that is, the sharp farthest to the right in the signature. The last sharp is *ti* in the scale, and *do* is just above *ti*.

Reading Pitch

The keynote of a flat key is always the same as the next-to-last flat, that is, the flat second from the right in the signature. The last flat in the signature is *fa,* and *do* also can be located by counting down the scale from the last flat: *fa, mi, re, do*. This system must be used for F major, which has only one flat.

The following table gives the commonly used major key signatures and their names and keynotes. Key signatures with more than four sharps or flats are rare in school music.

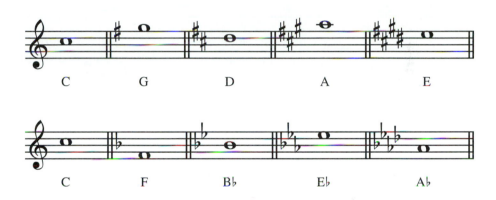

The Bass Clef

The low pitches sung by bass voices and played by the left hand on the piano cannot be written conveniently in the treble clef. For the pitches in this range another clef sign is used, the *bass clef*. This clef circles around the note F.

𝄢

The bass clef is also used for tenor voices when they are written on the same staff with the basses and for the large (low-pitched) instruments.

The function of the bass clef is most easily understood as a continuation downward from the treble clef. The note written on the first ledger line below the treble staff and the one written on the first ledger line above the bass staff are the same, *middle C*. Middle C is the C near the center of the piano keyboard and just below the lock or trademark.

A treble staff and a bass staff are combined to notate music for piano and mixed voices. The notes in the treble clef are played by the right hand on the piano and those in the bass clef by the left hand. For voices, the soprano and alto (women's) parts are in the treble clef, and the tenor and bass (men's) parts are in the bass clef. The same music can be used for piano and mixed voices, and this is usual in collections of familiar songs and hymns. The bar lines extend through both staffs in piano music except when there are words between the staffs.

Exercise 12

The notation for *Joyful, Joyful We Adore Thee* is typical of multipurpose music intended for both singing and playing. Sing the song, in parts if possible, with the piano. The soprano and bass lines can be reinforced by melody instruments or played independently as a duet.

JOYFUL, JOYFUL, WE ADORE THEE

Henry van Dyke

Ludwig van Beethoven

1. Joy - ful, joy - ful, we a - dore Thee, God of glo - ry, Lord of love;
2. All Thy works with joy sur - round Thee, Earth and heav'n re - flect Thy rays,
3. Thou art giv - ing and for - giv - ing, Ev - er bless - ing, ev - er blest,

Hearts un - fold like flow'rs be - fore Thee, Op - 'ning to the sun a - bove.
Stars and an - gels sing a - round Thee, Cen - ter of un - brok - en praise.
Well - spring of the joy of liv - ing, O - cean - depth of hap - py rest!

Melt the clouds of sin and sad - ness; Drive the dark of doubt a - way;
Field and for - est, vale and mount - ain, Flow - 'ry mead - ow, flash - ing sea,
Thou our Fa - ther, Christ our Broth - er— All who live in love are Thine;

Giv - er of im - mor - tal glad - ness, Fill us with the light of day!
Sing - ing bird and flow - ing foun - tain Call us to re - joice in Thee.
Teach us how to love each oth - er, Lift us to the joy di - vine.

Exercise 13

Sing the Revolutionary War ballad *Johnny Has Gone for a Soldier*. Notice how different it sounds from the songs you have been singing.

JOHNNY HAS GONE FOR A SOLDIER

IRISH/AMERICAN FOLK SONG

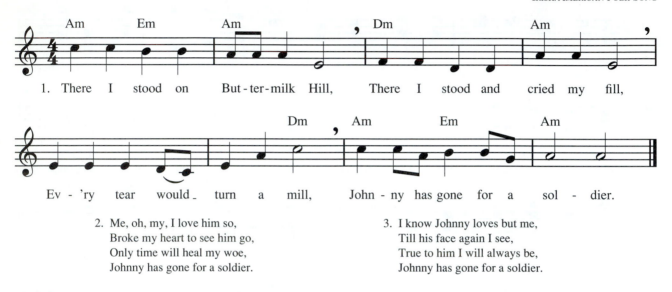

1. There I stood on But-ter-milk Hill, There I stood and cried my fill,

Ev-'ry tear would turn a mill, John-ny has gone for a sol-dier.

2. Me, oh, my, I love him so,
Broke my heart to see him go,
Only time will heal my woe,
Johnny has gone for a soldier.

3. I know Johnny loves but me,
Till his face again I see,
True to him I will always be,
Johnny has gone for a soldier.

Minor Songs and Scales

The sound of *Johnny Has Gone for a Soldier* is different from that of the songs in the preceding section because it is in a minor key, A minor. The notes of the melody (arranged as a scale starting on A) have the pattern of whole steps and half steps shown. The scale with this pattern of whole steps and half steps is a *natural minor* scale. The A natural minor scale is written without sharps or flats and is played on the white keys of the piano. Play the scale ascending and descending.

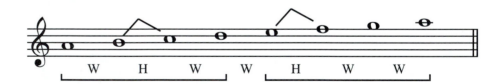

Exercise 14

Sing *Johnny Has Gone for a Soldier* again, and listen for the distinctive minor quality produced by the descending line—C, B, A—in the first two measures and the embellished repetition of the same line in the last two measures.

The key signature for A minor is the same as for C major—no sharps or flats. The major key and the minor key with the same signature are *relative keys*. C is the *relative major* of A minor; A is the *relative minor* of C major. The same syllables are used for relative keys. Any natural minor scale is like its relative major scale starting on *la* (6).

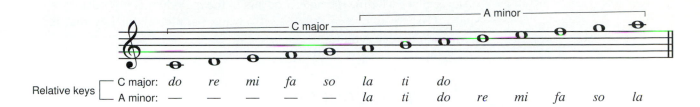

Relative keys	C major:	*do*	*re*	*mi*	*fa*	*so*	*la*	*ti*	*do*					
	A minor:	—	—	—	—	—	*la*	*ti*	*do*	*re*	*mi*	*fa*	*so*	*la*

The minor key and the major key with the same keynote are *parallel keys*. For example, A minor is the parallel minor of A major, and A major is the parallel major of A minor. Since parallel scales have the same keynote, it would seem logical to use the same syllables for the corresponding scale degrees and to change the vowel sound for the third degree from *mi* in major to *me* (pronounced "may") in minor, as shown. This system has the advantage of calling the keynote *do* in both major and minor and the other notes with similar functions by the same syllable names.

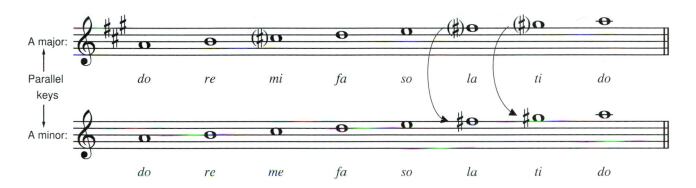

The syllables for natural minor are given in both systems. In natural minor the third, sixth, and seventh degrees of the scale are a half step lower than the corresponding degrees of the parallel major scale, and the vowel sounds are changed accordingly to *me, le,* and *te* (see the chromatic scale, p. 52).

Exercise 15

Sing the A natural minor scale ascending and descending with both sets of syllables, and discuss the relative merits of the two systems.

	la	*ti*	*do*	*re*	*mi*	*fa*	*so*	*la*	*la*	*so*	*fa*	*mi*	*re*	*do*	*ti*	*la*
	do	*re*	*me*	*fa*	*so*	*le*	*te*	*do*	*do*	*te*	*le*	*so*	*fa*	*me*	*re*	*do*

Exercise 16

Sing *Dame Get Up,* or listen while it is played. The key is A minor, but observe that each time the note G occurs in the melody it is preceded by a sharp. G-sharp is one of the notes from the parallel major key that is frequently used in A minor.

DAME, GET UP

ENGLISH CAROL

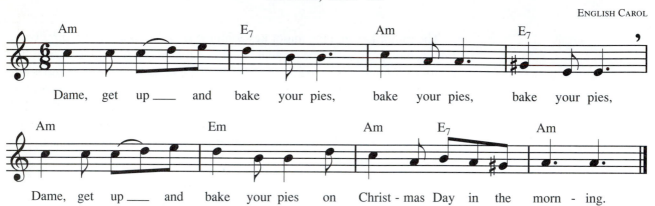

Dame, get up ___ and bake your pies, bake your pies, bake your pies,

Dame, get up ___ and bake your pies on Christ - mas Day in the morn - ing.

G-sharp is used consistently in the melody and also in the chords indicated for *Dame Get Up.* When only the seventh degree of the parallel major key is used in a minor key, the form of minor is *harmonic minor.* The syllables for harmonic minor are given in both systems. Sing the A harmonic minor scale ascending and descending with both sets of syllables or with the one adopted for class use.

| la | ti | do | re | mi | fa | si | la | | la | si | fa | mi | re | do | ti | la |
| do | re | me | fa | so | le | ti | do | | do | ti | le | so | fa | me | re | do |

Exercise 17

Follow the notation while the teacher plays *Charlie Is My Darling* until the melody is familiar. Then, sing the song.

CHARLIE IS MY DARLING

ENGLISH FOLK SONG

Char - lie   is   my   dar - ling,   my   dar - ling,   my   dar - ling,

Char - lie   is   my   dar - ling,   the   young   chev - a - lier. _____

Verse

'Twas   on   a   Mon - day   morn - ing   right   ear - ly   in   the   year, _____

When _ Char - lie came   to   our ____ town, the _ young _ chev - a - lier. _____

Charlie Is My Darling begins and ends on A and is in the key of A minor, but it contains more different notes than have been found in any scale previously. Write all of the notes used in *Charlie Is My Darling* on the staff in ascending order between the C below the staff and the C on the staff.

The melody of *Charlie Is My Darling* uses all of the notes of the A natural minor scale plus F-sharp and G-sharp borrowed from the parallel major scale. The notes between A and E are the same in all forms of the A minor scale. The notes ascending between E and A in *Charlie Is My Darling* are F, F-sharp, G, and G-sharp. The scale containing all of the notes in *Charlie Is My Darling* is the *melodic minor* form of the A minor scale. Melodic minor scales are not regarded as nine-tone scales but as a seven-tone scale ascending and a different seven-tone scale descending. The descending melodic minor scale is the same as the descending natural minor scale. Sing the melodic minor scale on A ascending and descending with the syllables of your choice.

Melodic Minor

| la | ti | do | re | mi | fi | si | la | | la | so | fa | mi | re | do | ti | la |
| do | re | me | fa | so | la | ti | do | | do | te | le | so | fa | me | re | do |

E Minor

Minor keys other than A minor have one or more sharps or flats in the key signature. The key signature for E minor is one sharp, the same as for G major.

Exercise 18

All the Pretty Little Horses is in the key of E minor. As you sing the song, notice the prominence of the keynote at the beginning and ending of the phrases.

ALL THE PRETTY LITTLE HORSES

AMERICAN LULLABY

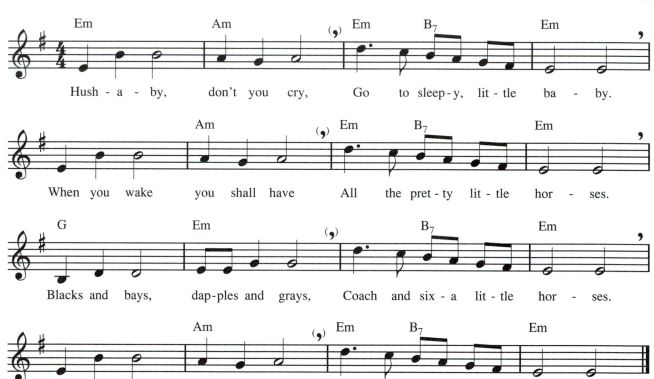

Hush - a - by, don't you cry, Go to sleep-y, lit - tle ba - by.

When you wake you shall have All the pret - ty lit - tle hor - ses.

Blacks and bays, dap-ples and grays, Coach and six - a lit - tle hor - ses.

Hush - a - by, don't you cry, Go to sleep-y, lit - tle ba - by.

Exercise 19

Write the key signature for E minor on the staff, and then write in scale order the notes used in *All the Pretty Little Horses*. What is the form of minor?

The distinctions between the various forms of minor exist more in theory than in practice, especially when the melodies are considered without reference to harmony. Minor melodies often have only five or six different notes, and the scale tones omitted are often the ones that distinguish the various forms of minor.

G Minor

When Johnny Comes Marching Home is in the key of G minor. The key signature for G minor is two flats (B-flat and E-flat), and that key signature is used even though there is no E, flat or natural, in the melody or chords. There are F-naturals, agreeing with the key signature, and F-sharps, borrowed from the parallel major, in both the melody and chords. Listen for the effect of these features as you sing the song, preferably with an accompaniment.

WHEN JOHNNY COMES MARCHING HOME

Louis Lambert   Louis Lambert

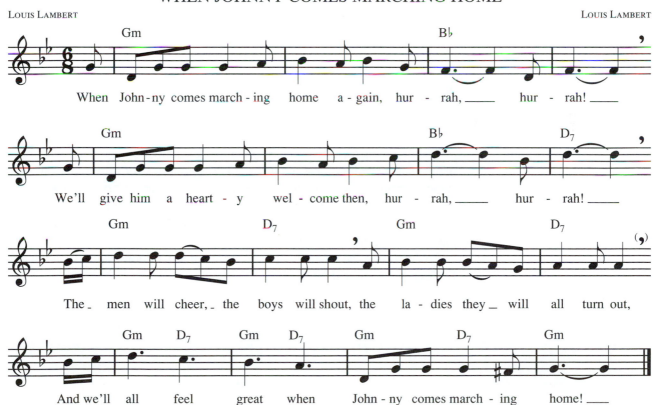

When John-ny comes march-ing home a - gain, hur - rah, ___ hur - rah! ___

We'll give him a heart - y wel - come then, hur - rah, ___ hur - rah! ___

The _ men will cheer, _ the boys will shout, the la - dies they _ will all turn out,

And we'll all feel great when John - ny comes march - ing home! ___

Since *When Johnny Comes Marching Home* has both F-naturals and F-sharps in the melody and harmony and these two notes occur only in the melodic form of G minor, the key of the song is G melodic minor.

Minor Key Signatures

Songs in minor keys can be distinguished from those in major keys by comparing the last note of the melody with the key signature. In terms of major key signatures, songs in major keys end on *do,* and songs in minor keys end on *la,* with very few exceptions.

The same arrangements of sharps and flats are used for both major and minor key signatures. When the keynote of a major key is on a line, the keynote of the relative minor key—the one with the same key signature—is on the next line below. When the keynote of a major key is in a space, the keynote of the relative minor key is in the next space below. If a sharp or a flat in the key signature applies to the keynote, the sharp or flat becomes part of the name of the key. Capital letters indicate major keys and small letters indicate minor keys when they are not otherwise modified.

The following table gives the commonly used minor key signatures with their names and keynotes. Observe that the key signatures for minor keys are the same as for major keys but that the keynotes are different. Also, sharps and flats are (and must be) placed on specific lines and spaces in specific order. As sharps and/or flats increase in number in the key signature, they continue to be placed in the same order each time.

To determine the notes in all three forms of any minor scale, use the Scale Builder in the endleaf pocket.

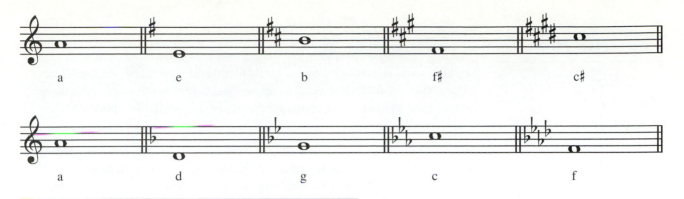

Modes

Major and minor are sometimes referred to as *modes*, the *major mode* and the *minor mode*. *Modal music* usually implies music based on one of the other seven-tone scales with five whole steps and two half steps. Each modal scale has a distinctive pattern of whole steps and half steps and a corresponding distinctive quality. Early liturgical music was modal, as are many folk songs. *Old Joe Clark* is a representative example of the latter.

The keynote of *Old Joe Clark* is D, and it is notated with the key signature for D major—two sharps. However, every time the note C occurs, it is preceded by a natural sign canceling the sharp in the signature. C-natural is also used consistently in the chords. The scale on D with F-sharp and C-natural and half steps between 3–4 and 6–7 is a modal scale (Mixolydian). The striking effect produced by this scale will be apparent immediately when you sing *Old Joe Clark*.

OLD JOE CLARK

AMERICAN FOLK SONG

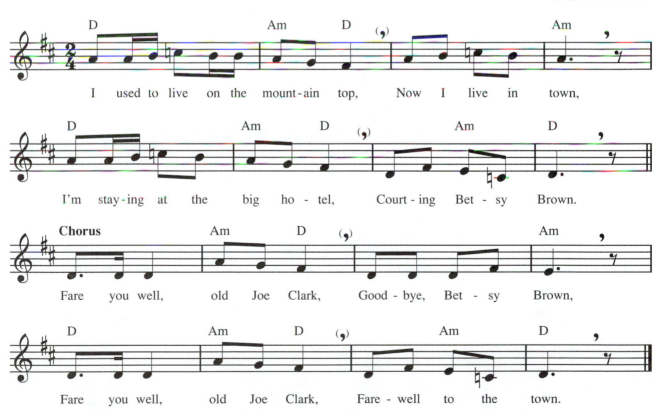

Exercise 20

Adding new verses to traditional melodies is a time-honored custom. Make up additional verses fitting the sprightly mood and rhythms of *Old Joe Clark*. Then, sing the melody several times using the new words to become thoroughly acquainted with the unique quality of this particular mode.

Each of the other modes has a similar characteristic quality resulting from the one note in its scale that distinguishes it from major or minor. Songs you sing and hear that differ from the major, minor, and pentatonic models are based on one of the modal scales.

Familiar tunes can be changed easily from major to minor by using the parallel minor key.

Exercise 21

Sing *The Pumpkin Man*, which is composed here in the key of F minor. Now sing *The Muffin Man* words (p. 328) and change the tune to F major.

K–4, 6c
5–8, 6c

THE PUMPKIN MAN

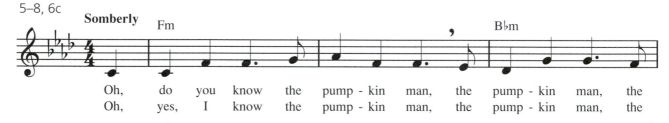

Oh,   do   you   know   the   pump - kin   man,   the   pump - kin   man,   the
Oh,   yes,   I   know   the   pump - kin   man,   the   pump - kin   man,   the

pump-kin man. Oh,   do   you know the pump-kin man that lives in Scar - y   Lane?
pump-kin man. Oh,   yes,   I   know the pump-kin man that lives in Scar - y   Lane.

Exercise 22

Do the same with *Oh, My Darling Clementine* (p. 58, in the key of F). Change the words to *Monster Frankenstein* and sing in the key of F minor.

K–4, 6c
5–8, 6c

MONSTER FRANKENSTEIN

Mary Lou Frierdich

Tune: *Darling Clementine*

1. In a cas - tle   in a   mount - ain,   near the dark   and murk - y   Rhine,
2. In a   grave - yard   near the   cast - le,   when the moon   re - fused to   shine,

Dwelt a   doc - tor,   the con - coct - or   of   the   mon - ster   Fran - ken - stein.
He dug for   nos - es   and   for "toes - es"   for   his   mon - ster   Frank - en - stein.

Chorus

Oh   my   mon - ster,   oh   my   mon - ster,   oh   my   mon - ster,   Frank - en - stein,

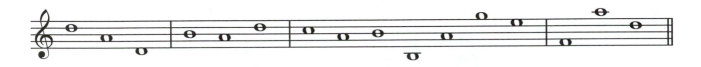

You   were   built   to   last   for - ev - er.   Dread - ful   scar - y   Frank - en - stein.

Suggested Assignments

K–4, 5b, 5d
5–8, 5c, 6c

1. Write the line notation for *Are You Sleeping*. If you do not remember the tune, refer to the notation in this chapter.
2. Give the appropriate hand signal for each note as you sing ascending and descending major scales with the syllables.
3. When the teacher establishes a key and gives hand signals, respond with the corresponding syllables and pitches.
4. Give the hand signals for the pitches as you sing familiar songs. Begin with songs that are slow and in which stepwise motion predominates.
5. The following note patterns spell words. Write the words.

6. Write the following words as note patterns on the staff.

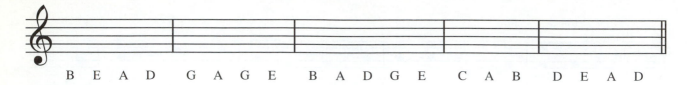

B E A D   G A G E   B A D G E   C A B   D E A D

7. Write five additional words as note patterns.

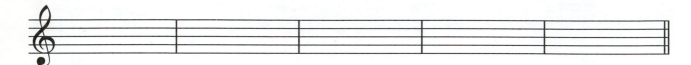

8. On a separate sheet of staff paper, write the melody of *Are You Sleeping* in the key of C major. Use the syllable and number names given with the notation on page 56 as a guide in the process of changing the key and pitch level, or—to use the technical term—*transposing* the melody from the key of G major to the key of C major.

9. Mark the half steps in the following major scales.

10. Add sharps or flats to the following notes as required to make major scales.

11. Write the key signatures for D major and E-flat major.

12. Name the following major keys, and write the keynotes on the staff.

13. Mark the half steps in each minor scale, and name the form of minor.

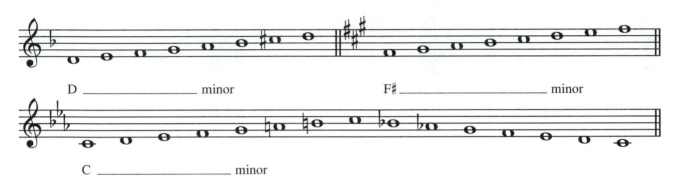

D _____ minor   F♯ _____ minor

C _____ minor

14. Provide the key signature and add sharps, flats, or naturals as required for the scales indicated.

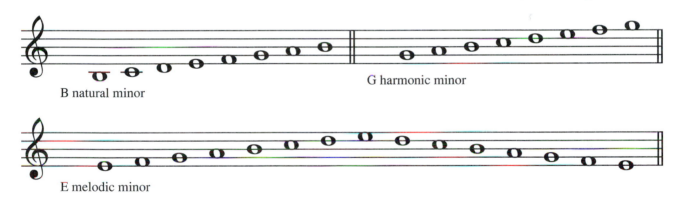

B natural minor

G harmonic minor

E melodic minor

15. Give the syllable names (in the system designated by the teacher or of your choice) and the number names for the notes in the following minor scale.

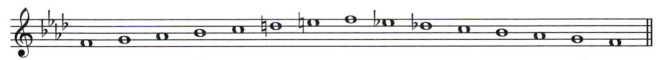

Syllables:

Numbers:

16. Find three songs in minor keys, name the songs, and identify the source. Copy the key signatures and write the first and last notes on the staff provided. Give the key and indicate whether the form of minor is natural, harmonic, or melodic.

1. Name _____ Source _____
2. Name _____ Source _____
3. Name _____ Source _____

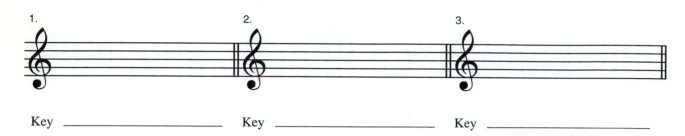

1.   2.   3.

Key _____   Key _____   Key _____

17. Identify the quality of *Sakura* (p. 320) and write the notes used in the melody as a scale.

CHAPTER 4

Combining Musical Sounds

Musical sounds are combined in a variety of ways. In succession, musical sounds become melodies. Melodies joined together, as they are in rounds and partner songs, produce *counterpoint*. Three or more notes sounding together form a *chord*, and successions of chords result in *harmony*. Musical sounds are also organized into small structural units and larger musical forms. The smallest combination of musical sounds consists of just two notes.

Intervals

An *interval* is the distance in pitch between two notes. Two notes written or sounded in succession form a *melodic interval*. Two notes aligned vertically or sounded together form a *harmonic interval*. The names of both melodic and harmonic intervals are determined by the number of scale degrees spanned by the two notes, including those occupied by the notes. Play the following intervals on the piano, and associate the sounds with the interval names. The two notes can be played with the index finger of each hand.

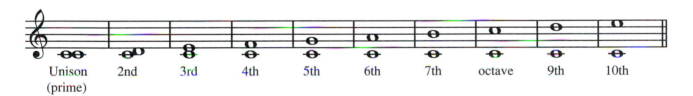

| Unison (prime) | 2nd | 3rd | 4th | 5th | 6th | 7th | octave | 9th | 10th |

The basic interval names are modified by terms indicating the type and the exact size or *quality* of the intervals. The intervals above the keynote in a major scale—above C in C major, for example—are *major* (M) or *perfect* (P) as indicated. The numbers in parentheses indicate the number of half steps (semitones) within the specified intervals.

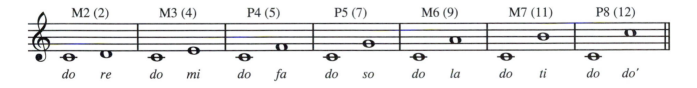

| M2 (2) | M3 (4) | P4 (5) | P5 (7) | M6 (9) | M7 (11) | P8 (12) |

| *do* | *re* | *do* | *mi* | *do* | *fa* | *do* | *so* | *do* | *la* | *do* | *ti* | *do* | *do'* |

Exercise 1

Sing the preceding melodic intervals with the syllables, and associate the sounds with the interval names. Observe that when singing the intervals in succession, each interval except the octave is sung both ascending and descending.

In natural minor scales the third, sixth, and seventh degrees are a half step lower than the corresponding degrees in major scales. Intervals that are a half step smaller than the corresponding major interval are *minor* (m) intervals. Fourths, fifths, and octaves are called *perfect* intervals in both major and minor scales. The syllable names of the minor scale notes are given in both systems for C minor.

M2 (2)	m3 (3)	P4 (5)	P5 (7)	m6 (8)	m7 (10)	P8 (12)
do re	do me	do fa	do so	do le	do te	do do'
la ti	la do	la re	la mi	la fa	la so	la la'

Exercise 2

Sing the intervals between the notes of the C minor scale using the syllables of the designated system or the one you prefer. If the pitches are insecure, assist the singing with the piano or any other available instrument.

The intervals of the C major and C natural minor scales are located on the piano keyboard as shown.

Minor

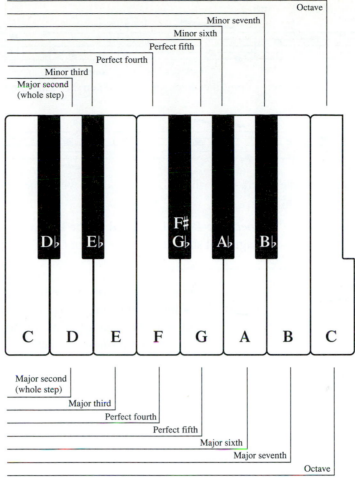

Octave

Minor seventh

Minor sixth

Perfect fifth

Perfect fourth

Minor third

Major second
(whole step)

Db Eb F# Gb Ab Bb

C D E F G A B C

Major second
(whole step)

Major third

Perfect fourth

Perfect fifth

Major sixth

Major seventh

Octave

Major

5–8, 6c

Exercise 3

The numbers 2 (second), 3 (third), etc., used to identify intervals are determined by counting the number of lines and spaces spanned by the two notes. The lines and/or spaces occupied by the notes are included in the count. The quality of the intervals—major (M), minor (m), or perfect (P)—is determined by the number of half steps (semitones) spanned by the two notes (see the major and minor scale examples). Write above the staff the number identifying the interval between each pair of notes in the melody of *Rockabye Baby.* More advanced students can add the letter indicating the quality of each interval. The first five intervals have been named to serve as models.

ROCKABYE, BABY

Rockabye Baby is notated in the key of C for the interval analysis. For singing, it should be in the key of G, a fourth lower.

Interval Chart

It is important to learn the concept of intervals and their characteristic sounds because everything that is sung and played—every pitched musical composition—is based upon the distance from note to note and interval to interval. The following chart will help students visualize intervals in succession.

Interval Chart

Interval	Number of Half Steps
PU (unison)	0
m2	1
M2	2
m3	3
M3	4
P4	5
A4/d5 (augmented or diminished)	6
P5	7
m6	8
M6	9
m7	10
M7	11
PO (octave)	12

Exercise 4

Using the chart above, measure the size of each interval by counting half steps, and place the correct answer underneath. (The first two examples have been done.) Use the keyboard here or the one found in the back pocket of the textbook to complete the exercise.

Combining Musical Sounds

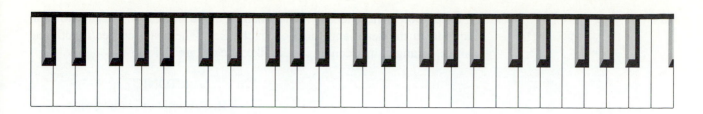

7 half steps = P5   1 half step = m2

Triads

5–8, 6c

Any three notes written vertically or sounded together constitute a chord, but the most usual chord structures contain three alternate scale tones that can be written on consecutive lines or in consecutive spaces of the staff. Three-tone chords of this type are called *triads*—the basic units of harmony.

Triads written with all three notes on lines or in spaces are identified by the letter name of the lowest note—the *root* of the chord. The letter name by itself indicates a *major triad* consisting, from the root up, of a major third and a minor third. The letter name followed by a small "m" indicates a *minor triad* consisting of a minor third and a major third. The letter name followed by "dim" indicates a *diminished triad* consisting of two minor thirds. A triad is associated with each degree of the scale. The type of triad depends on the location in the scale and the mode—major, minor, etc. The triads of C major are identified by letter name and type and by scale degree, written as a Roman numeral.

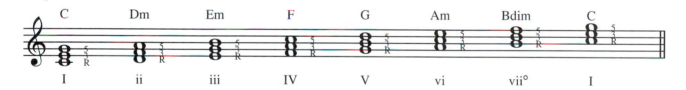

The notes of a given triad are always the same, but they can be arranged in any order. A triad is in *root position* when the root is the lowest note. A triad is *inverted* when one of the other notes is lowest. The letter name and number identifying a triad are the same no matter how its notes are arranged. Listen while the teacher plays the following C triads on the piano with the sustaining (right) pedal down to emphasize their similarity.

In addition to the letter and number names, chords have names related to their location in the scale and function in the key. The scale-degree/functional names, arranged in ascending order like a scale, are as follows:

I. TONIC

VII. Subtonic or leading tone

VI. Submediant

V. DOMINANT

IV. SUBDOMINANT

III. Mediant

II. Supertonic

I. TONIC

All of the chords are used, but those built on the first, fourth, and fifth degrees of the scale with their names (TONIC, SUBDOMINANT, DOMINANT) in full capitals predominate. These are the *primary chords*. Though other chords occur incidentally in the harmonies indicated for the songs, only the three primary chords are considered further in this study.

The primary triads (I, IV, and V) are major in major keys and minor in natural minor, but the harmonic form of minor is ordinarily used for chords. In harmonic minor the dominant (V) chord is major, as it is in major keys. The primary triads of C, F, and G major and A harmonic minor are given with their letter and number names.

Notice that the same triad occurs in different keys. For example, the C chord is I in the key of C, IV in the key of G, and V in the key of F.

Dominant Seventh Chords

Another third is frequently added to triads. The added note is a seventh above the root (bottom note) of triads arranged in thirds. Four-note chords built in thirds are called *seventh chords,* and the one on the fifth degree of the scale is the *dominant seventh chord*. A dominant seventh chord is indicated by a 7 following the Roman numeral V or the letter name of the triad. The V7 chords in the keys of C major, F major, and G major are shown.

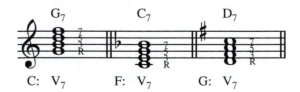

The V7 chords in the harmonic form of the parallel minor keys, C minor, F minor, and G minor would be the same, but the key signatures would be different, and the next note above the root of the chords would require a natural or a sharp.

The V7 chords can be played more easily without changing the effect appreciably by leaving out one note. The name and symbol for the chord are not affected by the omission of this note. Whenever V7 is indicated or required, this form of the chord may be used. Compare the sound of the complete and incomplete V7 chords. Acoustically, the difference is very difficult to discern!

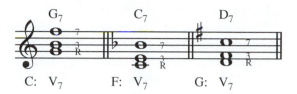

The notes in incomplete V7 chords can be rearranged and the chords inverted, as shown below.

Chord Progressions

In chord *progressions*—that is, going from one chord to another—the individual notes move smoothly and logically from chord tone to chord tone. Notes common to two chords ordinarily are repeated, and the other notes move stepwise to a note in the second chord. These principles are illustrated in all of the usual primary chord progressions in C major. If the study of chapter 7, Playing Keyboard Instruments, has been integrated with the study of this chapter, you may be able to play the following progressions by this point.

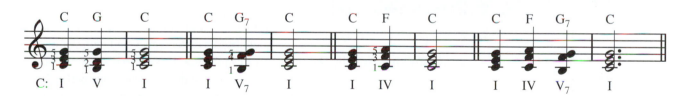

Exercise 5

Use a set of ToneChimes, Chimettes, or handbells to play the following chord-progression exercise. Individuals can ring one chime/bell to represent a member or note of one chord, or ring one chime/bell with each hand to represent different notes of one or more chords. If the set of bells or chimes has multiple octaves, the sound will be enhanced.

5–8, 6c

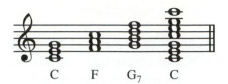

C   F   G₇   C

Exercise 6

Identify the notes in each chord of *Twinkle, Twinkle, Little Star* (p. 158). Practice ringing each chord several times by using ToneChimes, Chimettes, or handbells. Once the sequence or chord progression becomes easy to play, ring it in block chords to accompany the melody of *Twinkle, Twinkle, Little Star*. Other students can sing the melody of the song or it can be played on various melody instruments.

Phrases and Sentences

In music, as in language, ideas are expressed in *phrases* and *sentences*, also called *periods*. In this book *sentence* is used because it parallels the usage in language. Sentences are complete, more or less independent, units of musical form that most often consist of two four-measure phrases. The two phrases in a typical sentence have an antecedent-consequent relationship. An incomplete idea in the first phrase is brought to a satisfactory conclusion in the second or final phrase.

Each phrase ends with a *cadence*. A cadence is a closing effect created by appropriate melodic, rhythmic, and harmonic formulas that function like the corresponding vocal inflections in speech and the punctuation in written language. Just as there are commas and periods in language, in music there are *incomplete cadences* (i.c.) and *complete cadences* (c.c.). The final phrases of sentences end with complete cadences. Other phrases end with incomplete cadences.

In the following examples typical musical sentences are diagrammed. A line extending under the words of a phrase turns up at the cadence, and the type of cadence is indicated. Phrases are identified by lowercase letters. When two phrases begin alike but end differently, the second is assigned a different letter, but the letter of the first is added in parentheses to show the relationship.

K–4, 6c

Exercise 7

Bow, Belinda is a concise two-phrase sentence in which the two phrases begin alike and end differently. Sing *Bow, Belinda* and observe the different effect of the incomplete and complete cadences.

         Combining Musical Sounds

BOW, BELINDA
SINGING GAME

AMERICAN

1. Bow, bow, bow, Be - lin - da; Bow, bow, bow, Be - lin - da;

a   i.c.

Bow, bow, bow, Be - lin - da; Won't you be my dar - ling?

b(a)   c.c.

    2. Join right hands, Belinda, etc.   4. Promenade, Belinda, etc.
    3. Join left hands, Belinda, etc.   5. Circle, all, Belinda, etc.

Exercise 8

Barbara Allen illustrates a two-phrase sentence in which the two phrases are essentially different, though they share certain rhythmic features, which is usual. When the first phrase begins with an upbeat, subsequent phrases generally begin with an upbeat of the same value. Sing the song and notice how the ascending motion from low D to high D in the first phrase is answered by the descending motion from high D to low D in the second phrase.

BARBARA ALLEN

SCOTTISH BALLAD

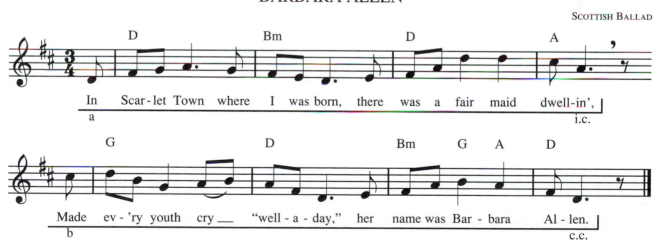

In Scar - let Town where I was born, there was a fair maid dwell - in',

a   i.c.

Made ev - 'ry youth cry — "well - a - day," her name was Bar - bara Al - len.

b   c.c.

Bow, Belinda and *Barbara Allen* illustrate the two most prevalent types of musical sentences. Both consist of two balanced phrases and have an incomplete cadence in the middle and a complete cadence at the end. A high percentage of the sentences in familiar songs and popular music have this basic design.

God Rest You Merry, Gentlemen illustrates some of the irregularities that occur in sentence structures. It has five phrases and four incomplete cadences before the complete cadence at the end. The second phrase is an exact repetition of the first, though with different words. The third phrase introduces new material, which appears only once. The fourth phrase begins on the third beat of the measure, in contrast to the previous phrases, which begin on the fourth beat. A cadence point is reached after only three measures, but the tonic chord is avoided and the phrase is extended to the normal four-measure length. The words "comfort and joy" are repeated to accommodate the extension in the melody. The final phrase is similar to the fourth, but with essential differences. The first full measure is modified, and the extension is dropped. Without the extension, the phrase is only three measures long. The final E is harmonized with the tonic (Em) chord, and the cadence is final.

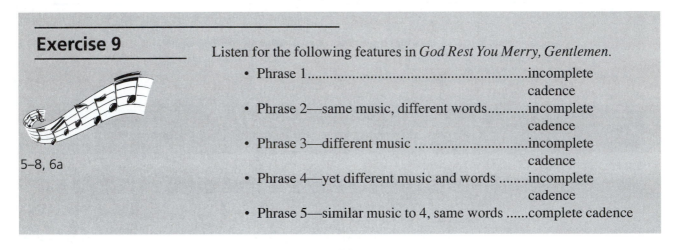

Exercise 9

5–8, 6a

Listen for the following features in *God Rest You Merry, Gentlemen*.

- Phrase 1...incomplete cadence
- Phrase 2—same music, different words...........incomplete cadence
- Phrase 3—different music ....incomplete cadence
- Phrase 4—yet different music and words ....incomplete cadence
- Phrase 5—similar music to 4, same words ......complete cadence

GOD REST YOU MERRY, GENTLEMEN

ENGLISH CAROL

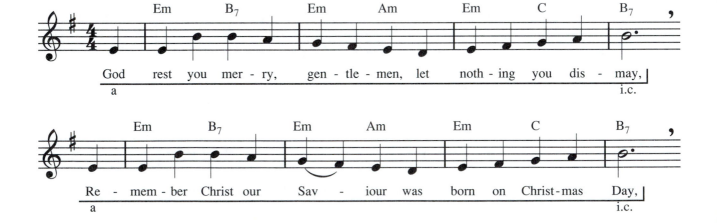

Combining Musical Sounds

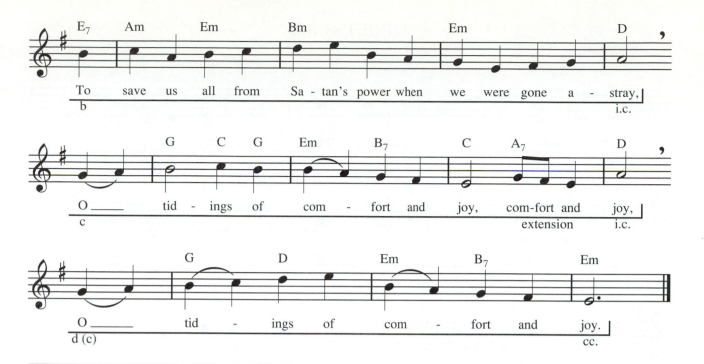

To save us all from Sa - tan's power when we were gone a - stray,

b   i.c.

O ____ tid - ings of com - fort and joy, com-fort and joy,

c   extension   i.c.

O ____ tid - ings of com - fort and joy.

d (c)   cc.

One-Part Form

In music certain structural elements are stated, repeated, restated after contrasting material, and/or varied in patterns perceived as *musical form.* The patterns that occur in simple songs are often classified as *song forms,* though the same patterns also occur in instrumental music where they are more properly called *small forms* or *part forms.* The smallest musical form is a *one-part form.*

When a song consists of a single musical sentence, it contains only one complete idea and is, therefore, a one-part form. The second and any subsequent phrases may begin like the first phrase or have rhythm and pitch figures (motives) derived from it, providing a high degree of unity.

Exercise 10

Bow, Belinda, Barbara Allen, and *God Rest You Merry, Gentlemen,* analyzed in the preceding section, are examples of one-part form. Other examples of one-part form are, in order of complexity, *The Muffin Man* (p. 328), *If You're Happy* (p. 124), *Silent Night* (p. 163), and *When Johnny Comes Marching Home* (p. 69). Sing these songs, and observe how the rhythmic flow and melodic contour interact at cadence points to create closing effects with varying degrees of finality.

Two-Part Form/Binary

The form resulting when two sentences are joined is *two-part form* or *binary form,* though binary sometimes implies a particular pattern of key relationships and repeats. The two sentences must be sufficiently different to provide a degree of contrast, but they typically have many elements in common.

Annie Laurie is a clear example of a two-part form. In form diagrams, sentences are identified by capital letters, phrases by lowercase letters. Phrases may divide into *subphrases,* as they do in this song, but units smaller than a phrase are usually ignored in diagramming musical forms.

ANNIE LAURIE

WILLIAM DOUGLASS

LADY JOHN SCOTT

The two sentences of *Annie Laurie* not only share rhythm patterns; they end similarly. This "rhyming" of parts is an effective unifying device. There is no convenient way to reflect it in form diagrams, but an explicit and descriptive name for binary forms with this feature is *rhymed binary*.

Song forms and their parts may be repeated individually and collectively without altering the basic concept of the form or the name for it. The musical design represented by A A A, which results when a one-part melody is used for a song with three verses, is still regarded as a one-part form.

Songs with a chorus or refrain usually have two parts, both beginning and ending in the same key. *The Big Corral* is typical of two-part form. The song contains a repeated A section; each A section contains two phrases—a and b. It also contains a repeated B section; each B section contains two phrases—a and b.

THE BIG CORRAL

AMERICAN COWBOY SONG

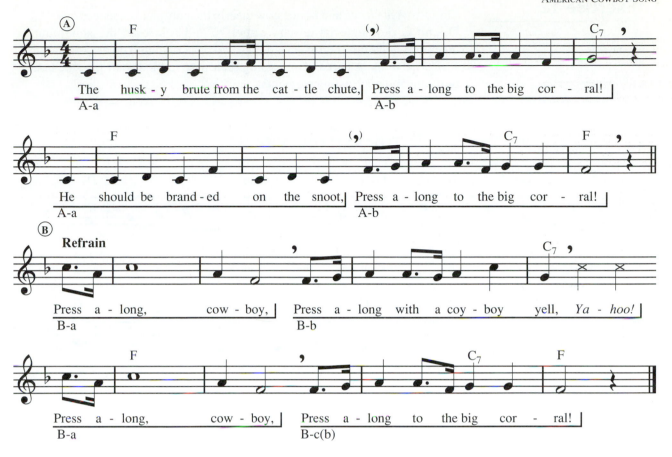

Ⓐ F (,) C₇ ,

The husk-y brute from the cat-tle chute, Press a-long to the big cor - ral!
A-a   A-b

F (,) C₇ F ,

He should be brand-ed on the snoot, Press a-long to the big cor - ral!
A-a   A-b

Ⓑ **Refrain** C₇ ,

Press a - long, cow - boy, Press a-long with a coy-boy yell, *Ya - hoo!*
B-a   B-b

F , C₇ F

Press a - long, cow - boy, Press a - long to the big cor - ral!
B-a   B-c(b)

O Come All Ye Faithful (pp. 216–217) is an example of two-part/binary form in which the A sentence modulates (changes key) from the tonic key (G) to the dominant key (D) before returning to the tonic key for the B sentence.

Exercise 11

K–4, 6a

Sing *Come All Ye Faithful* and listen for the unifying and contrasting elements in the A and B parts.

Three-Part Form/Ternary

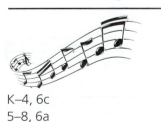

K–4, 6c
5–8, 6a

The musical form with three parts in a statement-departure-return relationship is *three-part form* or *ternary form*. The basic ternary design is represented by the letters A B A; but, more often than not, the first A is repeated immediately. The repetition of A can be written out or indicated by a repeat sign, as in *The Ash Grove*. With the repeat, the song has a total of thirty-two measures (called *bars* in popular music) in an AA B A pattern, the standard length and form of popular songs and much jazz improvisation.

Sing *The Ash Grove* and notice how clearly the complete cadences on G, G, D, and G delineate its ternary structure and reinforce the statement-repetition-departure-return design. The two pairs of eighth notes descending scalewise in the A part and ascending scalewise in the B part provide both unifying and contrasting elements.

THE ASH GROVE

WALES

The ash grove, how ___ grace - ful, how plain - ly ___ 'tis ___ speak - ing,
When o - ver its ___ branch - es the sun - light ___ is ___ break - ing,
A-a   i.c.

The wind through ___ it ___ play - ing has lan - guage for me.
A host of ___ kind ___ fac - es is gaz - ing at me.
A-b   c.c.

The ___ friends of ___ my ___ child - hood a - gain are ___ be - fore me,
B-a   i.c.

Each step wakes ___ a ___ mem - 'ry, as free - ly I roam.
B-b   c.c.

With soft whis - pers ___ lad - en, its leaves rust - le ___ o'er me;
A-a   i.c.

The ash grove, ___ the ___ ash grove that shel - tered my home.
A-b   c.c.

The typical ternary design represented by *The Ash Grove* is modified in many ways. Minimally, a ternary form consists of an opening phrase or sentence, with or without repetition, followed by a contrasting phrase or sentence and a return of the opening idea, which may be varied and abridged. Some of the possible modifications are illustrated in *Simple Gifts*. The first A is not repeated, and the contrasting part is only a phrase. The eight-measure sentence with which the melody begins is reduced to a four-measure phrase when it returns, but the essence of the initial statement is preserved. The melody of *Simple Gifts* is used as one of the themes in Aaron Copland's ballet *Appalachian Spring*. Compare the song with the version of the melody in Copland's orchestral composition.

SIMPLE GIFTS

Most folk and familiar songs have one, two, or three parts and a plan of organization closely related to one of the forms discussed in this chapter. As you sing and listen to songs, consciously strive to recognize their structures.

1. Analyze the intervals between the two parts in *Chopsticks* (p. 209) according to the instructions given for exercise 1 on page 78.
2. Using the primary chord progressions in C major on page 83 as a model, write the following progressions in F major and G major.

5–8, 6c

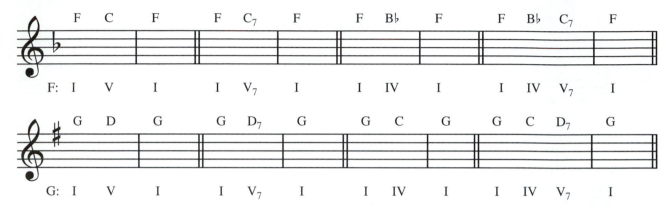

| | F | C | F | | F | C₇ | F | | F | B♭ | F | | F | B♭ | C₇ | F |

F: I V I | I V₇ I | I IV I | I IV V₇ I

| | G | D | G | | G | D₇ | G | | G | C | G | | G | C | D₇ | G |

G: I V I | I V₇ I | I IV I | I IV V₇ I

3. Write the phrase and cadence analysis below the words of *Johnny Has Gone for a Soldier*. The notation is on page 64. Use the analysis of *Barbara Allen* on page 85 as a model.

   There I stood on Buttermilk Hill, There I stood and cried my fill,

   Ev'ry tear would turn a mill, Johnny has gone for a soldier.

4. Write the phrase and cadence analysis below the words of *When Johnny Comes Marching Home*. The notation is on page 69. Use the analysis of *God Rest You Merry, Gentlemen* on pages 86–87 as a model.

   When Johnny comes marching home again, hurrah, hurrah!

   We'll give him a hearty welcome then, hurrah, hurrah!

   The men will cheer, the boys will shout, the ladies they will all turn out,

   And we'll all feel great when Johnny comes marching home!

5. Analyze and name the form of *Joyful, Joyful We Adore Thee* (p. 63). Use the analysis of *Annie Laurie* on page 88 as a model.

   Joyful, joyful we adore Thee, God of glory, Lord of love;

   Hearts unfold like flow'rs before Thee, op'ning to the sun above.

   Melt the clouds of sin and sadness; drive the dark of doubt away;

   Giver of immortal gladness, fill us with the light of day!

6. Analyze and name the form of *We Wish You a Merry Christmas*. The notation is on page 214. It is necessary to make the repeat from the beginning (*D.C.*) to complete the form. Use the analysis of *The Ash Grove* on page 90 and *Simple Gifts* on page 91 as models.

We wish you a merry Christmas, We wish you a merry Christmas,

We wish you a merry Christmas, and a happy New Year!

Good tidings to you, and all of your kin,

Good tidings for Christmas, and a happy New Year!

We wish you a merry Christmas, We wish you a merry Christmas,

We wish you a merry Christmas, and a happy New Year!

7. Analyze and name the form of *Twinkle, Twinkle, Little Star* (p. 158).

Twinkle, twinkle, little star, how I wonder what you are!

Up above the world so high, like a diamond in the sky,

Twinkle, twinkle, little star, how I wonder what you are!

CHAPTER 5

Developing the Singing Voice

Singing is generally recognized as the core of the elementary school music program. Nearly all musical skills and knowledge can be developed through worthwhile singing experiences in the classroom. Therefore, it is important for the elementary teacher to be able to use the singing voice effectively. The purpose of this chapter is to help teachers develop singing skills.

Perhaps the greatest obstacle of the semester for the future teacher is overcoming *the fear of singing.* Everyone who has a larynx has the ability to phonate sound—to sing! Elementary children do not judge their teacher's singing voice as critically as the teacher may. If the classroom teacher can sing enthusiastically and in tune from a given pitch with a pleasant voice quality, he or she will be able to work with students given all of the other teaching aids available.

The self-conscious college student needs to gain confidence through knowledge and experience in order to be comfortable with and well-prepared in his/her own singing voice and in his/her teaching of singing to children in the classroom. If the teacher possesses a basic understanding of both adult and children's voices, his/her fear should turn into the production of positive and pleasurable group (and individual) classroom singing activities.

We all possess the following "voices":

1. Speaking
2. Shouting
3. Singing (humming)
4. Laughing and crying
5. Whispering
6. Whistling

All of us (children and adults alike) are capable of great flexibility with our voices. Just try each of the above entries in or out of sequence. First, we must realize, however, that with each of the "voices," we have the ability to imitate high and low sounds by utilizing various aspects of the vocal mechanism called voice registers.

Voice Registers

Even though voice teachers rarely agree and have not developed a common vocabulary about vocal registration, most concur that essentially there are two voice registers in singing—the head and chest registers. One set of throat muscles controls the vocal mechanism for the upper register, while the resonating head cavities are used to resonate the tone. The other set controls the lower register, with the chest cavities as resonators. The former is frequently referred to, especially in children's singing, as *head voice* and the latter as *chest voice.* The *approximate* range of these two registers follows (for treble voices):

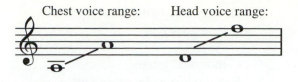

Chest voice range: Head voice range:

The Child's Singing Voice

K–4, 1a
5–8, 1a

The ideal singing voices of children have a light, high, flutelike quality. The sound becomes noticeably more beautiful as they sing higher on the treble staff when they are singing freely and easily. This is evidence that the children are using head voice. Head-voice singing is a desired goal for classroom singing in all the grades.

The trend today, however, is to write children's songs in their easiest singing range (middle C to C), probably to encourage more participation from boys and some girls. As the children gain experience, it is recommended that these songs be transposed upward to facilitate beautiful *head-voice* singing (when feasible).

One of the most important procedures for teachers to remember in developing the head voice is to pitch the songs accurately in the written keys, especially since these have been selected carefully by the nation's leading music educators. It also helps if the classroom singing is light, free, and unforced at all times. Current research indicates that boys' voices are starting to change as early as fifth grade. These young men may be unstable singers, and it is at this time that the *cambiata* voice needs understanding, encouragement, and guidance to sing wherever most comfortable—in the head voice *or* an octave below.

The Classroom Teacher's Singing Voice

Because of a lack of experience in "finding" their vocal registers, many female elementary school teachers are more comfortable singing in the alto range, using throaty chest tones. Male teachers, more often than not, like to pitch songs in the low baritone or bass range. Children's songs, however, are written within the easy range of the soprano voice. The most successful female teachers *can* sing from the middle B to the top of the treble staff with a light free tone, and the men can do likewise an octave lower. Male teachers may sing in falsetto, which is easier for both teacher and student. This technique is not difficult for the majority of teachers, even those with limited singing ability. The most important skills to master are the use and control of the head register and the projection of the voice high and forward into the head resonators for the upper tones.

Ways to "Find" the Vocal Registers

By speaking with various voice inflections, the adult and child learner can "find" his or her own vocal registers. Try the following exercises (CD example 1).

1. Imitate common sounds to find the *head voice:*
    —hoot owls
    —wind
    —puppy-dog "whine"
    —Mickey Mouse, etc.

2. Do the same in the *chest registers:*
   —bear growl
   —"jaws"
   —monster "grunts"
3. Blend registers by repeating:
   —high and low siren sounds over and over
   —"The dog runs up the hill and down the hill and up the hill and down the hill," etc., moving up and down with voice inflection as you go higher or lower.
4. Use physical actions as visuals to accompany any of the previous exercises.
5. Play musical examples of today's singers who effectively incorporate both the head and chest voices. Suggestions include "popular" artists Babyface, Harry Connick Jr., Gloria Estefan, Whitney Houston, and Leann Rimes.
6. Have students imitate favorite songs or song-sections with their own voices.
7. With those who continue to have trouble matching pitch, other suggestions for success include:
   a. Place the individual(s) beside (a) strong singer(s)
   b. Have listening and instrument-playing stations available in the classroom to encourage stronger listening or recall skills
   c. Work with the individual alone more than once
   d. Become comfortable singing one very easy song. For example, if the student can sing even the first phrase of "America" with ease, pitch it in various high and low keys to help him experience quick register changes and vocal flexibility.

The following suggestions and exercises are designed specifically to assist teachers in singing children's songs effectively. No attempt has been made to write a complete vocal method, nor is it our aim to develop solo singers. Teachers who find it impossible to sing songs in the written keys may choose to teach them with song bells, the recorder, or by playing the melody line on a keyboard.

Posture and Breathing

K–4, 1a
5–8, 1a

During the singing of the forthcoming exercises and songs, the student will become aware of the need for breath support, especially if asked to sing complete phrases in one breath. Posture and breathing are interrelated in the singing act—without good posture it is impossible to breathe properly.

Exercise 1

Stand erect and poised with heels slightly apart, right foot slightly ahead of the left, weight on the ball of the right foot. Keep the head high and the chin in. Now lift the back part of the top of the head. This exercise tends to straighten the back and lift the chest. It discourages the common bad habit of raising the shoulders and projecting the chin. Think a "high chest" without tightening or crowding the neck.

Exercise 2

Standing

Stand firmly against a door or wall with heels, calves, hips, shoulder blades, and back of head touching. Then step away, trying to keep the line. Have someone check for a perpendicular line extending from earlobe to heel.

Sitting

Sit with both feet placed firmly on the floor (legs are never crossed in singing class), spine straight, chest up, chin in, *body tilted slightly forward*. Be free but poised. When a book is used, hold it upright on the desk. Never bow the head to read music. The ideal situation would be to remove desks from the music area and place music on a sturdy music stand, where students could read at eye level, not having to hold the music.

Exercise 3

Deep breathing is the key to good singing. Poor tone quality, out-of-tune singing, and forced high tones usually result from a lack of breath control. The following suggestions will help develop proper breath support.

Breathing

Place hands firmly on hips with thumbs pressing into the back. Take four short breaths, hold the breath for four counts, exhale in four counts with four impulses. Increase this entire exercise to six and then eight counts or more. You should feel expansion at both the front and back of the waist. If not, and the shoulders and chest rise, reach arms straight up above the head. Try the exercise. Then try again, this time with hands on hips. Repeat until the lower breath impulse is felt.

Inhaling

Whenever there is time in singing, breathe through the nose. This encourages lower rib expansion and depresses the diaphragm, increasing chest capacity for breath intake. Rounding the lips and pronouncing a big "oh" when inhaling through the mouth produces about the same result. Shoulders must remain motionless.

Exhaling

To exhale correctly is more difficult than to inhale correctly. Chest and shoulders must be kept in position during exhalation and never allowed to collapse. In singing, a steady stream of breath must be exhaled with no sudden expulsion of air. An even flow of air continuously pressing against the vocal cords is necessary for the best vocalization.

Visualizing

Bring a sleeping bag to class and have a student lie on it on the floor. Place a book or similar object on the student's diaphragm area (about waist level) and have him/her move it up and down with his/her breath. It will be obvious that other parts of the body—especially the high chest—do *not* need to move during breathing.

Exercise 4

With hands on hips, practice panting. This should give the "feel" of the breath impulse at waist level.

Exercise 5

Take a deep breath and expand at the waist. Exhale slowly and steadily to the end of the breath with a hissing sound, "sss." Turn the head gently back and forth to release any possible tension. Keep a "high chest" to the end of the breath.

Exercise 6

With hands firmly pressed into the waist, take a deep breath and say "hmp," then "ha," sharply; then sing "ha" on G to the end of the breath. A definite impulse should be felt at the waist on all three sounds. Keep the breath against the tone.

The Singing Tone

The high forward placement of head tones is best achieved through the soft, flexible humming of scale passages and easy melodies. The most used hum, "hm," is produced with the lips gently closed. The correct position for this hum is made by singing "ah" and then closing the lips but not the jaw. The singer will feel a slight vibrating sensation at the lips if the placement is correct. This practice helps the student to discover head tones. Make certain that all humming is free and easy, never pinched.

Exercise 7

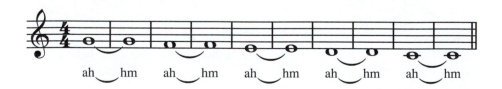

Developing the Singing Voice

Exercise 8

Transpose up by semitones (half steps) and sing softly. To *transpose* music is to change the key from that in which it is written. Each note must be written or performed a certain fixed distance higher or lower, occupying the same position in the new scale that it held in the original one.

ah _____ hm _____

Exercise 9

Transpose upward by semitones.

hm _____

These vocalises should be sung on "ee" and "oo" vowels for additional practice in head resonance focus. The bright vowel sound "ay" can also be used.

Exercise 10

Now practice the entire descending scale with repeated tones. Try to carry a light tone to the last note of the scale. Transpose upward by semitones.

etc.

Ming, ming, ming, ming, ming.	Ming, ming, ming, ming, ming.	Ming, ming, ming, ming, ming.
Zing, zing, zing, zing, zing.	Zing, zing, zing, zing, zing.	Zing, zing, zing, zing, zing.
Moo, mee, moo, mee, moo.	Moo, mee, moo, mee, moo.	Moo, mee, moo, mee, moo.
Nee, nay, nah, noh, noo.	Nee, nay, nah, noh, noo.	Nee, nay, nah, noh, noo.

Develop the sensation of head resonance further by singing familiar, easy songs. Hum lightly, sing on "mee," "moo," "loo," or "la," etc. When using "la," be sure to open the mouth and drop the jaw. Always think an "open throat." Imagine your mouth and throat just before a yawn!

Range and Flexibility

1–8, 5a

Range, flexibility, and tone quality are closely related. The singer who has a wide range and a flexible voice usually can produce a lovely free tone, both high and low. These accomplishments require systematic voice building and development of the vocal organ, the larynx. The following exercises will help develop both range and flexibility. Transpose them upward by semitones to the highest comfortable pitch. Use a bright "ah" sound. Open the mouth and drop the jaw.

Exercise 11

This exercise is especially good for women's voices.

ha ha ha	ha ha ha	ha ha ha	ha	ha _____
ah ah ah	ah ah ah	ah ah ah	ah	ah _____
ho ho ho	ho ho ho	ho ho ho	ho	ho _____
oh oh oh	oh oh oh	oh oh oh	oh	oh _____

Exercise 12

Continue singing on the descending scale.

ah _____   ah _____   ah _____   etc.

Exercise 13

Continue singing on the descending scale.

ah _____   ah _____   ah _____   etc.

Vowels

In singing, the tone is sustained on the vowel. Beauty of tone is dependent largely on correct vowel formations. The fundamental vowel sounds are *ee, ay, ah, oh,* and *oo.* The pure, natural vowel form, not too bright and not too dark, is the main objective.

Some voices require vowel coloring. If a voice is too bright, the "e" as in *he*, the "a" as in *hate*, and the "a" as in *and* very often are shrill and nasal. The vowel form needs to be rounded; "oo," "oh," and "ah" sounds help to round the vowel, and "ee," "eye," and "ay" provide resonance and brightness. Practice saying the sequence ee, ay, ah, oh, oo. The lips are open the widest with the "ah" vowel. The "ay" and "oh" vowels require less lip opening, "ee" and "oo" the least. Sing songs on these vowel forms as necessity dictates. Also practice the following exercises.

Exercise 14

For roundness, round and slightly purse the lips.

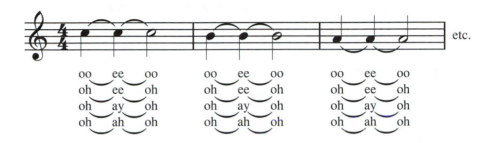

Exercise 15

For brilliance, do not allow "ah" to become "uh." This dulls the tone and flats the pitch.

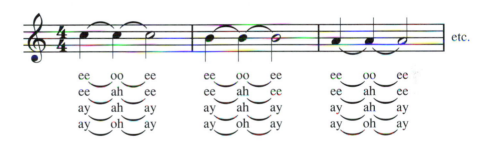

Diphthongs

A diphthong is a double vowel sound. For example, the *e* in *few* is pronounced "feeoo," and the *i* in *mine* is pronounced "maheen." The shorter vowel must be sung quickly. The longer vowel is sustained, as in "feeoo" and "maheen." Practice singing:

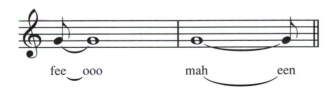

Consonants

Clear, distinct articulation of consonants is necessary for good diction. Remember the following basic principles in articulating consonants.

1. Sing the consonant very quickly.
2. Try to keep an open throat (the sensation experienced just before a yawn).
3. Think the consonant at the same pitch level as the vowel to which it is attached, with a minimum change of the vowel form used.
4. Emphasize slightly the final consonants. Try not to close the mouth on these.
5. Articulate only one of the consonants when one word ends and the next begins with the same consonant, as in *and dear.*

The consonants *t, d, s, z,* and *r* are troublesome for many inexperienced singers. Frequently the letters *t* and *d* are blurred and dropped, especially at word endings. The tendency is to sing "an" for *and,* "liddle" for *little,* and so on.

The consonants *s* and *z* must be articulated very quickly and without accent to avoid a hissing effect. The letter *r* must not be sustained at any time. Emphasize the adjacent vowel sound and pronounce the *r* quickly. The letter *r* at the end of a word may be dropped. Thus *father* is sung "fathuh," not "fathrr."

Consonants are also often classified as *voiced* or *unvoiced* (*voiceless*). With those that are voiced, the larynx must vibrate or phonate. With unvoiced, the larynx is silent and the teeth, tongue, lips, and air produce the sound together.

Exercise 16

Speak the following consonant *sounds* followed by the *words* in each example. Compare the two columns for sound production. Concentrate on listening to the *ending* consonants of the words.

Examples of Voiced Consonants	Examples of Unvoiced Consonants
B (as in Bob)	P (as in pop)
D (as in dad)	T (as in tot)
G (as in ugh)	K (as in kick)
V (as in Viv)	F (as in fluff)

Exercise 17

Now repeat the sounds of the previous consonants in rhythm. Each time repeat the sounds more quickly. Diaphragmatic action can be felt and an aural comparison can be made easily between voiced and unvoiced consonant sounds.

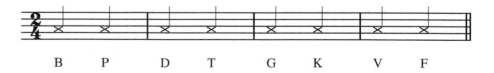

B   P   D   T   G   K   V   F

Developing the Singing Voice

Singing Songs

K–4, 1c
5–8, 1c

Sing the following songs, applying the recommended principles. These songs can also be sung with Autoharp, guitar, and simple piano chording as accompaniment. The chord symbols are provided where each chord change occurs.

HELLO SONG

SHIRLEY McRAE

SHIRLEY McRAE

Hel - lo, hel - lo. I'm so ver - y glad to see you.

Hel - lo, hel - lo. How are you to - day?

TWO, FOUR, SIX, EIGHT

ENGLISH NURSERY RHYME

MARILYN DAVIDSON

Two, four, six, eight, Meet me at the gar-den gate.

If I'm late, don't wait. Two, four, six, eight.

MAIL MYSELF TO YOU

Woody Guthrie

Woody Guthrie

Refrain

I'm gon-na wrap my-self in pa-per, I'm gon-na daub my-self with glue.

End (Fine)

Stick some stamps on top of my head. I'm gon-na mail my-self to you. _____

Verse

1. I'm a-gon-na tie me up in a red string, I'm gon-na tie blue rib-bons, too;
2. When _ you _ see me in your _ mail-box, Cut the _ string and let me out;
3. Take _ me _ out of my wrap-ping _ pa-per. Wash the _ stamps _ off my head;

Go back to the beginning and sing to the End.
(Da Capo al Fine)

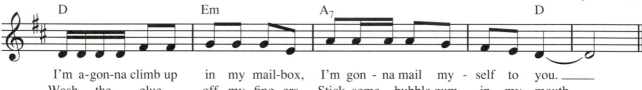

I'm a-gon-na climb up in my mail-box, I'm gon-na mail my-self to you. _____
Wash _ the _ glue _ off my fing-ers, Stick some _ bubble gum in my mouth. _
Pour _ me _ full of ice-cream so-dies, Put me _ in my nice warm bed. _____

LONE STAR TRAIL

American Cowboy Song

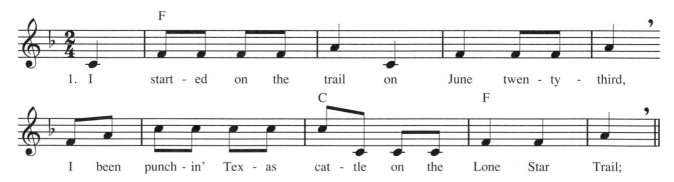

1. I start-ed on the trail on June twen-ty-third,

I been punch-in' Tex-as cat-tle on the Lone Star Trail;

Sing - in' ki yi yip - pi yip - pi yay, yip - pi yay!

Sing - in' ki yi yip - pi yip - pi yay! _____

2. I'm up in the mornin' before daylight,
And before I sleep the moon shines bright. *Refrain*

3. Oh, it's bacon and beans 'most every day,
I'd as soon be a-eatin' prairie hay. *Refrain*

4. My feet are in the stirrups and my rope is on the side,
Show me a horse that I can't ride. *Refrain*

ANIMAL FAIR

AMERICAN FOLK SONG

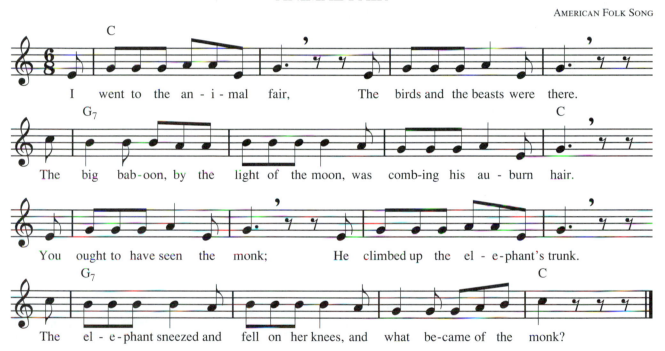

I went to the an - i - mal fair, The birds and the beasts were there.

The big bab - oon, by the light of the moon, was comb-ing his au - burn hair.

You ought to have seen the monk; He climbed up the el - e-phant's trunk.

The el - e-phant sneezed and fell on her knees, and what be-came of the monk?

A RAM SAM SAM

MOROCCAN FOLK SONG

① A ram sam sam, a ram sam sam. Gu - li gu - li gu - li gu - li gu - li ram sam sam.

② A ra - fi, a ra - fi, Gu - li gu - li gu - li gu - li gu - li ram sam sam.

SARASPONDA

Dutch Spinning Song

Sa - ra - spon - da, Sa - ra - spon - da, Sa - ra - spon - da, Ret - set - set! Sa - ra -

spon - da, Sa - ra - spon - da, Sa - ra - spon - da, Ret - set - set! Ah - do - ray - oh! Ah -

do - ray-boom-day - oh! Ah - do - ray-boom-day, Ret - set - set! Ah - say - pa - say - oh!

SIMPLE GIFTS

Shaker Song

Verse

'Tis the gift to be sim - ple, 'tis the gift to be free, 'Tis the

gift to come down where we ought to be. And when we find our-selves in the

place just right, 'Twill be in the val - ley of love and de - light.

Refrain

When true sim - plic - i - ty is gained, To bow and to bend we shan't be a-shamed.

To turn, turn will be our de-light, Till by turn - ing, turn - ing we come 'round right.

Developing the Singing Voice

GO, MY SON

Carnes Burson and Arliene Nofchissey Williams

Carnes Burson and Arliene Nofchissey Williams

1. Practice good singing posture and deep breathing in front of a full-length mirror.
2. Listen to recordings of the songbook series adopted by your state and local elementary school. Carefully study the vocal style and habits of the performing artist. Sing along with the recordings.
3. Sing songs from the various chapters of this book, applying the principles of singing stressed in this chapter.

The classroom teacher should strive in every way to be as good a singer as possible for elementary school children to imitate and follow. It is not necessary to possess a strong solo voice. The aim is to develop a free musical tone, good diction, and an overall enthusiasm for classroom singing activities. With reinforcement and encouragement, classroom teachers may seek additional private or group lessons from a qualified teacher. Most teachers can do it!

CHAPTER 6

Singing for Fun Is Learning!

K–4, 1a, 1c
5–8, 1a, 1c

Singing familiar melodies and fun songs is one of the most enjoyable and effective musical activities of the elementary school program. The value of informal group singing in stimulating interest in vocal music has been demonstrated many times by teachers, camp directors, recreation leaders, and church choir coordinators.

The purpose of this chapter in teacher education classes is threefold: it serves to put musically inexperienced and timid students at ease through informal singing; it helps future teachers, through enjoyable singing, to acquire a repertory of interesting classroom song materials and lesson plan ideas; and it introduces a wide variety of singing topics available for today's classrooms. These well-known and semi-familiar tunes can be taught easily by rote (ear imitation) to both adults and children. Above all, the instructor should cultivate a joyful spirit of singing for pleasure *while* learning.

Most of a child's musical experiences are and should continue to be developed through singing. Somewhere along education's pathway, however, if confidence is not instilled with singing, judgment of this form of self-expression can erode the individual's desire to sing. A student can become increasingly resistant to singing when, for example, a teacher says to him, "You can't sing!" and asks him to quit and "mouth" the words only. This discouraging attitude is destructive to both the student and the others in the classroom. If the teacher has patience and the acquired skills to "sing for fun" first, many hours of *esprit* can be experienced, learning will occur, and self-esteem can be elevated to new levels.

Future classroom teachers may be the only music teachers their students ever have. Therefore, it is important to sing carefully chosen songs to put those at ease who are lacking in vocal confidence and inexperienced in singing—teachers and students alike!

Graded series textbooks developed by the major publishing companies and many other source books incorporate in their indexes a wide variety of topics that can be integrated into the classroom through singing. Each of the songs in this chapter has been chosen to accomplish specific goals through purposefully fun singing! The use of Omnichord, guitar, and piano accompaniments will add to the pleasure of singing. To facilitate accompaniment, chord names are indicated above the melody line directly over the note where the chord change occurs. Breath marks are shown by apostrophes. The teacher is welcome to sing the songs without accompaniment, if they are pitched in the correct key or one that is near to the original.

Hello songs, get-acquainted pieces, and songs of friendship help to begin the year with singing.

HELLO

Teresa Jennings

Teresa Jennings

Bouncy

Group Echo Group Echo Group Echo

Hel - lo! *(Hel - lo!)* Hel - lo! *(Hel - lo!)* It's good to say "hel - lo!" *(Hel - lo!)*

Group A₇ Echo

Put on your grin and come right in! Hel - lo! Hel - lo! Hel - lo! *(Hel - lo!)*

Group D Echo Group Echo Group Echo

Hel - lo! *(Hel - lo!)* Hel - lo! *(Hel - lo!)* To ev - 'ry - one we know! *(We know!)*

Group A₇ D

A friend - ly way to start the day: Hel - lo, hel - lo, hel - lo! *Hel - lo!*

MAKE NEW FRIENDS

ROUND

Make new friends, but keep the old, One is sil - ver and the oth - er's gold.

GIVE ME YOUR HAND

DONNE-MOI LA MAIN

Charlotte Diamond and Guy Auger

Guy Auger

Don - ne - moi la main, give me your hand;

Don - ne, don - ne, don - ne, donne, don - ne - moi la main.

pronunciation: do na mwa la mɛ̃

Popular and Patriotic Songs

Songs in this section are important examples of history and tradition. They help to preserve our cultural heritage.

IT'S A SMALL WORLD

RICHARD M. SHERMAN AND ROBERT B. SHERMAN

RICHARD M. SHERMAN AND ROBERT B. SHERMAN

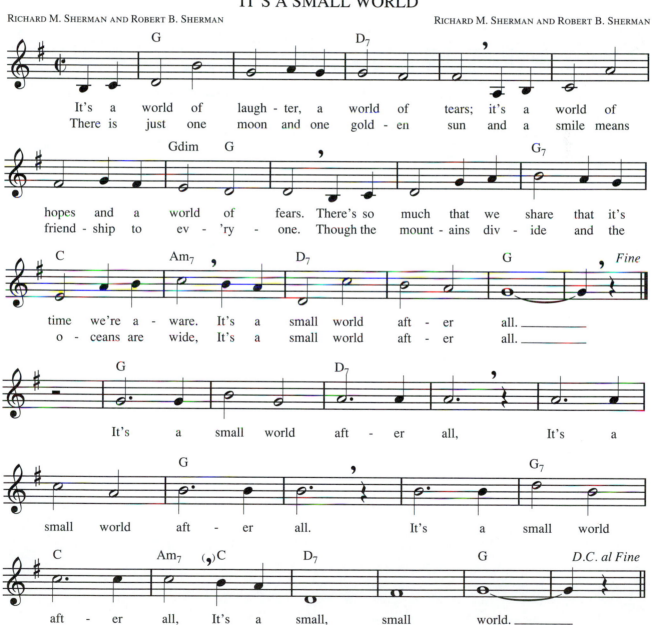

YANKEE DOODLE DANDY

George M. Cohan

George M. Cohan

I'm a Yan-kee Doo-dle Dan - dy, A Yan - kee Doo-dle, do or die; _____ A real live neph-ew of my Un - cle Sam, Born on the Fourth of Ju - ly. _____ I've got a Yan-kee Doo-dle sweet - heart, She's my Yan-kee Doo-dle joy. _____ Yan-kee Doo-dle came to Lon-don, just to ride the po - nies, I am a Yan - kee Doo-dle boy. _____

Also sing and play *America* (p. 335) and *The Star-Spangled Banner* (pp. 336–337).

Singing for Fun Is Learning!

THIS LAND IS YOUR LAND

WOODY GUTHRIE

WOODY GUTHRIE

This land is your land, _____ This land is my land, _____ From Cal - i -

for - nia _____ to the New York is - land, _____ From the red - wood for - est ____

_____ to the Gulf Stream wa - ters; _____ This land was made for you and me. _____

THIS LAND IS YOUR LAND Words and Music by Woody Guthrie TRO © Copyright 1956 (renewed), 1958 (renewed) and 1970 Ludlow Music, Inc., New York, NY. Used by permission.

Spirituals

K–4, 1c, 9c, 9d
5–8, 1c, 9a, 9c

Spirituals are an important part of the great heritage of American folk music and were developed largely by African Americans in the South as deeply emotional religious expression. The texts of many spirituals contain hidden messages that were passed among the slaves. The simple melodic style, syncopation with the occasional use of modes or the pentatonic scale served to lay the foundation for American jazz, the blues, and rock music as we know it today.

MICHAEL, ROW THE BOAT ASHORE

GEORGIA ISLANDS SPIRITUAL

1. Mich - ael, row the boat a - shore, al - le - lu - ia.

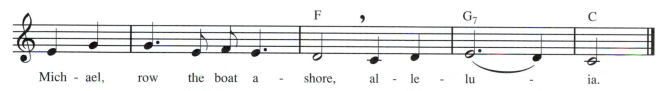

Mich - ael, row the boat a - shore, al - le - lu - ia.

2. Sister, help to trim the sail, alleluia, *(twice)*

(repeat verse 1 after each verse)

3. River Jordan's deep and wide, alleluia, *(twice)*

4. River Jordan's chilly and cold, alleluia, *(twice)*

CHATTER WITH THE ANGELS

AFRICAN-AMERICAN SPIRITUAL

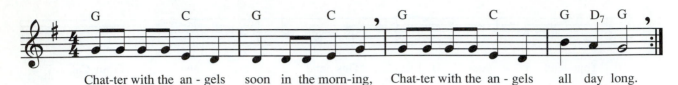

Chat-ter with the an-gels soon in the morn-ing, Chat-ter with the an-gels all day long.

I hope to join that band and chat-ter with the an-gels all day long.

WHO BUILT THE ARK?

AFRICAN-AMERICAN SPIRITUAL

Who built the ark? No-ah, No-ah, Who built the ark? Broth-er No-ah built the ark.

1. Now didn't old No-ah build the ark? __ Built it out of a hick-o-ry bark. __
2. He built it long, both wide and tall __ Plenty of room for the large __ and small. __
3. Now in come the ani-mals two by two, __ Hippo-pota-mus and __ kang-a-roo. __
4. Now in come the ani-mals three by three, __ Two big cats and a bum-ble-bee. __ *Sing Refrain*

5. Now in come the animals four by four,
   Two through the window and two through the door.

6. Now in come the animals five by five,
   Four little sparrows and the redbird's wife.

7. Now in come the animals six by six,
   Elephant laughed at the monkey's tricks.

8. Now in come the animals seven by seven,
   Four from home and the rest from heaven.
   Refrain

9. Now in come the animals eight by eight,
   Some were on time and the others were late.

10. Now in come the animals nine by nine,
    Some was a-shouting and some was a-crying.

11. Now in come the animals ten by ten,
    Five black roosters and five black hens.

12. Now Noah says, "Go shut that door,
    The rain's started dropping and we can't take more."
    Refrain

Singing for Fun Is Learning!

DO, LORD

AFRICAN-AMERICAN SPIRITUAL

Refrain

Do, Lord, oh do, Lord, oh do re-mem-ber me, Do, Lord, oh

do, Lord, oh do re-mem-ber me. Do, Lord, oh do, Lord, oh

do re-em-ber me, Look a - way be - yond ___ the blue.

Verse

I got a home in glo - ry - land that out - shines the sun,

I got a home in glo - ry - land that out - shines the sun.

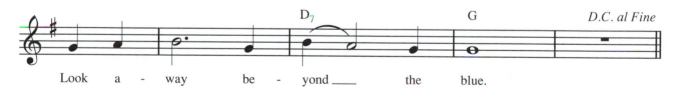

I got a home in glo - ry - land that out - shines the sun,

Look a - way be - yond ___ the blue.

Singing for Fun Is Learning!

115

Here is a recorder part for "Do, Lord" that uses only three notes. Can you play it while your class sings the song?

For additional beautiful African American spirituals, sing and play *Jacob's Ladder* (p. 184), *Joshua Fit the Battle of Jericho* (p. 245), *When the Saints Go Marching In* (p. 148), *He's Got the Whole World in His Hands* (pp. 282–283), and *Rocka My Soul* (p. 284).

Folk and Global Songs

K–4, 1c, 9c
5–8, 1c

The majority of the songs selected to teach music skills in this text can be classified as folk songs. These songs were handed down orally from generation to generation, expressing the emotions, feelings, aspirations, and varied geographic characteristics of the peoples of many lands. Through the message of music, the singing and playing of folk songs will help children appreciate and understand *all* of their classmates, regardless of race, color, or creed.

OLD DAN TUCKER

AMERICAN FOLK SONG

Old Dan Tuck-er was a might-y man, He washed his face in the fry-ing pan,

Combed his hair with a wag-on wheel, Had a tooth-ache in his heel;

Refrain
So get out the way, Old Dan Tuck-er; Get out the way, Old Dan Tuck-er;

Get out the way, Old Dan Tuck-er, You're too late to get your sup-per.

2. Old Dan Tucker came to town,
   Riding a billy goat, leading a hound;
   Hound dog barked, then billy goad jumped;
   Dan fell off and landed on a stump; *Refrain*

LONE STAR TRAIL

AMERICAN COWBOY SONG

1. I start - ed on the trail on June twen - ty - third,
I been punch - in' Tex - as cat - tle on the Lone Star Trail;

Refrain

Sing - in' ki yi yip - pi yip - pi yay, yip - pi yay!

Sing - in' ki yi yip - pi yip - pi yay! _____

2. I'm up in the mornin' before daylight,
   And before I sleep the moon shines bright. *Refrain*

3. Oh, it's bacon and beans 'most every day,
   I'd as soon be a-eatin' prairie hay. *Refrain*

4. My feet are in the stirrups and my rope is on the side,
   Show me a horse that I can't ride. *Refrain*

Also sing and play the cowboy song *Old Texas* (p. 276).

LADIES OF CHIAPAS
CHIAPANECAS

English text by M.M.H.

Mexican Folk Song

1. Now that the night has ar - rived, un - der a
1. *Cuan - do la no - che lle - gó,* *y con su*
   kwan do la no che ye go i kon su
2. Un - der the moon shin - ing white, I will go
2. *El blan - co ran - cho cu - brió,* *a - le - gre el*
   el βlang ko ɾan cho ku βɾyo α le gɾel

man - tle of blue, Dance, now, my *chia - pa - ne - ca.*
man - to de a - zul *Bai - la, mi chia - pa - ne - ca.*
man to ðea sul bai la mi chya pa ne - ka
danc - ing with you.
bai - le em - pe - zó.
βai lem pe so

Dance with grace and en - chant-ment. Dance, now, with the moon
Bai - la, bai - la con gar - bo. Bai - la, sua - ve ra -
bai la bai la kon gaɾ βo bai la swa βe ɾa
Dance, my gen - tle one,
que en el bai - le rei -
ken el bai le ɾei

1.
shin - ing bright. 2 You will
- yo de luz. - *na e - res*
yo ðe lus nɑe res

2.
soon be the queen of the dance!
tú, chia - pa - ne - ca gen - til.
tu chya pa ne ka xen til

The birthday serenade *Las Mañanitas* usually is sung early in the day as a
beginning to the birthday celebration. The melody is a Mexican folk tune.

LAS MAÑANITAS

Mexico

As of old, we bring a song, a greet-ing gay at ear-ly
dawn; Wak-en, friend, and join our sing-ing, O hear the mu-sic we bring.
I'll step out of doors at dawn-ing, I'll climb up a mag-ic
stair, And bring down the stars of morn-ing to make a crown for your hair.

Estas son las mañanitas que cantaba el Rey David,
Per no eran tanbonitas como las cantan aquí.
Despierta, mi bién, despierta, mira que ya amaneció;
Ya los pajarillos cantan, la luna ya se metió.

Despierta, mi bién, despierta, mira que ya amaneció;
Ya los pajarillos cantan, la luna ya se metió.
Estas son las mañanitas que cantaba el Rey David,
Pero no eran tanbonitas como las cantan aquí.

DON GATO

English Words by Margaret Marks

Mexican Folk Song

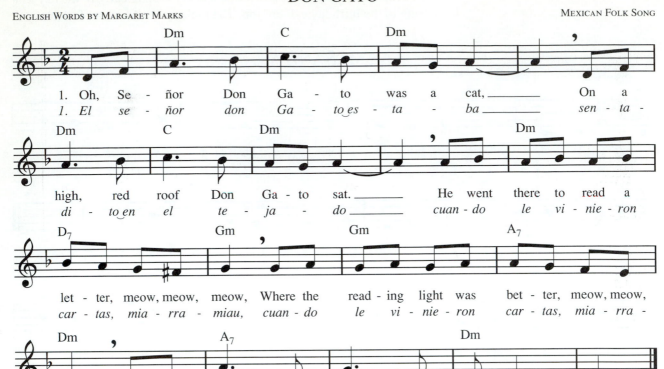

1. Oh, Se - ñor Don Ga - to was a cat, _____ On a
1. *El se - ñor don Ga - to es - ta - ba _____ sen - ta -*

high, red roof Don Ga - to sat. _____ He went there to read a
di - to en el te - ja - do _____ cuan - do le vi - nie - ron

let - ter, meow, meow, meow, Where the read - ing light was bet - ter, meow, meow,
car - tas, mia - rra - miau, cuan - do le vi - nie - ron car - tas, mia - rra -

meow, 'Twas a love note for Don Ga - to! _____
miau, si que - rí - a ser ca - sa - do. _____

2. "I adore you!" wrote the lady cat,
   Who was fluffy, white, and nice and fat.
   There was not a sweeter kitty, . . .
   In the country or the city, . . .
   And she said she'd wed Don Gato!

3. Oh, Don Gato jumped so happily,
   He fell off the roof and broke his knee,
   Broke his ribs and all his whiskers, . . .
   And his little solar plexus, . . .
   "¡Ay caramba!" cried Don Gato!

4. Then the doctors all came on the run
   Just to see if something could be done,
   And they held a consultation, . . .
   About how to save their patient, . . .
   How to save Señor Don Gato!

5. But in spite of ev'rything they tried,
   Poor Señor Don Gato up and died,
   Oh, it wasn't very merry, . . .
   Going to the cemetery, . . .
   For the ending of Don Gato!

6. When the funeral passed the market square,
   Such a smell of fish was in the air,
   Though his burial was slated, . . .
   He became re-animated! . . .
   He came back to life, Don Gato!

2. *Con una gatita blanca,*
   sobrina de un gato pardo,
   que no la había más linda, . . .
   que no la había más linda, . . .
   en las casas de aquel barrio.

3. *Don Gato con la alegría,*
   se ha caído del tejado;
   ha roto siete costillas, . . .
   ha roto siete costillas, . . .
   las dos orejas y el rabo.

4. *A visitar lo venían,*
   médicos y cirujanos;
   todos dicen que se muere, . . .
   todos dicen que se muere, . . .
   que don Gato está muy malo.

5. *El gatito ya se ha muerto,*
   ya se ha muerto el buen don Gato;
   a enterrar ya se lo llevan, . . .
   a enterrar ya se lo llevan, . . .
   todos las gatos llorando.

6. *Cuando pasaba el entierro,*
   por la plaza del pescado,
   al olor de las sardinas, . . .
   al olor de las sardinas, . . .
   don Gato ha resucitado.

Singing for Fun Is Learning!

Also sing *La Raspa,* an excellent example of Mexican folk rhythm (p. 175).

SEVEN STEPS
SIEBEN STEPS

German Folk Song

Eins, zwei, drei vier,   fünf, sechs, sieben,   Eins, zwei, drei, vier,   fünf, sechs, sieben,   Eins, zwei, drei,
aıns tsvaı draı fir   fünf zɛks zibn   aıns tsvaı draı fir   fünf zɛks zibn   aıns tsvaı draı

eins, zwei, drei,   Eins, zwei, drei,   eins, zwei, drei,   Eins, zwei, drei, vier,   fünf, sechs, sieben.
aıns tsvaı draı   aıns tsvaı draı   aıns tsvaı draı   aıns tsvaı draı fir   fünf zɛks zibn

HELLO TO ALL THE CHILDREN OF THE WORLD

Nancy Klein

Nancy Klein and Pam Beall

Hel - lo,   *bon jour,** bue - nos   di - as,**   G' - day,** gu - ten Tag,**

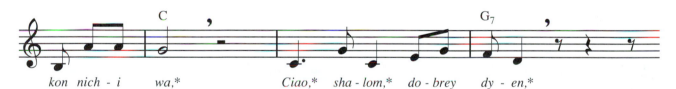

kon nich - i   wa,**   Ciao,** sha - lom,** do - brey   dy - en,**

Hel - o   to   all   the   chil - dren   of   the   world!

*There are greetings from the following countries:

bon jour—good day (French)	*kon nichi wa*—hello (Japanese)
buenos dias—good day (Spanish)	*ciao*—hi, good-bye (Italian)
g'day—good day (Australian)	*shalom*—hello, good-bye, peace (Hebrew)
guten Tag—good day (German)	*dobrey dyen*—good day (Russian)

1. We live in dif-f'rent plac-es from all a-round the world, We speak in man-y dif-f'rent ways __ Tho' some things might be dif-f'rent, we're chil-dren just the same, And we all like to sing and play.

2. There are children in the deserts
   And children in the towns
   And children who live down by the sea,
   If we could meet each other
   To run and sing and play,
   Then what good friends we all could be. *Chorus*

YANKEE DOODLE

DR. RICHARD SCHUCKBURGH   TRADITIONAL MELODY

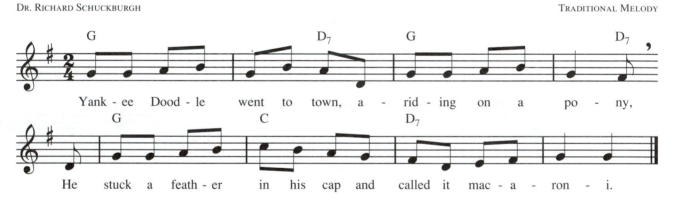

Yank-ee Dood-le went to town, a-rid-ing on a po-ny,

He stuck a feath-er in his cap and called it mac-a-ron-i.

JIM ALONG, JOSIE

AMERICAN FOLK SONG

With movement

Hey, jim a-long, jim a-long, Jo-sie, Hey, jim a-long, jim a-long, Joe!

Hey, jim a-long, jim a-long, Jo-sie, Hey, jim a-long, jim a-long, Joe!

Go back to the beginning and sing to the End.
(Da Capo al Fine)

(same words each time)

| D | | G | D, | G | A₇ | D | A₇ | D, |

Face to the cen-ter,   hands on your knees,   Clap three times and   turn a-round, please!

2. Tiptoe along, . . .   4. Jump, jump along, . . .

3. Jog, jog along, . . .   5. Do what you want, . . .

For additional folk songs refer to chapter 14 (pp. 316–322), *"Folk Songs Around the World."*

Recreational Songs

Action, movement, game, stunt, and camp songs provide spontaneous opportunities for informal class participation and enjoyment for any age level from kindergarten upward. As well, these songs can be classified in other categories, such as folk or patriotic songs.

K–4, 1c
5–8, 1c

YANKEE DOODLE

CAMP SONG

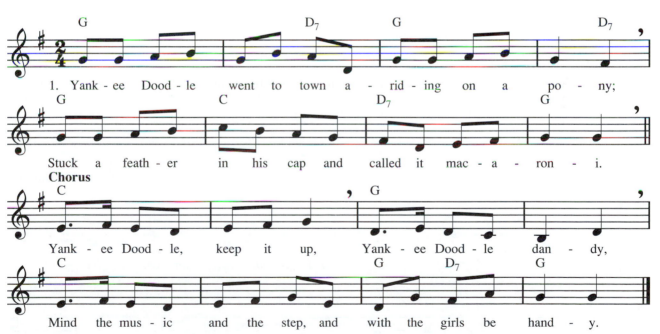

1. Yank - ee Dood - le   went to town a - rid - ing on a po - ny;
Stuck a feath - er in his cap and called it mac - a - ron - i.

Chorus

Yank - ee Dood - le,   keep it up,   Yank - ee Dood - le   dan - dy,
Mind the mus - ic   and the step, and   with the girls be hand - y.

2. Father and I went down to camp
Along with Captain Gooding,
And there we saw the men and boys
As thick as hasty pudding. *Chorus*

3. There was Captain Washington
Upon a slapping stallion,
A-giving orders to his men,
I guess there was a million. *Chorus*

IF YOU'RE HAPPY

Camp Song

If you're hap - py and you know it, clap your hands. *(clap clap)*

If you're hap - py and you know it, clap your hands. *(clap clap)*

If you're hap - py and you know it, then you real - ly want to show it,

If you're hap - py and you know it, clap your hands. *(clap clap)*

If you're happy and you know it, touch your head . . .

If you're happy and you know it, touch your ears . . .

If you're happy and you know it, do all three . . .

Create additional words and actions.

Also sing the camp songs *Three Cornered Hat* (p. 221), *Upidee* (p. 223), and *Upward Trail* (pp. 325–326).

ACITRÓN

Spanish Stone-Passing Game

A - ci - trón de un fan - dan - go, zan - go, zan - go, sa - ba - ré.
α si tɾon de um fan dan go san go san go sa βa ɾe

Sa - ba - ré de far - an - de - la, con su tri - qui, tri - qui tran.
sa βa ɾe ðe faɾ an de la kon su tɾi ki tɾi ki tran

COTTON-EYED JOE

AMERICAN DANCE SONG

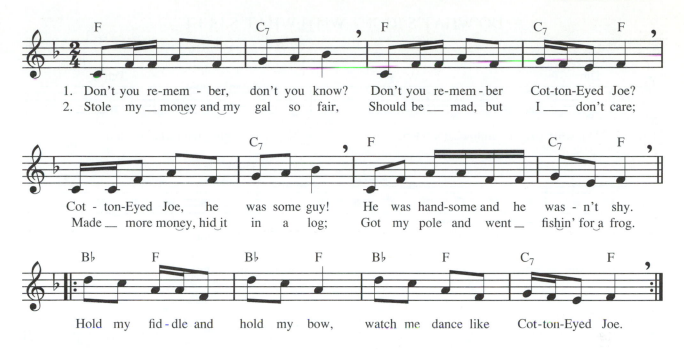

1. Don't you re-mem - ber, don't you know? Don't you re-mem - ber Cot-ton-Eyed Joe?
2. Stole my __ money and my gal so fair, Should be __ mad, but I __ don't care;

Cot - ton-Eyed Joe, he was some guy! He was hand-some and he was - n't shy.
Made __ more money, hid it in a log; Got my pole and went __ fishin' for a frog.

Hold my fid - dle and hold my bow, watch me dance like Cot-ton-Eyed Joe.

Note: College students who are especially interested in teaching primary grade children should refer to chapter 14 (pp. 327–331), for recreational song materials at that level.

Additional Songs

K–4, 8b
5–8, 8b

Many other topics can be incorporated into the music classroom for fun and to accomplish a specific purpose. Suggestions include:

1. Songs for holidays and celebrations
2. Songs with current societal topics (like environmental preservation)
3. Songs from favorite musicals or Broadway plays
4. Songs for developing confidence and higher self-esteem
5. Songs for relaxation, tension relief, or getting attention
6. Songs that incorporate lessons in spelling, geography, math, science, etc.

DO WHAT'S RIGHT WITH WHAT'S LEFT

Carmino Ravosa   Carmino Ravosa

SAVE THE PLANET

Gene Grier

Gene Grier and Lowell Everson

Save the plan - et and ev-'ry-thing on ___ it. We've got to do ___ it to - day. ___

Last time to Coda

___ Save the plan - et and ev - 'ry - thing on ___ it.

We've got to start ___ right a - way! ___

Verse

There are some prob-lems for you ___ and me ___ to solve with-out ___ de - lay. ___

We'll set ex - am-ples for all ___ to see ___ and we will show ___ the way. ___

Coda

We've got to start, all do our part, we've got to start ___ right a - way! ___

I CAN'T SPELL HIPPOPOTAMUS

J. Fred Coots

J. Fred Coots

1. I can spell *Hat,* H - A - T, I can spell *Cat,* C - A - T,
   I can spell *Dog,* D - O - G, I can spell *Log,* L - O - G,

I can spell *Fat,* F - A - T, ___ But I can't spell *Hip - po - pot - a - mus.*
I can spell *Hog,* H - O - G, ___

H - I - P - P - O I know, and then comes P - O - T.

But that's as far as I can go, and that's what both - ers me. Gee!

2. I can spell *Top,* T-O-P,
   I can spell *Hop,* H-O-P,
   I can spell *Mop,* M-O-P,
   But I can't spell *Hippopotamus.*
   H-I-P-P-O I know,
   and then comes P-O-T.
   But that's as far as I can go,
   and that's what bothers me. Gee!
   I can spell *Ban,* B-A-N,
   I can spell *Man,* M-A-N,
   I can spell *Fan,* F-A-N,
   But I can't spell *Hippopotamus.*

3. I can spell *Tag,* T-A-G,
   I can spell *Bag,* B-A-G,
   I can spell *Sag,* S-A-G,
   But I can't spell *Hippopotamus.*
   H-I-P-P-O I know,
   and then comes P-O-T.
   But that's as far as I can go,
   and that's what bothers me. Gee!
   I can spell *Sat,* S-A-T,
   I can spell *Rat,* R-A-T,
   I can spell *Mat,* M-A-T,
   But I can't spell *Hippopotamus.*

WABASH CANNON BALL

TRADITIONAL

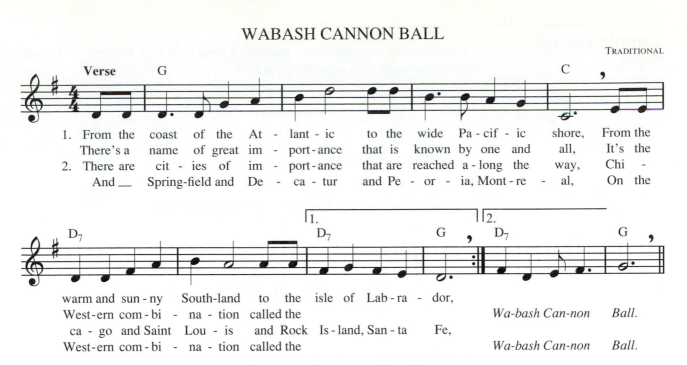

Verse G / C /

1. From the coast of the At - lant - ic to the wide Pa - cif - ic shore, From the
   There's a name of great im - port - ance that is known by one and all, It's the
2. There are cit - ies of im - port - ance that are reached a - long the way, Chi -
   And __ Spring-field and De - ca - tur and Pe - or - ia, Mont - re - al, On the

1. D7 / D7 G / 2. D7 G /

warm and sun - ny South - land to the isle of Lab - ra - dor, Wa-bash Can-non Ball.
West - ern com - bi - na - tion called the Wa-bash Can-non Ball.
ca - go and Saint Lou - is and Rock Is - land, San - ta Fe,
West - ern com - bi - na - tion called the Wa-bash Can-non Ball.

Refrain G / C /

Just list - en to the jing - le, the rum - ble, and the roar

D7 / G /

Of the might - y lo - co - mo - tive as she streams a - long the shore,

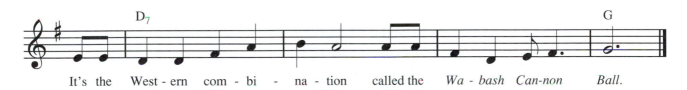

G / C /

Hear the thun - der of the en - gine, hear the lone - some whis - tle call,

D7 / G

It's the West - ern com - bi - na - tion called the Wa - bash Can-non Ball.

Sample Lesson Plans

K–4, 1a, 1b
5–8, 1a

The following suggestions for teaching a song by rote in lesson-plan format can be modeled with other songs as well.

SONG TITLE:

1. TITLE OF LESSON:

2. SPECIFIC OBJECTIVES: (you need at least two)

    a.

    b.

3. MOTIVATION or MANIPULATIVE (a visual aid to draw the students into the lesson)

4. TEACHING PROCEDURE

    a. Listen to a recording of the song or sing the song in live performance once. Accompany yourself with the Omnichord, guitar, or piano, or play the song yourself on a melody instrument. The song may also be sung a cappella (without instrumental accompaniment).

    b. Discuss the mood and tempo of the song.

    c. Learn to sing the song by phrase recall or "call and response." The teacher can alternate singing and listening to each phrase. Short songs may be learned as a whole. ALWAYS remember to establish tempo by counting out loud at least one measure (i.e., in 4/4 "one, two, three, go"). ALWAYS play the starting pitch(es) BEFORE the singing starts so that the teacher and students can hear the correct tones and key of the music.

    d. Correct mistakes in pronunciation (diction), notes, and rhythm.

    e. Add dynamics, if they are not already included in the music.

    f. Drill the song by singing it in its entirety several times—expressively.

    g. Difficult passages may be repeated several times using hand cues or other visual pictures for pitch direction.

5. FOLLOW-UP ACTIVITIES

    a. Sing additional verses

    b. Create new verses

    c. Add actions, movement, or dramatization to the song

    d. Add classroom instruments

6. MATERIALS USED (for ease in later retrieval)

    a. List publisher of song, page number, and specific grade level

    b. List CD or recording number

    c. List additional instruments used—piano, recorder, etc.

    d. List motivational materials needed

K–4, 6c

1. TITLE OF LESSON: High and Low Sounds

2. SPECIFIC OBJECTIVES:

    a. Develop the awareness that sounds are relatively high or relatively low.

    b. Children who have explored environmental sounds before may have developed some understanding of the meaning of high and low pitch. Explain the meaning of PITCH vs. VOLUME of sound, as confusion may occur as a result of comments such as "Turn down the TV; it's too high."

3. MOTIVATION:

Show the class pictures of several animals. Ask them to imitate the sounds these animals make and tell whether the sounds are high or low.

4. PROCEDURE:

    a. Sing the song "The Animal Band" to have the students find out which animals are mentioned and to acquaint themselves with the tune.

    b. Have the children list the animals in the order they are heard in the song.

    c. Have them imitate the sounds made by the animals.

    d. Listen again, identifying which sounds are high and which are low.

    e. LEARN TO SING THE SONG, phrase by phrase, correcting mistakes, by following the sample procedure and then FINISH the song by singing it several times.

5. FOLLOW-UP ACTIVITIES:

    a. Discuss other animals and the kinds of sounds they make.

    b. Create new verses about these animals.

    c. Dramatize the song with individuals or small groups making the animal sounds.

    d. Talk about and imitate other high and low environmental sounds.

6. MATERIALS USED:

    a. "The Animal Band" found in *The Spectrum of Music*, MacMillan Publishers, 1984, pp. 59–60, grade level: Kindergarten

    b. Piano

    c. Stuffed animals and pictures of animals

THE ANIMAL BAND

Schröder Wieke

Schröder Wieke

1. Mist - er Drake con - duct - ed the an - i - mal band, __ The
2. Mist - er Drake con - duct - ed the an - i - mal band, __ The

ver - y best band in all the land. __ There were ducks on the left and
ver - y best band in all the land. __ There were cows on the left and

mice on the right, And this was the tune they played all night:
sheep on the right, And this was the tune they played all night:

Singing for Fun Is Learning!

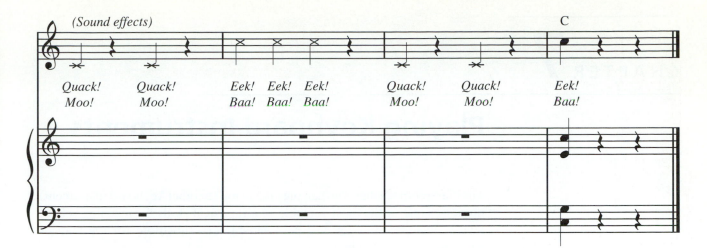

(Sound effects)

C

Quack!   Quack!   Eek! Eek! Eek!   Quack!   Quack!   Eek!
Moo!   Moo!   Baa! Baa! Baa!   Moo!   Moo!   Baa!

3. Mister Drake conducted the animal band,
   The very best band in all the land.
   There were pigs on the left and birds on the right,
   And this was the tune they played all night:
   "Oink, oink, Tweet, tweet, tweet! Oink, oink, Tweet!"

4. Mister Drake conducted the animal band,
   The very best band in all the land.
   There were some on the left and some on the right,
   And this was the tune they played all night:
   (Create your own animal sounds.)

CHAPTER 7

Playing Keyboard Instruments

The classroom teacher who can play the piano (or other keyboard instrument) possesses one of the most valuable of all musical skills for teaching school music. The stereo never will be a satisfactory substitute for the teacher performing live at the piano.

Anyone with a sense of rhythm can learn to play the piano well enough for classroom music activities. Technical facility at the keyboard is desirable but not necessary. The teacher who can play simple melodies, easy accompaniments, and basic rhythms with accuracy will succeed well with his/her students.

Uses for the Piano in the Classroom

The piano has numerous uses in the classroom:

- To help teach the melody, especially when the teacher cannot sing well.
- To give the keynote, key chord, and starting notes of songs.
- To provide accompaniments, introductions, and codas to songs.
- To provide rhythmic music for marching, skipping, hopping, and other interpretative activities.
- To help teach part singing and harmonic skills.
- To introduce musical notation.
- To introduce keyboard appreciation to children and encourage their study of it.

It is not necessary to have a regular, upright piano on which to learn keyboard skills. It is advisable, however, to have some kind of keyboard instrument with at least 52 *full-size* keys (mini-keys do not fit well or maneuver easily with the adult hand). In addition, most keyboards take up less space than traditional pianos, are portable, and never need tuning. Any piano in satisfactory condition or keyboard that meets the criteria mentioned above would be a good "starter" instrument. Additional information about electronic keyboards will be discussed at the end of this chapter.

Naming and Playing the Piano Keys

The black keys are grouped alternately in twos and threes on the piano keyboard. The white keys, named with the first seven letters of the alphabet (A B C D E F G), can be located quickly in relation to these groups of black keys:

1. The white key C is located directly to the left of the group of two black keys. Find and play all the C keys on the piano. Notice especially the fourth C, counting from left to right on the keyboard—the twenty-fourth white key. This is called *middle C,* falling about the middle of the keyboard, slightly to the left of the piano maker's label. Middle C is midway between the treble and bass staffs. If another instrument is being used, locate the middle of it and look underneath the brand label, if one is there. Middle C should "split" the keyboard.

Chart of the complete piano keyboard.

2. The white key D is located between the group of two black keys. Find and play all the D keys.

3. The white key E is located directly to the right of the group of two black keys. Find and play all the E keys.

4. The white key F is located directly to the left of the group of three black keys. Find and play all the F keys.

5. The white key B is located directly to the right of the group of three black keys. Find and play all the B keys.

6. Locate and play all the G and A keys in the same manner in relation to their position among the black keys. Then, practice finding all the notes at random with increasing speed.

7. The black keys get their names from the white keys on either side of them using the term sharp (♯) or flat (♭) added to the name of the white key. For example, the black key between C and D can be either C-sharp moving upward to the nearest key to the right or D-flat moving downward to the nearest key to the left.

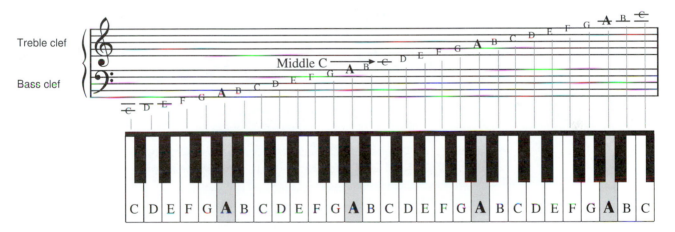

The right hand usually plays the notes on the treble staff, and the left hand plays the notes on the bass staff. Because of our unique, mirrored anatomy, each hand works differently, or inversely, in playing correct pitches on the piano keyboard.

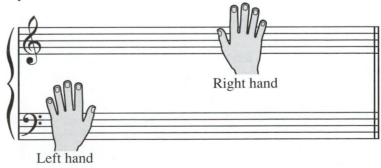

Playing Keyboard Instruments

Playing with the Right Hand

K–4, 2b

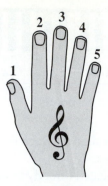

Right-hand finger numbers

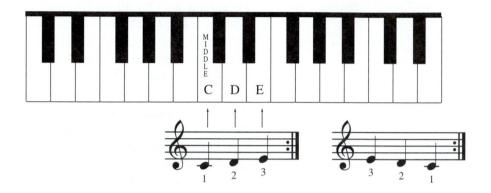

WALTZ TIME

Playing Keyboard Instruments

Playing with the Left Hand

K–4, 2b

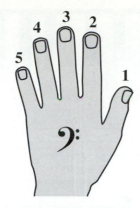

Left-hand finger numbers

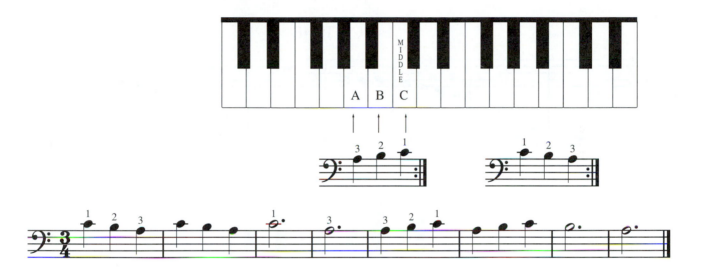

Playing with Both Hands

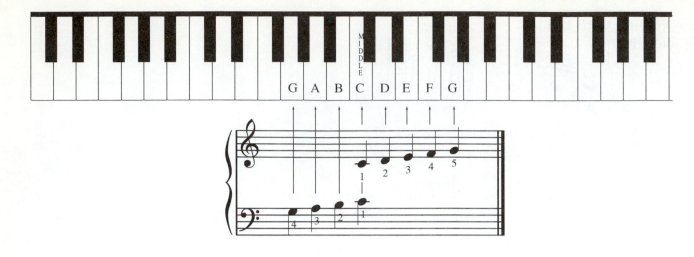

MARCH TIME

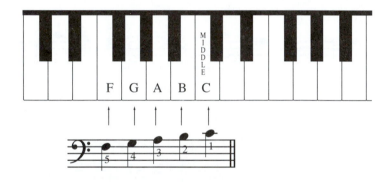

CAMPTOWN RACES

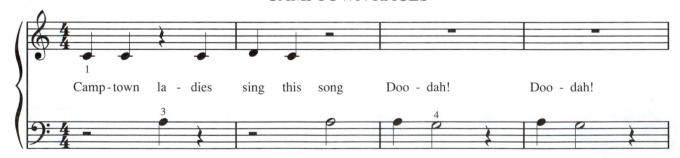

Camp - town la - dies   sing this song   Doo - dah!   Doo - dah!

Playing Keyboard Instruments

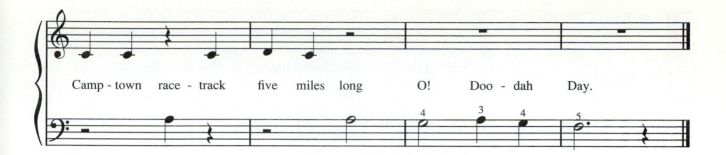

Camp - town race - track five miles long O! Doo - dah Day.

Five-Finger Positions

K–4, 2b
K–5, 2a

The Right-Hand C Position

Take the piano chart from the endleaf pocket, and place it above and align it with the piano keys for reference while practicing.

1. Place the right thumb on middle C and play up the scale to the G on the right. Curve and raise the fingers. Strike the keys; do not press them.

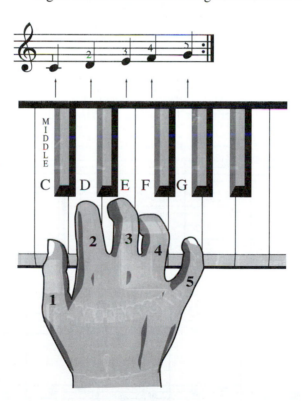

2. Keeping your hand in the same place, play these five notes *up and down* repeatedly to learn the "feel" of the position of the right hand in relation to the keyboard. Try not to look at your hands; learn to visualize the keyboard. Also play with your eyes closed.

The Left-Hand C Position

Place the fifth finger of the left hand on C below middle C and play up the scale to the G on the right. As with the previous exercise for the right hand, hold your left hand still while you play the five notes up and down repeatedly to learn the "feel" of the position of the left hand in relation to the keyboard.

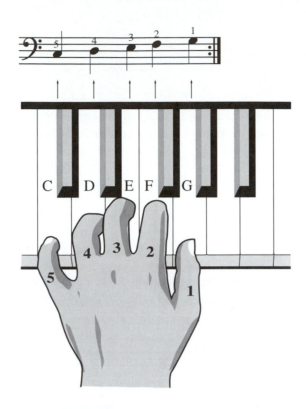

Practice the following exercises with each hand separately when necessary.

Playing Keyboard Instruments

Play each hand of *The Woodchuck* separately several times before attempting to play both hands together. This basic practice technique will build the student's confidence in his/her ability to learn to play unfamiliar pieces of music.

THE WOODCHUCK

AMERICAN

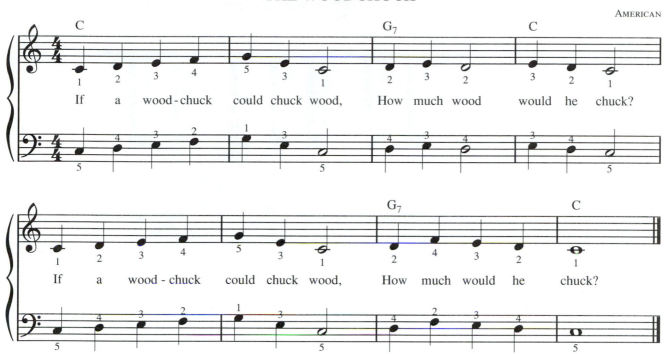

If a wood-chuck could chuck wood, How much wood would he chuck?

If a wood-chuck could chuck wood, How much would he chuck?

CHORALE THEME

J.S. BACH

The Right-Hand G Position   Place the right thumb on G above middle C. Play from G up the scale to D several times. Play from D down to G as well.

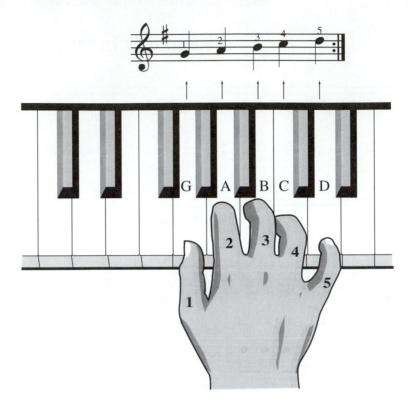

Playing Keyboard Instruments

The Left-Hand G Position

Place the fifth finger of the left hand on G just below middle C. Play up the scale to D several times. Play from D down to G as well.

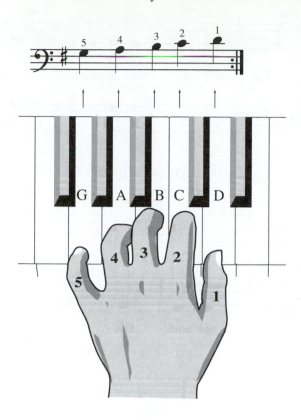

Practice the following exercises with each hand separately when necessary. Play both hands together when more confidence is assumed.

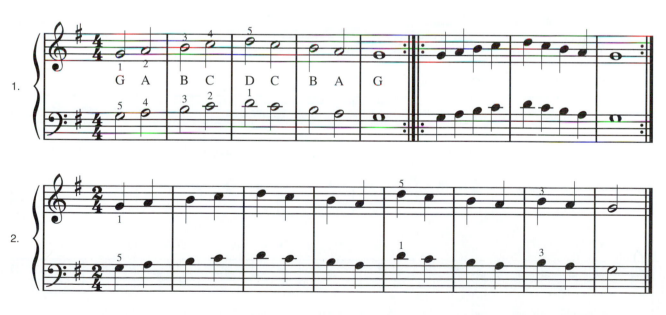

HOT CROSS BUNS

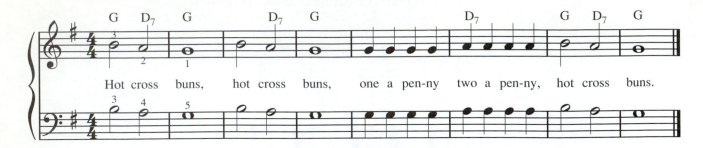

Hot cross buns, hot cross buns, one a pen-ny two a pen-ny, hot cross buns.

Preparatory exercise for *Lightly Row*

LIGHTLY ROW

GERMANY

Light-ly row, light-ly row, o'er the shin-ing waves we go; Smooth-ly glide,

smooth-ly glide, on the si-lent tide. Let the winds and wa-ters be

min-gled with our mel-o-dy, Sing and float, sing and float, in our lit-tle boat.

The Right-Hand F Position   Place the right thumb on F above middle C. Play from F up to C, extending the fourth finger slightly forward to strike B-flat. Repeat the exercise several times, playing up to the right and down to the left.

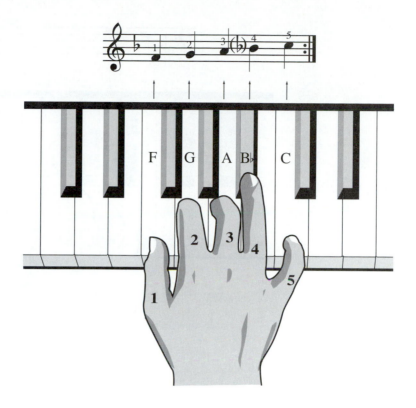

The Left-Hand F Position

Place the fifth finger of the left hand on F below middle C. Play from F up to C, extending the second finger slightly forward to strike B-flat. Repeat the exercise several times, playing up to the right and down to the left.

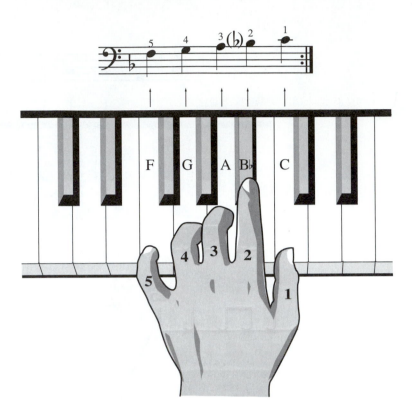

Remember to play the following exercises with each hand separately before attempting to play both hands together.

Playing Keyboard Instruments

SINGING ON THE PLAYGROUND

GERMANY

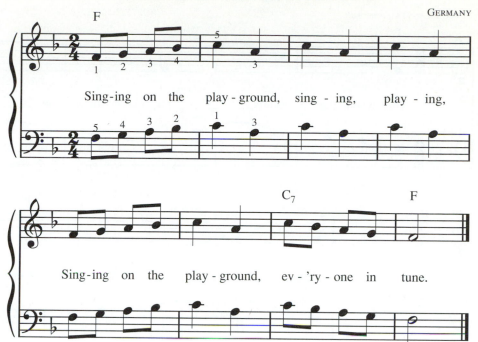

Sing-ing on the play-ground, sing-ing, play-ing,

Sing-ing on the play-ground, ev-'ry-one in tune.

GO TELL AUNT RHODIE

UNITED STATES

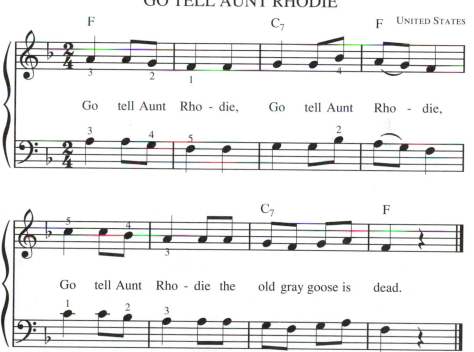

Go tell Aunt Rho-die, Go tell Aunt Rho-die,

Go tell Aunt Rho-die the old gray goose is dead.

WHEN THE SAINTS GO MARCHING IN

Oh, when the saints _____ go march-ing in, _____ oh, when the

saints go march-ing in, _____ how I want to be in that

num - ber, _____ when the saints go march - ing in. _____

Accompanying and Harmonizing Melodies

Bass accompaniment exercise

THEME FROM THE SURPRISE SYMPHONY
(ADAPTED)

JOSEPH HAYDN

K–4, 2b

GERMAN FOLK TUNE
(ADAPTED)

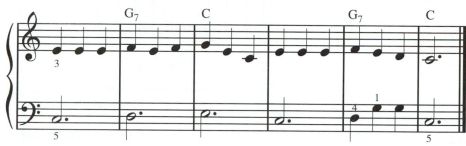

AIR

Mozart

Chording Melodies in Major Keys

Playing Basic Chords in C Major

K–4, 2b

Play the notes of the chord separately, and then sound them simultaneously.

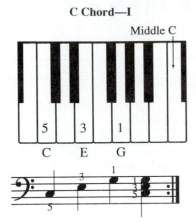

PLAYGROUND TUNE

Eventually, through practice and experience, the hands begin to play more independently. Any chord can be inverted and played through the various registers of the keyboard, as the following example illustrates.

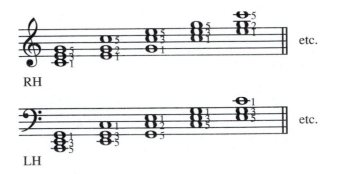

Playing Keyboard Instruments

G_7 Chord—V_7

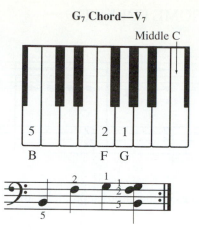

Practice the chords below several times before playing the songs that follow. Play the chords with your eyes closed. Practice with each hand separately. The notation 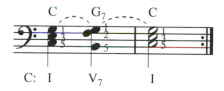 indicates notes and fingering in common. Keep finger in position. The G_7 chords used here are placed in inversion with the fifth of the chord eliminated (see chapter 4, "Combining Musical Sounds," p. 77).

MERRILY WE ROLL ALONG

TRADITIONAL

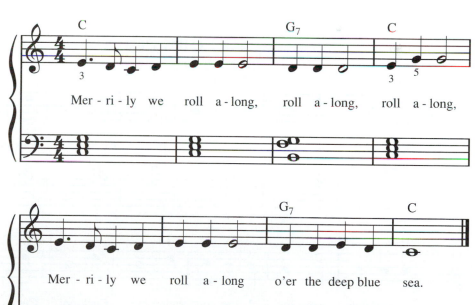

Mer - ri - ly we roll a - long, roll a - long, roll a - long,

Mer - ri - ly we roll a - long o'er the deep blue sea.

Playing Keyboard Instruments

SOME FOLKS DO

Stephen Foster

Playing Basic Chords in G Major

Play the notes of the chord separately, and then sound them simultaneously.

G Chord—I

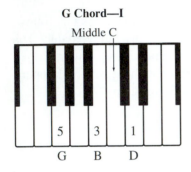

D₇ Chord—V₇

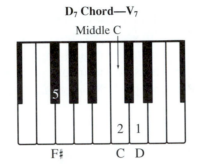

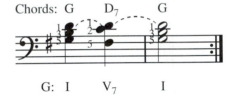

THE CUCKOO

Germany

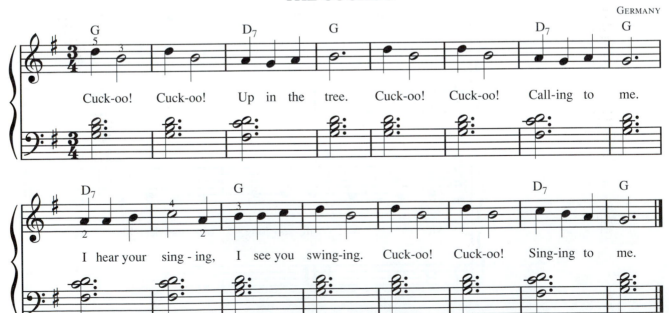

Cuck-oo! Cuck-oo! Up in the tree. Cuck-oo! Cuck-oo! Call-ing to me.

I hear your sing - ing, I see you swing-ing. Cuck-oo! Cuck-oo! Sing-ing to me.

Playing Basic Chords in F Major

Play the notes of the chord separately, and then sound them simultaneously.

AUF WIEDERSEHEN

GERMANY

Auf Wie - der - sehen, Auf Wie - der - sehen, Now that our school's at an end

we'll say good - bye to our friends. Auf Wie - der - sehen, Auf Wie - der - sehen.

Chording Melodies in Minor Keys

Playing Basic Chords in A Minor

The hand positions, common notes, and fingerings in the chord progressions are the same for both major and minor keys. Note, however, the addition of sharps and/or flats.

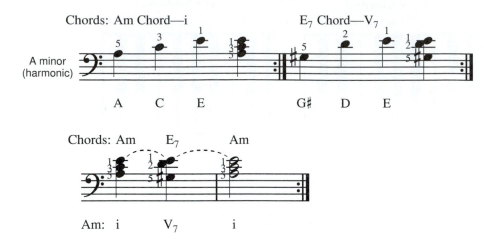

FOLK TUNE

Playing Basic Chords in E Minor

E minor (harmonic)

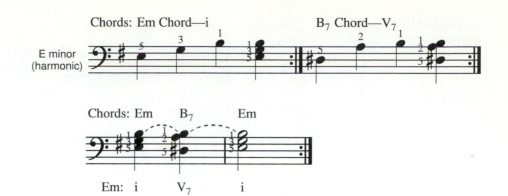

Em: i   V₇   i

SLEEP, MY BABY

Eve-ning time is com-ing soon, Birds have hushed their _ sing - ing, Shad-ows gent - ly

fill the _ room, Send your cares a - wing - ing, Sleep, oh, sleep, my _ ba - by.

Playing Basic Chords in D Minor

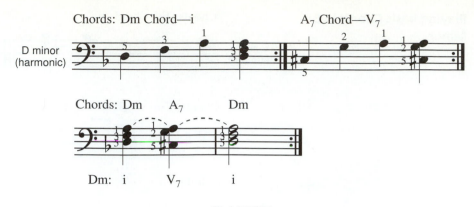

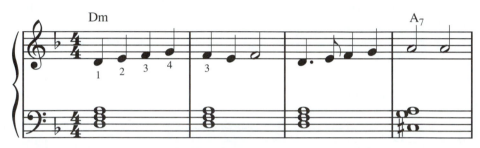

DANCE

HUNGARY

Note: Practice all of the piano chords in Appendix 3 in both treble and bass clefs (pp. 349–350).

Playing Keyboard Instruments

Using the IV Chord with I and V₇ in C Major

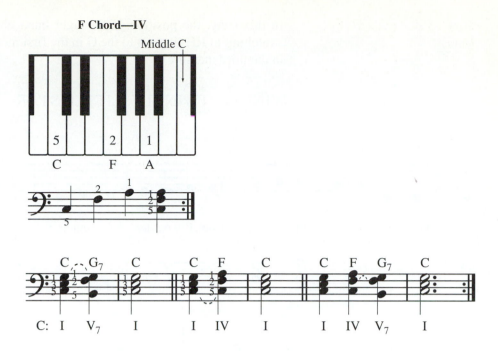

F Chord—IV

Extending the Five-Finger Position

The range of notes can be extended by expanding the hand position. *Fingerings involving a change of hand position are circled.*

LAVENDER'S BLUE

ENGLAND

Lav - en - der's blue, dil - ly, dil - ly, Lav - en - der's green.

When I am king, dil - ly, dil - ly, You shall be queen.

In this song, the position of the right hand changes to accommodate the stretching of RH finger 4 to the G in the first measure and the return to the F in the third measure.

TWINKLE, TWINKLE, LITTLE STAR

FRANCE

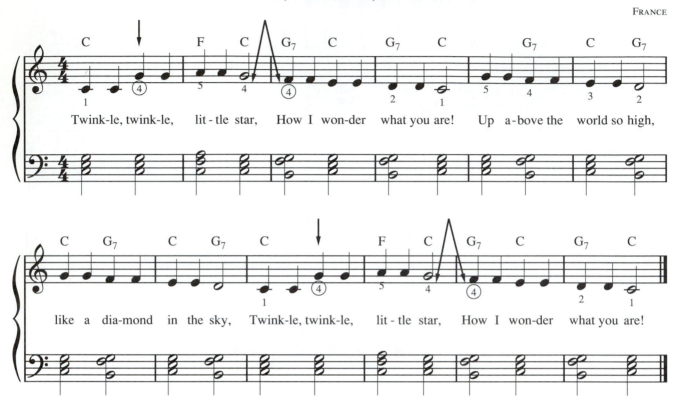

The technique of *bass chanting* is covered in chapter 12, "Singing in Harmony," p. 293. The same technique can be applied to piano playing in a similar manner. Try playing the *roots* of the chords of *Twinkle, Twinkle, Little Star* to get a flair for this easy method of producing simple harmony.

Playing Accompaniment Patterns

Chords can be played in various patterns to make more interesting accompaniments. The following are particularly useful in playing accompaniments for familiar songs.

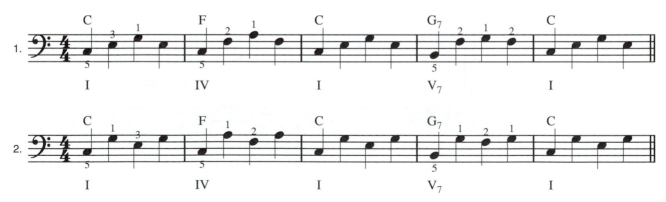

JINGLE BELLS

J.S. Pierpont

Repeat using patterns 1 and 4 (pp. 158 and 159).

Note: Play this song with each hand separately first. Observe right-hand fingering.

DU, DU, LIEGST MIR IM HERZEN

German Folk Song

liegst mir im Sinn; Du, du, machst mir viel Schmerz - en;

Weiss nicht wie gut ich dir bin; _____ Ja, ja,

ja, ja, weiss nicht wie gut ich dir bin. _____

(Translation: You are my heart's love; you are the love of my mind; you make me feel pained, for I do not know what I am to you.)

Accompanying Singing and Playing with Bass Accents (>) and Chords (Oompah Style)

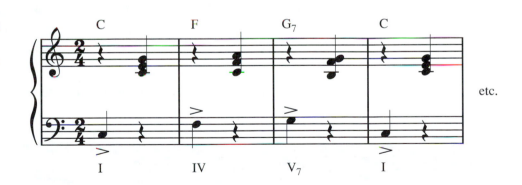

etc.

I   IV   V₇   I

Creating Accompaniments

Improvise chord, bass accent, and broken-chord accompaniments for the following melodies.

K–4, 3b
5–8, 3a

NORWEGIAN DANCE

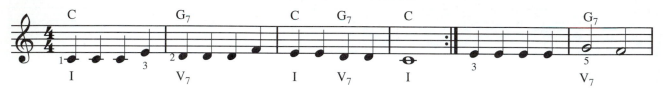

A-HUNTING WE WILL GO

ENGLAND

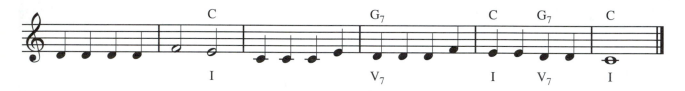

Oh, a - hunt - ing we will go, a - hunt - ing we will go. We'll

catch a lit - tle fox and put him in a box and nev - er let him go.

A broken-chord accompaniment is very effective with *Silent Night*.

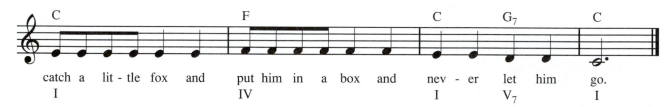

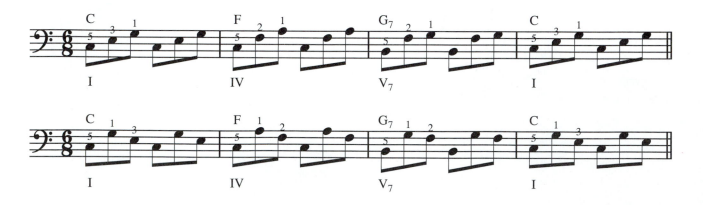

SILENT NIGHT

JOSEPH MOHR

FRANZ GRUBER

Si - lent night! ho - ly night! All is calm, all is bright.

Round yon vir - gin Moth - er and Child, Ho - ly In - fant, so ten - der and mild,

Sleep in heav - en - ly peace, ___ Sleep ___ in heav - en - ly peace. ___

Electronic Keyboards

The advancements in scientific and entertainment technology are evident all around us, and nowhere more than in the modern classroom. After the computer, by far the most useful and successful technological advancement is the *electronic keyboard and synthesizer,* available in a variety and range of sizes, sounds, and computer tie-ins. Some instruments are stand-alone units, while others require external speakers or headphones, or stands, and can be linked to computers to work complex MIDI files. No matter how simple, complex, or intimidating an electronic keyboard may appear, the basic piano skills already practiced in this chapter will be a more than adequate beginning to a lifetime of musical promise. The electronic keyboard affords exciting possibilities beyond those of the acoustic piano:

1. With one button these keyboards can produce rhythms and percussion combinations for all types of traditional and world music, including singing games, folk songs, rock, country, big band, Latin, Caribbean, and African.

2. Pressing one key can produce a full chord of three or more notes.

3. Accompaniments can be produced to fit the chord progressions of a chosen piece. These accompaniments can be block or broken chords, or a combination of both.

4. Bass patterns can be automatically generated to accompany the melody of the right hand, and stylized bass patterns, such as walking basses, are available in some keyboards.

Example of electronic keyboard

5. The sound produced by the keyboard can be changed at the touch of a button. Typical sounds include piano, organ, flute, guitar, violin, vibes, harp, and saxophone. Many keyboards also offer mixtures such as strings and "fantasia" (usually a vocal/choral "ah" sound).

6. Some keyboards will allow an expanded number of sampled instrumental sounds and digital effects through the addition of a sound module or through computer CD-Rom.

7. Some keyboards will allow a complex pattern of melody, harmony, and rhythm to be constructed—line by line, layering one part upon another—so that the finished product is quite elaborate and fascinating, while the procedure is much more simple than teacher or student might expect.

8. Some keyboards will store information on a floppy disk or other storage device, enabling children to encounter the intriguing world of musical composition and arranging, allowing the teacher to create and store an ever-increasing library of rhythms and accompaniments.

9. No tuning is necessary on electronic keyboards.

Children by nature are fascinated by the wide array of sounds around them, and the electronic keyboard allows them to explore the sounds of diverse musical instruments through a single keyboard. A teacher can use these vibrant and colorful instruments to accompany a wide range of musical activities.

Keyboards vary widely in price, yet many less-complicated but full-featured instruments are economically priced to fit the budgets of most schools. Prominent manufacturers include *Roland, Yamaha,* and *Suzuki.* Information, specifications, and pricing are available in most music stores, through music mail-order companies, and on the World Wide Web.

A keyboard laboratory multiplies the possibilities already found in a single keyboard. By linking keyboards, both teacher and students can create music together with the sounds of a complete band or orchestra. Each student can be given a simple part and unique sounds to produce; when everyone plays together, the sum is much greater than each individual part. Labs can be situated to teach children piano keyboard skills as time and teacher's skill permits.

The basis for playing the electronic keyboard is the same as for the acoustic piano, so the skills learned in this chapter will suffice for enabling one to navigate the keys. Methods exist for learning the specifics of electronic keyboards, complete with the special effects possible on these instruments. A successful and manageable method is *Alfred's Basic Electronic Keyboard Course* by Palmer, Manus, and Lethco, Alfred Publishing Co. For any particular instrument, familiarize yourself with the placement and variety of sound, rhythm, and other options, so that you need not hunt for them. Switching keyboards, or using one for the first time, can be as frustrating as changing word-processing programs—the function keys are all rearranged, but with a few minutes of extra study, a new keyboard will restore your self-confidence and ability to communicate the excitement of music to others.

K–4, 4c
5–8, 4c

K–4, 2e
5–8, 2a

Elementary student Amber Canava in a keyboard lab, Wichita Falls, Texas.

CHAPTER 8

Playing Classroom Percussion Instruments

Experience with percussion instruments is invaluable, not only for developing rhythmic sensitivity and coordination, but also for building other musical insights, such as a feeling for musical structure. In addition, it provides another interesting musical activity for teachers and children with limited musical background.

Playing Rhythm Instruments

K–4, 6d

Examples of rhythm instruments used in the classroom are shown here. Others include wrist- and hand-played bells, gongs, claves, guiros, coconut shells, temple blocks, wood blocks, and pom-poms. These, as well as instruments made by children themselves, bring added enjoyment to the music period.

Rhythm Sticks

One stick is struck against the other, producing a clicking sound. If one stick is notched, a gourd effect can be produced by rubbing the other over it.

Tone Blocks

Small, medium, and large tone blocks are available; they produce hollow tones of high, medium, and low pitch. The tone is sounded by striking the hollow barrel with the mallet midway between the two slots.

Sand Blocks

Sand blocks are rubbed together to produce a deep swishing sound.

Jingle Sticks (also called Jingle Clogs)

The jingle stick is struck against the palm of the hand for single beats. A roll is made by rotating the wrist. Five jingle sticks can be substituted for one tambourine.

Castanets

The castanet with a handle is struck against the palm of the hand for a single click. Roll effects are produced by rotating and snapping the wrist. Finger castanets are worn on the thumb of each hand and are played by the fingers with a crisp, short, tapping action.

Maracas

The Latin-American rhythm instruments called maracas are played by shaking easily, using the wrist as a pivot.

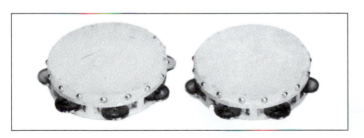

Tambourines

The tambourine is held with fingers in a slot of the wood frame. For light beats, strike the bottom edge of the tambourine with the open hand or tap with a striker or the fingers. For accented beats, strike with the knuckles. For a roll effect, rotate the wrist freely and shake.

Triangle

To produce a clear tone on a triangle, strike the side opposite the open corner with the straight end of the metal striker. A wood striker produces a softer ring. For a roll effect, rotate the beater in the corner against both sides, using free wrist action. The triangle should always be suspended with a cord loop for full vibration.

Courtesy of The World of Peripole, Inc., Browns Mills, New Jersey 08015.

Drums

All sizes and types of drums can be played with the hand or a mallet. To prevent muffling, drumheads must be completely free from contact with any object while being played. For this reason slings are provided with some drums.

Cymbals

Cymbals come in many different sizes. Crash effects with cymbals are produced by an up-and-down sweep of the arms. For single beats and gong effects, hold one cymbal with a sling and strike it with a mallet. Finger cymbals are fitted on the thumb and forefinger of each hand and played by clashing them together. The player can also hold one cymbal and strike it with a mallet.

Classifying the Rhythm Instruments

Rhythm or percussion instruments can be played in different ways, making countless numbers of sounds. They can be shaken, struck, tapped, rolled, plucked, rubbed, swished, and so forth. Woods often make clicking and scraping sounds. Metals can produce sounds of clanging, ringing, and tingling. Skins are struck, tapped, etc. Examples of instruments classified by the materials out of which they are made follow:

Woods	Metals	Skins
rhythm sticks	hand cymbals	drums of all sizes and
claves	finger cymbals	shapes:
wood blocks	suspended cymbals	tom-toms, congas,
tone blocks	gongs	bongos, snares, etc.
temple blocks	wrist bells	tambourines
coconut shells	sleigh bells	
castanets	triangles	
guiros	tambourines	
tap-a-taps	jingle sticks	

Some instruments are made out of more than one type of material like the tambourines, which include metal and/or wood and/or skin. Similarly, swishing instruments include sand blocks, maracas, pom-poms, and any other type of a *shaker* made out of various materials.

Arranging the Instrumentation

Which instruments produce the most appropriate sound effects for different types of music? Small instruments usually play the fastest rhythmic patterns, and large instruments provide basic beats and accents. The ringing or jingling instruments provide sound effects for light, higher-pitched music, while the drums produce background for deep, rhythmic music.

National characteristics of music can be enhanced by the selection of instruments used to play rhythmic patterns associated with various countries and peoples. For example, tambourines, shakers, and castanets suggest Mexican or Spanish music; tom-toms and drums, Native American music; bongo drums, claves, guiros, and maracas, Latin American music. Examples of various multicultural instruments that can be incorporated into the classroom follow:

1.

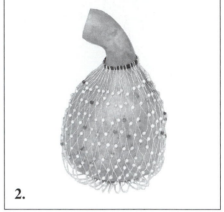

2.

4.

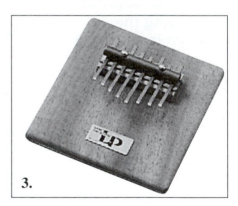

3.

5.

African

1. Agogo Bells are of African origin. The bells produce two distinct sounds when struck by a wood mallet.

2. Axatse is a beaded rattle widely used in Western Africa, especially by the peoples of Ghana. This instrument is used in percussion ensembles to produce a buzzing, rattling effect.

3. Mbira is an African thumb piano. This widely used instrument produces different scales and scale segments according to the number of tones available.

4. Squeeze Drum is a variety of Nigerian talking drum. It fits underneath the arm and is squeezed with various pressures while tapping with the other hand to vary the pitch.

5. Slit Log Drums are ancient African resonating chambers that are capable of producing different pitches or scale segments. They are played with soft mallets that do not wear away the wood surface of the drums.

1.

2.

South American

1. Rain Stick is a Chilean instrument produced from cactus. Enclosed pebbles produce a rainlike effect as the stick is gradually turned from one end to the other.
2. Samba Whistle is a blown instrument of Brazil that produces three distinctive tones.

1.

3.

2.

Far Eastern

1. Den Den is an instrument of Japanese origin. Played by placing the handle or stem between the two hands and rolling it back and forth, the instrument creates a rhythmic sound as the two plastic beads attached to strings hit the respective heads rhythmically.
2. Kokiriko is an ancient Japanese instrument. Wooden slats are strung together and strike each other in domino style.
3. Nipple Gong, with its various indentations, is a typical Burmese instrument that is handcrafted out of metal to produce traditional Asian gonglike sounds and overtones.

1.

2.

Native American and Native Hawaiian

1. Ankle Bells, produced by Native Americans and worn on the ankles or wrists, produce a jingling sound when the wearer walks or dances.
2. Uli Uli are Hawaiian feathered gourds attached to rattan handles. The feathers are of bright colors while the gourds are filled with beads to produce sound.

Rhythm Instrument Scores

K–4, 2b

For clarity of sound, only a few instruments are played at one time, especially when they are used to accompany classroom singing. A feeling for musical form and structure can be taught by having a different group of instruments play each phrase or section of the music.

Printed rhythm instrument scores are seldom used in the modern classroom. The following sample scores are provided to demonstrate typical uses for different instruments.

A simple score for *Yankee Doodle* (see p. 123 for melody) could be arranged as follows:

YANKEE DOODLE

Melody Pattern

Tambourines
Triangles
Finger cymbals

Underlying Beat

Rhythm sticks
Tone blocks

Accent

Drum
Hand cymbal

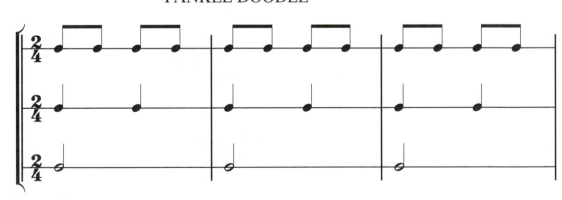

Playing Classroom Percussion Instruments

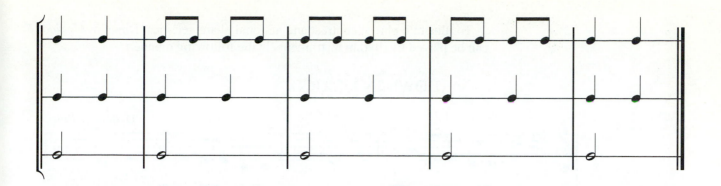

Exercise 1

Chant the following speech game and play a rhythm instrument in the rests.

'ROUND IN A CIRCLE

Margaret Campbelle-duGard   Margaret Campbelle-duGard

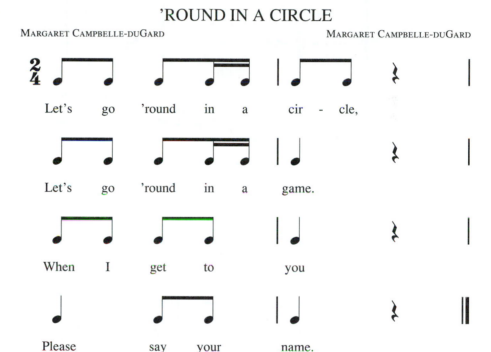

Let's go 'round in a cir - cle,

Let's go 'round in a game.

When I get to you

Please say your name.

To illustrate phrase contrast and national characteristics, *Down in Mexico* can be played by rhythm instruments in the following manner:

DOWN IN MEXICO

Playing Classroom Percussion Instruments

Play and sing *La Raspa* ("the sound of feet while dancing") and *Calypso Joe*. Create rhythmic patterns on castanets, tambourines, maracas, claves, and other instruments. Then, play the rhythmic pattern of the *melody* of each song on one instrument.

K–4, 2b, 2c, 4b
5–8, 2c

LA RASPA

TR. MAURICE TALBOT

MEXICO

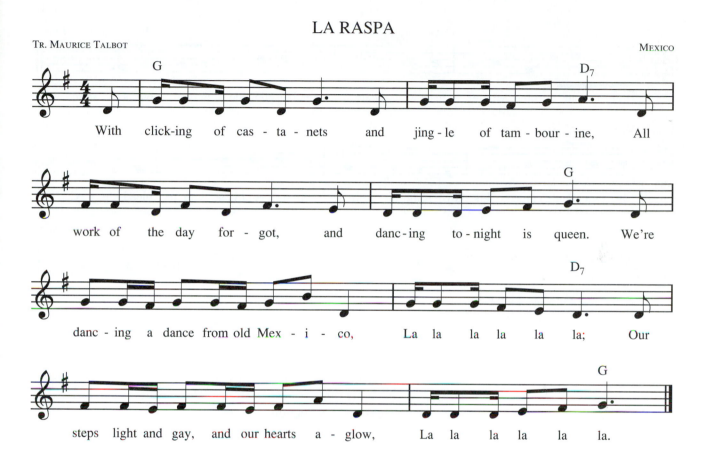

With click-ing of cas - ta - nets and jing - le of tam - bour - ine, All

work of the day for - got, and danc - ing to - night is queen. We're

danc - ing a dance from old Mex - i - co, La la la la la la; Our

steps light and gay, and our hearts a - glow, La la la la la la.

CALYPSO JOE

Refrain

I know a boy down on Nas-sau isle, Joe is his name, he's got a win-ning smile.

"How a-bout a shine, Mist-er, just a dime?" Sings lit-tle Joe in ca-lyp-so time.

Verse

If you should come to his town some-day, _ he'll cap-ture your heart with his plead-ing way, _

Sing-ing and clap-ping his tune so bright, _ He'll nev-er let you out of sight. _

Also play and sing *Las Pollitas* (p. 317), creating appropriate instrumentations.

The following typical calypso rhythmic patterns can be used to accompany *Calypso Joe* and many other Caribbean tunes. These patterns can be used as two- and four-measure introductions and codas (endings).

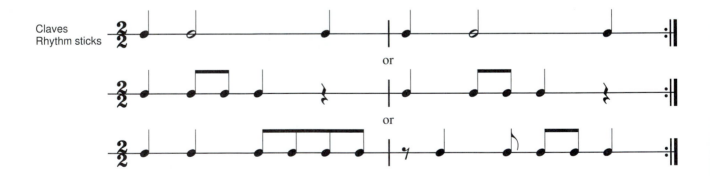

Claves
Rhythm sticks

or

or

Playing Classroom Percussion Instruments

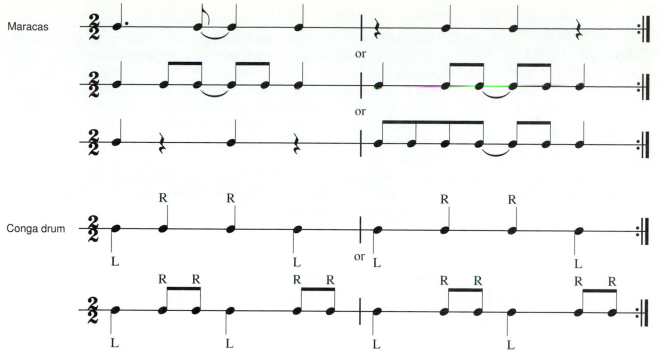

For pitch variation, play L (left hand) in the center of the drum and R (right hand) on the edge.

Exercise 2

Add the following ostinato accompaniment to *My Home's in Montana* (p. 285) in chapter 12, "Singing in Harmony," and repeat it throughout the song.

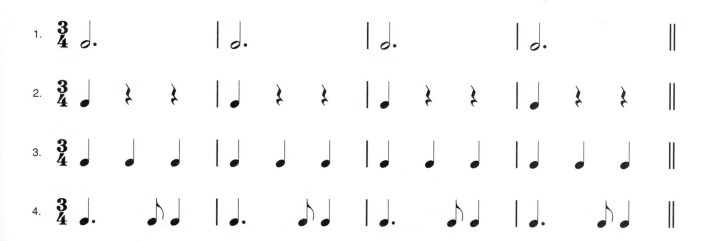

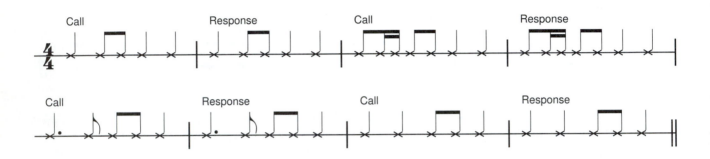

Playing Bells

Uses for Bells in the Classroom

K–4, 2b, 4b

Bells have proven to be an effective aid in teaching children to enjoy and understand music. For teachers and children with limited musical background, bells are especially helpful in learning simple melodies. Bells can be used as follows:

1. To teach rote songs to children. Teachers who choose not to sing or who have low-pitched voices can play the tune. Also, difficult tonal patterns and phrases can be learned quickly by having them played several times on the bells.
2. To pitch and start songs. In pitching the song, bells can be used to sound the keynote or first few pitches of the song, check the pitch at phrase and song endings, etc. Some teachers prefer the bells since the key chord, 1–3–5 (*do-mi-so*), can be played more easily. Interesting introductions can be made with bells. Also, the first or last phrase of the song or a simple tonal pattern can be used to start the piece.
3. To provide simple accompaniments, descants, and codas for children's songs.
4. To create special sound effects in the music, such as imitating chimes, clocks, church bells, and sleigh bells.

5. To provide creative opportunities by having children take turns constructing their own tunes.
6. To provide ear training through tone matching activities to help out-of-tune singers locate and sing pitches that have been played on the bells.
7. To create a classroom orchestra with recorder, percussion instruments, Omnichord, and piano.

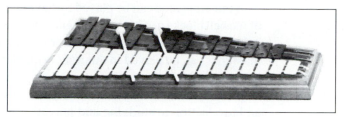

Courtesy of Wallberg & Auge, 86 Mechanic St., Worcester, Massachusetts.

Song Bells (Melody Bells)

Song bells are available in sets of various sizes, ranging from eight bars to the popular and very useful two-and-a-half octave set pictured above.

Step Bells

Step bells are available in two sizes—an eight-note C to C diatonic set, and a seventeen-note C to E chromatic set. These special bar bells are mounted on a staircase frame. They are used in the classroom to show visually the relationship between pitch, half and whole steps, and scale elevation. Step bells are an invaluable audiovisual aid for students who do not understand pitch direction.

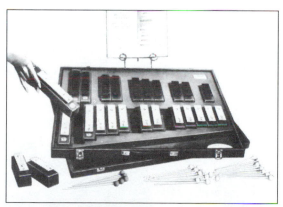

Courtesy of Scientific Music Industries, Inc., 1255 S. Wabash Ave., Chicago, Illinois 60805.

Tone Educator Bells

Tone Educator Bells are available in two sizes, a twenty-bell set (one-and-a-half octaves, C through G) and a twenty-five bell set (two octaves, G through G). These bells can be removed from the case and played individually or in various combinations. They can be used in any key since they are built chromatically. (Resonator Bells are similar to Tone Educator Bells; the two can be used interchangeably.)

Uses for Tone Educator Bells in the Classroom

A unique feature of Tone Educator Bells is that the player can choose from the set *only* the bells that are needed for any given song. For example, the beginner in music can start with as few as three bell blocks to play such tunes as *Hot Cross Buns* and *Merry Bells,* and then go to five-tone songs like *Jingle Bells* and *Lightly Row,* six-tone songs like *Twinkle, Twinkle, Little Star,* and so on, adding bells for wider range songs. This is a practical way to introduce sharps and flats one at a time.

A musical game can be played by having individual class members hold one of the bell blocks needed for a certain tune. Each plays the note for the bell block held when signaled by the teacher or student director. Both familiar and original tunes can be played in this way, with all children in the room taking turns in the activity.

It is important to note that Tone Educator Bells can be used effectively as an introduction to studying and playing harmony. These bells provide beautiful chordal accompaniments for classroom singing. Individual students are given single notes of a chord and all the notes of a given chord are sounded simultaneously to produce the required harmony. Refer to *Ring, Ring the Banjo* (p. 185) and chapter 4, "Combining Musical Sounds" (p. 77), where harmony created with Tone Chimes, Chimettes, and Handbells is discussed.

How to Play the Bells

The mallet should be held firmly. Use a bouncing blow, flexing the wrist quickly just as the bar is struck. The use of two mallets struck alternately facilitates playing fast passages. When two mallets are used, a roll can be made by a fast movement of the wrists and hands for sustained notes.

Courtesy of Karen Evans, Music Consultant, Bobier Elementary School, Vista, California.

Line Notation

Teachers and children who have little experience reading music can learn to play simple tunes on the bells through the use of *line notation.* (See chapter 3, p. 44.) The number or letter over a word indicates the bar to be struck to produce the melody note. These can be written on the bars with chalk or crayon. The approximate duration of the notes is indicated by the relative lengths of the lines. At first use songs that move stepwise, such as *Hot Cross Buns* and *Merry Bells.*

Playing Classroom Percussion Instruments

HOT CROSS BUNS

NURSERY SONG

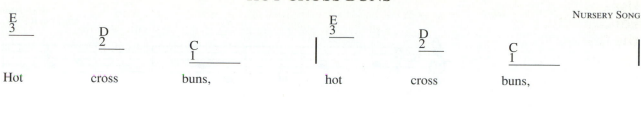

| E 3 | D 2 | C 1 | | E 3 | D 2 | C 1 | |
Hot — cross — buns, — hot — cross — buns,

| C 1 | C 1 | C 1 | C 1 | D 2 | D 2 | D 2 | D 2 | E 3 | D 2 | C 1 | |
One — a — pen - ny, — two — a — pen - ny, — hot — cross — buns.

MERRY BELLS

WALES

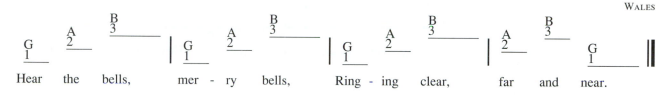

| G 1 | A 2 | B 3 | G 1 | A 2 | B 3 | G 1 | A 2 | B 3 | A 2 | B 3 | G 1 | |
Hear — the — bells, — mer - ry — bells, — Ring - ing — clear, — far — and — near.

Using Staff Notation

Note: Play the following exercises and songs using staff notation. Practicing the exercises and songs for piano right-hand position presented in chapter 7, starting on p. 136, will be helpful at this point.

K–4, 2a

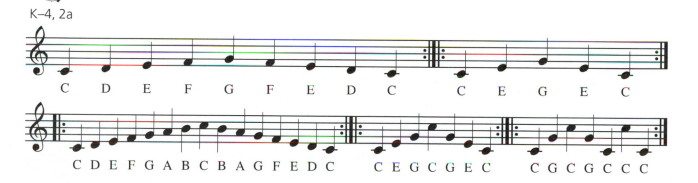

C D E F G F E D C   C E G E C

C D E F G A B C B A G F E D C   C E G C G E C   C G C G C C C

VALENTINE SONG

UNITED STATES
ADAPTED R.W.W.

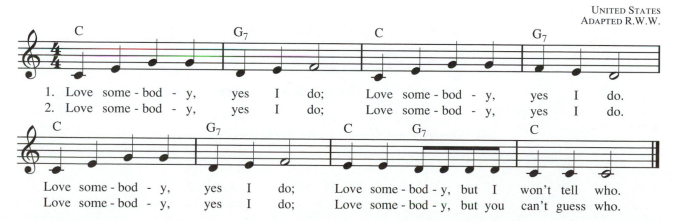

1. Love some-bod - y, yes I do; Love some-bod - y, yes I do.
2. Love some-bod - y, yes I do; Love some-bod - y, yes I do.

Love some-bod - y, yes I do; Love some-bod - y, but I won't tell who.
Love some-bod - y, yes I do; Love some-bod - y, but you can't guess who.

BIG BEN CLOCK

ENGLAND
ADAPTED R.W.W.

STEEPLE BELLS

FRANCE

Stee-ple bells are gent-ly ring-ing, Hear them ring - ing,

"Peace on earth" is what they're say-ing, Hear them ring - ing.

EVENING BELLS

NURSERY SONG

Those eve-ning bells, those eve-ning bells, how many a tale their

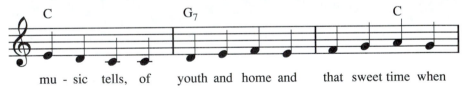

mu - sic tells, of youth and home and that sweet time when

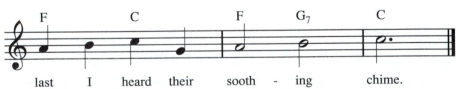

last I heard their sooth - ing chime.

Also play and sing *Joy to the World* (p. 220).

EBENEEZER SNEEZER

Lynn Freeman Olson   Lynn Freeman Olson

Eb - en - eez - er Sneez-er,   Top - sy - turv - y man,

Walks up - on his el - bows   Ev - 'ry time he can,

Dress - es up in pa - per   Ev - 'ry time it pours,

Whist-les "Yank - ee Dood - le"   Ev - 'ry time he snores.

Oh,   Eb - en - eez - er, what a   man!

WHITE CORAL BELLS

ROUND

England

①

1. White cor - al bells   up - on a slend - er stalk,
2. O, don't you wish that you could hear them ring?

②

Lil - ies of the val - ley deck my   gar - den walk.
That will hap - pen on - ly when the   fair - ies sing.

JINGLE BELLS

J. Pierpont

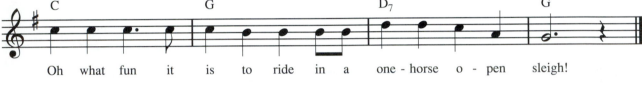

Jing - le bells, jing - le bells, jing - le all the way.

Oh what fun it is to ride in a one - horse o - pen sleigh, ___

Jing - le bells, jing - le bells, jing - le all the way.

Oh what fun it is to ride in a one - horse o - pen sleigh!

Playing in Harmony

The following songs can be performed by one or more players.

K–4, 2e

JACOB'S LADDER

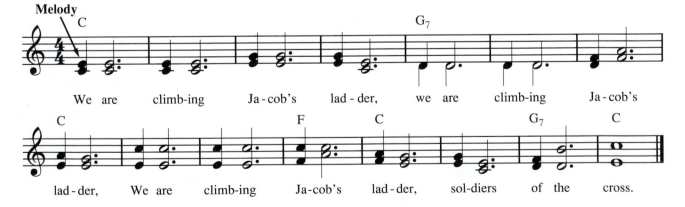

We are climb-ing Ja-cob's lad - der, we are climb-ing Ja-cob's

lad - der, We are climb-ing Ja-cob's lad - der, sol-diers of the cross.

Next, play and sing *De Colores* (p. 291).

RING, RING THE BANJO

Stephen C. Foster

Stephen C. Foster

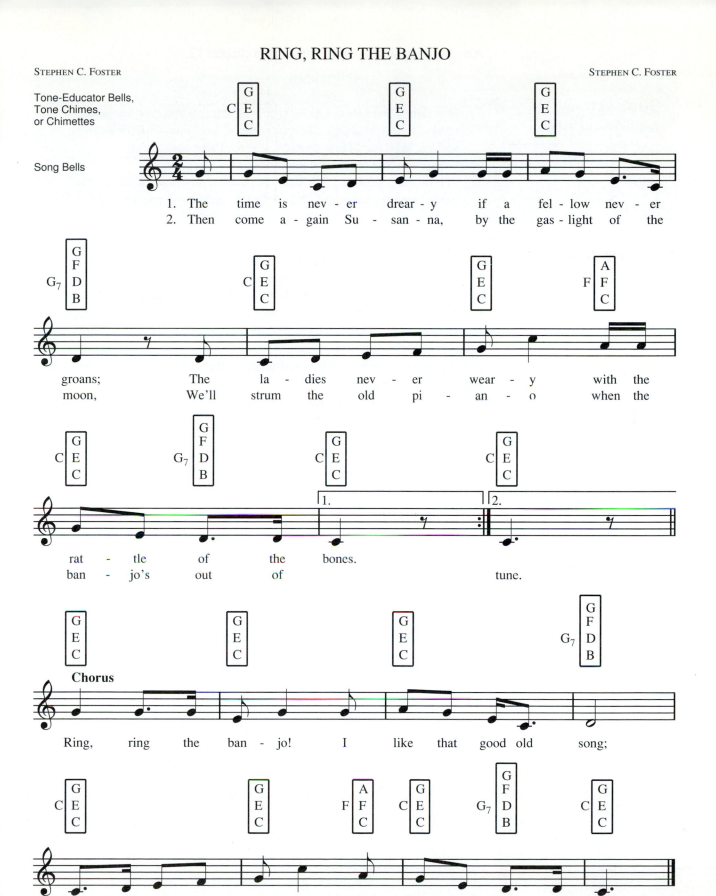

Also play and sing two-part songs from chapter 12.

Suggested Assignments

1. Play songs from state and local school songbook series. Include songs with several parts. Practice finding and sounding the keynote and the key chord (1–3–5–8–5–3–1) for these songs.
2. Create and play your own melodies.
3. Practice the chromatic scale on the bells up and down between the lowest and highest notes, and gradually increase the speed.

The Orff Approach

The Orff approach to teaching music is based on a program developed by *Carl Orff* (1895–1982) at the Guentherschule, a school of music, dance, and gymnastics in Munich, Germany. His ideas have won acclaim and acceptance by music educators throughout the world. Orff's uniquely creative approach introduces music to children through their own speech and rhythmic movement, and through singing and playing percussion and melody instruments. His belief proposes that the primary instrument is the body and that all other instruments extend from it.

A brief introduction to some of Carl Orff's approaches to music education and the skills involved is presented here. Teachers and students who wish to pursue this very important topic further should refer to the classic text *Elementaria,* by Carl Orff's longtime associate, Gunild Keetman.

Speech and Rhythmic Experiences

Chanting

Chanting results from the instinctive connection between speech and rhythm. Through the rhythm of the words, children naturally and delightfully relate to their carefree world of play and imagery, whether they are chanting traditional nursery rhymes or creating their own rhymes about their activities, their friends, or their pets.

Clapping

Clapping, the simplest form of bodily movement, occurs spontaneously as children begin to feel the rhythm of the words.

Chant and clap the rhythms of the following:

Tom - my, Mar - y, come and play with me.

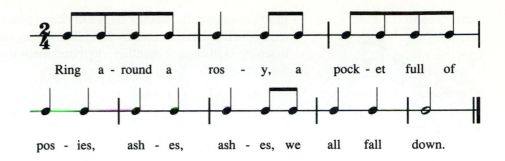

Ring a-round a ros - y, a pock-et full of pos - ies, ash - es, ash - es, we all fall down.

HEY, CHILDREN, WHO'S IN TOWN?

Carol Bitcon   Carol Bitcon

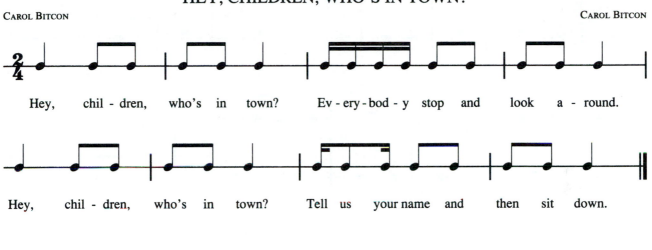

Hey, chil - dren, who's in town? Ev - ery - bod - y stop and look a - round.

Hey, chil - dren, who's in town? Tell us your name and then sit down.

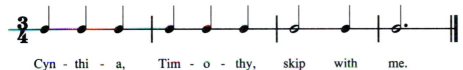

Cyn - thi - a, Tim - o - thy, skip with me.

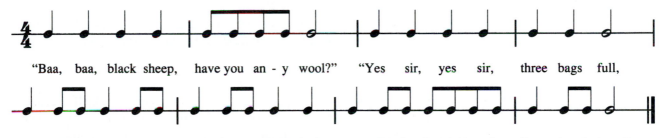

"Baa, baa, black sheep, have you an - y wool?" "Yes sir, yes sir, three bags full,

One for my mast - er and one for my dame, And one for the lit - tle boy that lives in the lane."

Orff teachers have found that, through repeated use in combinations of various rhythms, these patterns imprint themselves quickly and soon are readily recognized and reproduced in music reading and writing.

K–4, 5a

Echo Clapping

K–4, 4d

In *echo clapping,* the teacher claps a rhythmic pattern of one, two, or more measures, which is to be imitated by the children. This exercise is designed to develop listening skills, quick reaction, rhythmic memory, and feeling for form. Clap the following:

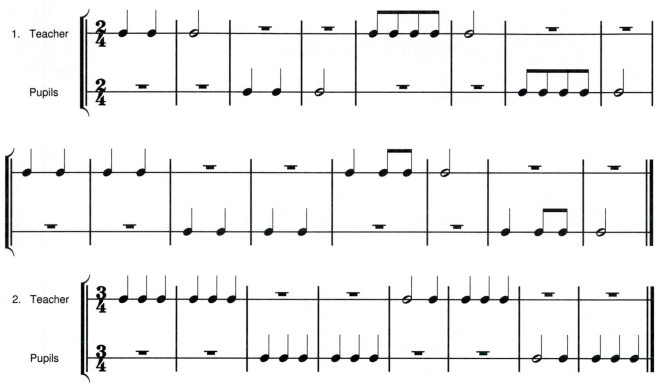

From Lawrence Wheeler and Lois Raebeck, *Orff and Kodály Adapted for the Elementary School,* 3d ed. Copyright © 1984 Wm. C. Brown Publishers, Dubuque, Iowa. All Rights Reserved. Reprinted by permission.

Improvise various other rhythmic patterns in duple and triple meter with gradually increased difficulty to include dotted rhythms, syncopation, triplets, and the like.

Other Bodily Movements (Patschen, Stamping, Finger Snapping)

In addition to chanting and clapping, a prominent feature of the Orff approach to rhythmic training is the use of various bodily movements such as patschen, stamping feet, and snapping fingers. Wheeler and Raebeck include many excellent exercises for rhythmic experiences in their valuable book, *Orff and Kodály Adapted for the Elementary School.*[1] A few of these exercises are shown here; practice the patterns indicated. For patschen, simultaneously pat the left thigh with the left hand and the right thigh with the right hand. (See pp. 28–29 for additional experiences with patschen.)

[1]Wheeler, Lawrence, and Raebeck, Lois, *Orff and Kodály Adapted for the Elementary School.* 3d ed. Dubuque, Ia.: Wm. C. Brown Company Publishers, 1984.

Playing Classroom Percussion Instruments

For Primary Grades

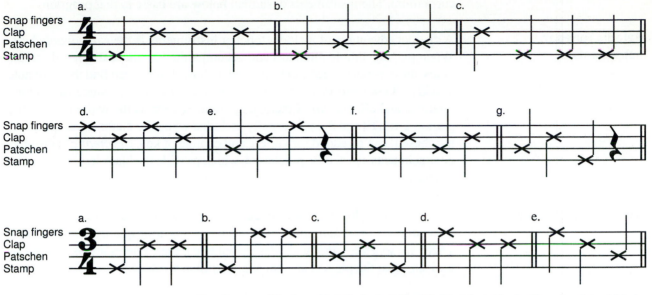

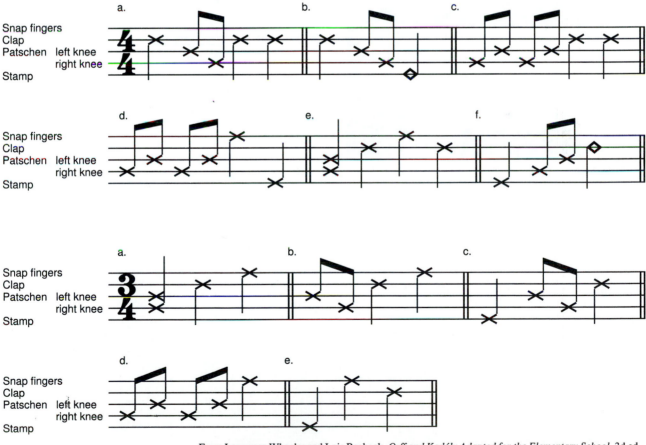

From Lawrence Wheeler and Lois Raebeck, *Orff and Kodály Adapted for the Elementary School,* 3d ed. Copyright © 1984 Wm. C. Brown Publishers, Dubuque, Iowa. All Rights Reserved. Reprinted by permission.

For Upper Grades

From Lawrence Wheeler and Lois Raebeck, *Orff and Kodály Adapted for the Elementary School,* 3d ed. Copyright © 1984 Wm. C. Brown Publishers, Dubuque, Iowa. All Rights Reserved. Reprinted by permission.

Playing Classroom Percussion Instruments

189

Playing Orff-Designed Instruments

The playing of these unique and fascinating instruments provides creative and joyful experiences in bridging the gap between rhythm and melody in the Orff curriculum. The instruments described below are basic to that program.

Melodic Tonebar Instruments

A distinct advantage of melodic tonebar instruments is their *removable* bars. When playing simple melodies and accompaniments that call for only a few notes, the bars not needed can be removed; thus, children can find the right note quickly. These instruments are made of wood or metal to produce varied tone qualities and effects. All of them are diatonic (same as the white keys of the piano). Extra F♯ and B♭ bars (usually included when the diatonic instrument is purchased) can be added for variety and change of key. *Chromatic* "add-ons" or attachments can also be purchased, which provide the black key (chromatic) pitches.

Wood-Barred Instruments

Tonebars for xylophones are made of rosewood or fiberglass and set on a resonator box or an aluminum tube resonator. The tone quality is *mellow-dry*. There are *soprano, alto,* and *bass* xylophones; their ranges are as follows (*8* indicates that the pitch is an octave higher than written):

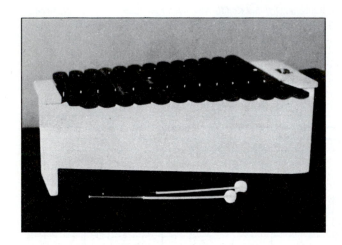

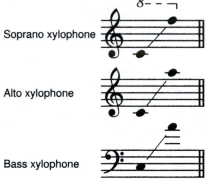

Metal-Barred Instruments

Metallophones

Tonebars for metallophones are also removable. They are made of metal alloy and set over box resonators. The tone quality is rich, mellow, and bell-like. Tone Educator Bells or Tone Chimes may be substituted for metallophones. There are *soprano, alto,* and *bass* metallophones; their ranges are as follows:

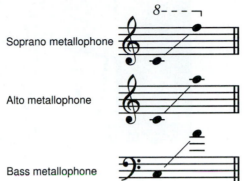

Glockenspiels

Tonebars for glockenspiels are made of tempered steel and are set on wooden resonator boxes. The tone quality is a bright, ringing, bell-like sound. Large sets of melody song bells (or Chimettes) may be substituted, if necessary. There are *soprano* and *alto* glockenspiels; their ranges are as follows (*15* indicates that the pitch is two octaves higher than written):

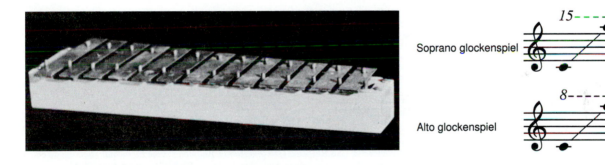

Xylophones, metallophones, and glockenspiels can be purchased as diatonic or chromatic instruments.

**Tuned Percussion
Instruments**

The drums shown below are used in pairs to give an octave range. They are usually tuned to *do* and *so* (scale steps 1 and 5), sometimes to *do* and *re* (steps 1 and 2), *so* and *la* (steps 5 and 6), or *do* and *la* (steps 1 and 6). The heads are made of skin or resonant plastic, and hand screws are used for tuning. They are

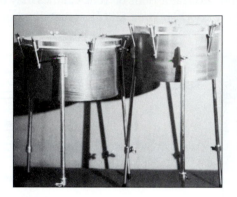

played with wool- or felt-headed mallets. Wheeler and Raebeck recommend the twenty- and sixteen-inch timbales to meet the needs of the average classroom.

These two drums are especially useful in accompanying songs pitched in the C, D, F, and G *pentatonic* scales, as shown below:

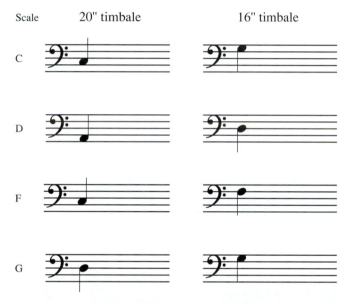

Pentatonic scales are based on a five-note scale—steps 1–2–3–5–6 of the major scale. All melodies used with Orff instruments are *pentatonic*, thereby avoiding clashing dissonant harmonies. C and G are the most commonly used in the Orff approach.

Also refer to pages 52–54, in chapter 3.

Playing Classroom Percussion Instruments

Untuned Percussion Instruments

See the beginning of this chapter for photographs and/or descriptions of the following percussion instruments.

triangles (several sizes)	rhythm sticks
tone blocks	rattles
sand blocks	maracas
finger cymbals	tambourines

Other Orff Instruments for the Classroom

String Instruments

viola da gamba
cello
guitar
ukulele (baritone)
Autoharp
dulcimer

Wind Instrument

recorder (soprano)

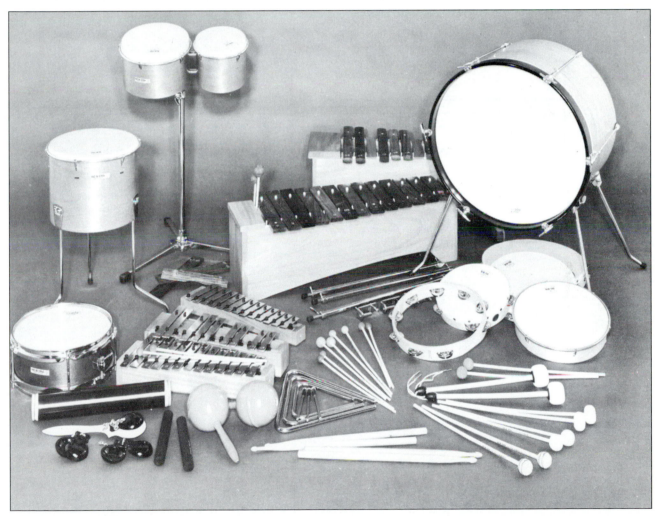

Courtesy of Selmer, Elkhart, Indiana.

Orff Percussion Instruments

Rhythmic and Melodic Ostinati

K–4, 3b

Another important purpose of the Orff school is to provide the student with copious experiences in creating rhythmic and melodic *ostinati* (musical patterns repeated to form accompaniments as well as melodies for movement, singing, and playing instruments). These develop a feeling for meter, form, and basic note values as well as melodic concepts and the natural, free use of the singing voice. The children chant first in two-note patterns, then in three-, four-, and five-note patterns, calling to their friends and imitating bird calls, street cries, familiar jingles, and nursery rhymes. A typical starting point is the child's play chant on a descending minor third interval (e.g., G–E, 5–3).

JOHNNY

John - ny,   where are you?   John - ny,   where are you?

CLAP, CLAP

Clap,   clap,   clap your hands,   clap   your hands to - geth - er.

Clap
Rhythm sticks

Playing Classroom Percussion Instruments

Rhythm sticks, triangle, and tambourine can be substituted for clapping rhythms, and drums can be substituted for stamping rhythms.

K–4, 2f

RAIN, RAIN

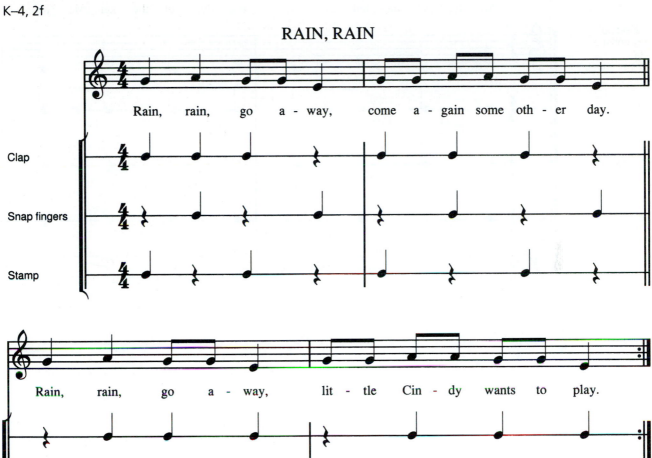

Rain, rain, go a - way, come a - gain some oth - er day.

Clap

Snap fingers

Stamp

Rain, rain, go a - way, lit - tle Cin - dy wants to play.

POLLY, PUT THE KETTLE ON

Pol - ly, put the ket - tle on, Pol - ly, put the ket - tle on,

Soprano xylophone or Resonator bells

Triangle

Tambourine

Drum

Timpani

Pol - ly, put the ket - tle on, We'll all have tea!

Five-Note Pattern (Pentatonic)

Any one or more of these ostinati may be used as a two- or four-measure introduction before the voice part enters. A concluding part (coda) may be added by having one or more of the ostinati continue for two or four measures after the melody has ended. One ostinato at a time may drop out with a gradual decrease in volume (diminuendo).

SOURWOOD MOUNTAIN

APPALACHIAN SONG
ARR. R.W.W.

① Voice or Recorder

Chick-en crow-in' on Sour-wood Mount-ain, Hey de ing dang did-dle al-ly day.
So many pret-ty girls, I can't count 'em, Hey de ing dang did-dle al-ly day.

② Soprano metallophone

③ Alto metallophone

④ Bass xylophone

⑤ Wood block or Rhythm sticks

⑥ Tambourine

My true love, she lives in Letch - er, Hey de ing dang did-dle al - ly day.
She won't come, and I won't fetch 'er, Hey de ing dang did-dle al - ly day.

Additional ostinati follow.

Try these melodic ostinati:

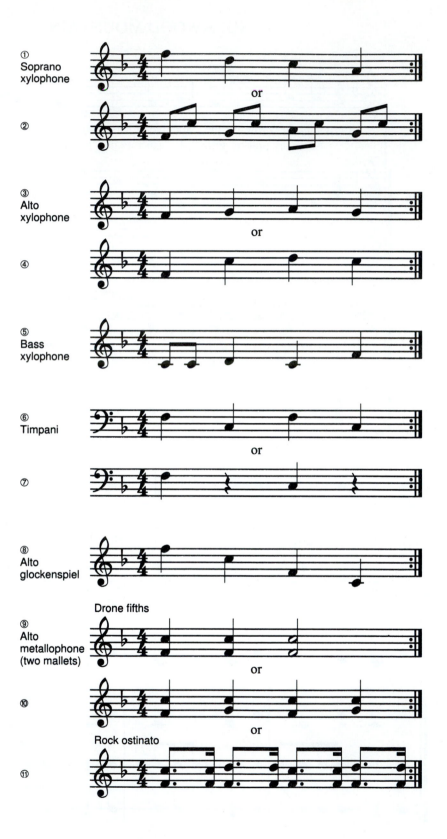

Playing Classroom Percussion Instruments

A basic hard rock beat, like that of the rock ostinato above, against any pentatonic folk tune or improvised melody provides a spirited classroom experience.

Now try these rhythmic ostinati. (Numerous others with bodily movement are given in this chapter on page 189.)

Clap
Patschen
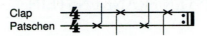

Clap
Stamp

Snap fingers
Clap
Patschen
Stamp
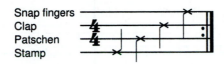

Outside left thigh
Left knee
Right knee
Outside right thigh
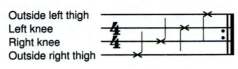

RH LH RH LH

Classroom Orchestra

Monster Frankenstein is the familiar *Oh, My Darling, Clementine* (p. 58) transposed into a minor key (using flats and naturals). This Orff arrangement calls for instruments such as metallophones, soprano and alto xylophones, and drums.

MONSTER FRANKENSTEIN

MARY LOU FRIEDRICH

1. In a castle on a mountain
   Near the dark and murky Rhine
   Dwelt a doctor, the concoctor
   Of the monster Frankenstein.

Chorus: Oh my monster, oh my monster,
   Oh my monster Frankenstein,
   You were built to last forever
   Dreadful scary, Frankenstein.

2. In a graveyard near the castle
   When the moon refused to shine,
   He dug for noses and for "toeses"
   For his monster Frankenstein.

3. *Etc., in the same bloodthirsty manner.*

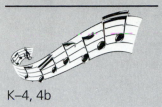

Suggested Assignment

K–4, 4b

Create your own ostinati and instrumentations for the following pentatonic melodies.

Li'l Liza Jane (p. 279)
Old Texas (p. 276)
Auld Lang Syne (p. 294)

Play this bell part during section A of *The Big Corral* (p. 89 of *Combining Musical Sounds*).

Play this pattern on a wood block in section B.

Sources for Orff Instruments

American Orff Schulwerk Assoc., P. O. Box 391089, Cleveland, OH 44139-8089. <www.aosa.org>.

De Gouden Brug (The Golden Bridge), distributed by Rhythm Band, Inc., P.O. Box 126, Fort Worth, Texas 76101. <www.degoudenbrug.com>.

Lefima Instruments, distributed by Custom Music Company, 1414 S. Main St., Royal Oak, Michigan 48067. <www.custommusiccorp.com>.

New Era Instruments, distributed by Rhythm Band, Inc., P.O. Box 126, Fort Worth, Texas 76101. <www.rhythmband.com>.

Peripole-Bergerault, Inc., 2041 State St., Salem, Oregon 97301. <www.pborff.com> and <www.peripolebergerault.com>.

Premier Instruments, distributed by Selmer, Box 310, Elkhart, Indiana 46515. <www.selmer.com> and <www.ludwig-drums.com>.

Sonor Instruments, distributed by Hohner, Inc., P.O. Box 15035, Richmond, Virginia 23227. <www.hohnerusa.com>.

Studio 49, distributed by Magnamusic-Baton, Inc., 10370 Page Industrial Blvd., St. Louis, Missouri 63132. <www.mmbmusic.com>.

Suzuki Instruments, P.O. Box 261030, San Diego, California 92196-1030. <www.suzukimusic.com>.

CHAPTER 9

Playing the Recorder

The recorder has been popular as a social instrument with young and old alike since the fifteenth century. The predecessor to the modern flute, the recorder is a recognized instrument of historical significance and is widespread in its use today. For many reasons, it occupies a place of real substance in the elementary classroom. The recorder:

- Has a pleasing flute-like tone.
- Has an accessible range of two octaves of well-tuned notes.
- Is relatively easy for children to learn.
- Has a wealth of great music written for it from the Renaissance period to the present day.
- Can serve as an aid in learning to read music.
- Can provide invaluable preband and preorchestra experience.
- Can be used as a melody instrument in teaching children's songs when men's and women's voices are extremely low.
- Can be played in harmony and used effectively with other instruments such as bells, Orff instruments, Omnichords, and guitars.
- Can help classroom teachers develop their own musical skills at the same time as their students.

Courtesy of Karen Evans, Music Consultant, Bobier Elementary School, Vista, California.

Kinds of Recorders

Four-part harmony (soprano, alto, tenor, and bass) can be played using C-Soprano, C-Tenor, F-Alto, and F-Bass recorders. The Sopranino recorder is a diminutive of the C-Soprano and is built in the key of F. In schools the C-Soprano is generally used, with the occasional addition of the F-Alto for low harmony parts. Instruction in this chapter is limited to the C-Soprano recorder.

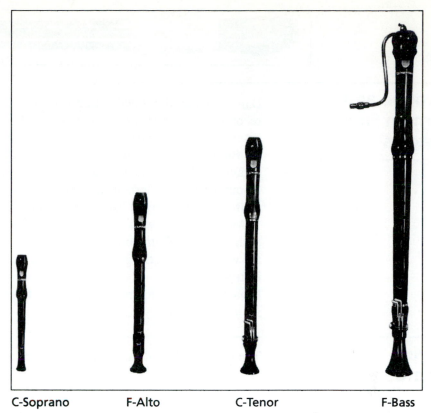

C-Soprano   F-Alto   C-Tenor   F-Bass

Courtesy of Trophy Music Co., 1278 W. 9th St., Cleveland, Ohio 44113.

Care of the Recorder

An all-plastic, two-piece recorder is available and recommended for use in the elementary classroom because of its economic price and practicality. The serious student of the recorder, however, should use one made of wood. Instruments similar to the soprano recorder, such as flutophones and tonettes, *should not* be purchased in place of a recorder.

The *wood* recorder requires greater care than the plastic recorder.

Wood

1. A new wood recorder should be oiled before it is played. Take the instrument apart and oil each part with a swab lightly moistened with woodwind oil. Do not oil the fipple or the aperture. Allow the oil to dry for about twelve hours before playing the recorder. Oil the instrument three or four times a year. Do not oil it just after playing; wait until it is dry.
2. A new wood recorder should not be played more than fifteen or twenty minutes at a time. The wood must become adjusted to moisture and warmth.
3. Hold the instrument in the hands until it is warm. A recorder should be warm before it is played to protect the wood from cracking.

Plastic and Wood

1. When playing, blow gently. Overblowing causes bad tone quality.
2. After playing, dry each section of the instrument with a swab. Do not touch the fipple or the aperture when drying the head piece.
3. When the recorder is not in use, keep it in its case. Never store it near heat or sunlight; avoid sudden changes of temperature.

Baroque and German Fingering Systems

Baroque (sometimes called English) fingering was the authentic fingering of recorders from the Baroque period until the early 1900s. The main difference between Baroque and German fingering systems lies in the fingering for F and F♯. Baroque fingering has the advantage of an easier F♯ in both low and high octaves, which facilitates passages involving this note (see the chart on p. 206). About 1920, the German fingering came into use, simplifying the forked (Baroque) fingering of low F and high F (see the chart on p. 206).

Music teachers who use the recorder as a preorchestral instrument for children prefer the German fingering because of its direct relationship to orchestral woodwind fingerings. Not only is the recorder an appropriate prewoodwind instrument, but also its usage can be transferred to string instruments. The note B on recorder is fingered with the first finger, likewise E or A on the D or G *strings,* respectively.

Playing the Recorder

The range of the C-Soprano recorder is as follows:

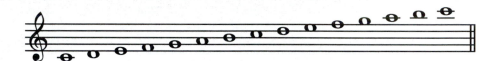

Holding and Fingering Positions

The first three fingers of the left hand are used to cover holes 1, 2, and 3. The hole on the underside is covered with the left thumb. Fingers 1, 2, 3, and 4 of the right hand are used to cover holes 4, 5, 6, and 7. The right thumb rests on the underside of the instrument. Play with flat, not rounded, fingers. Do not place too much of the mouthpiece in the mouth. In addition, do not hold the instrument too far away from the body like a trumpet. Fingers should *not* be watched while playing—only the music.

Producing the Tone

The mouthpiece is held with the lips. The tone is started by pronouncing the syllable "tu" (using the tongue) and sustained with a steady stream of air. Only a small amount of air is needed; *do not overblow.* In fact, the lower the note on the recorder, the lighter the blowing should be, as in blowing on a flower, or whispering.

Courtesy of Karen Evans, Music Consultant, Bobier Elementary School, Vista, California.

Courtesy of Colton Canava, McNiel Junior High School, Wichita Falls, Texas.

Fingering Chart for Soprano Recorder

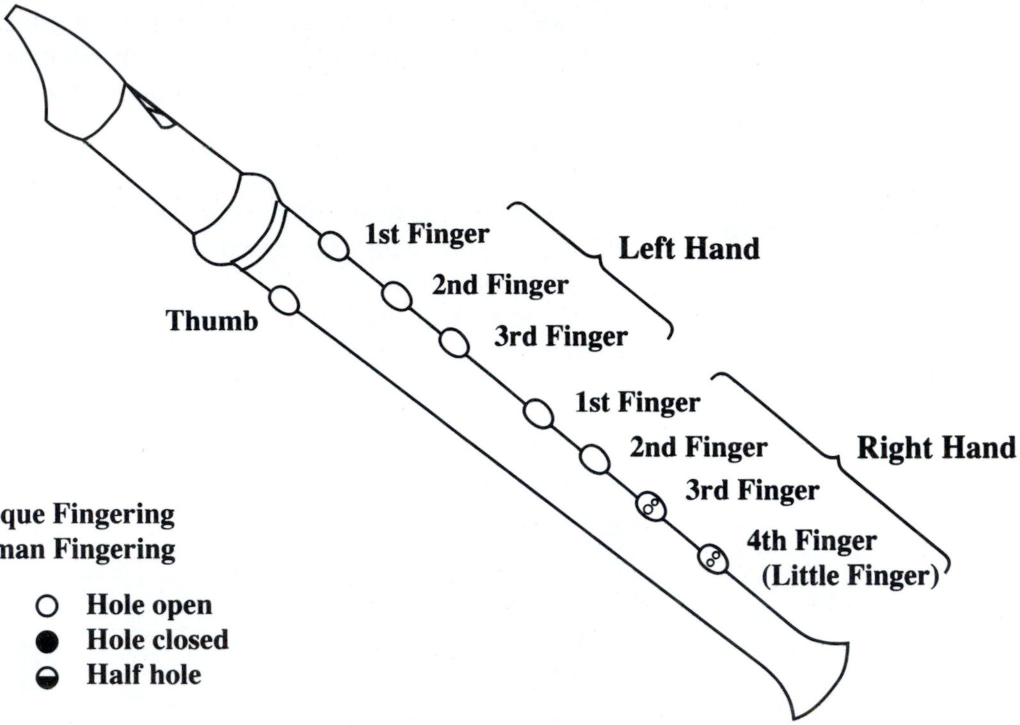

B – Baroque Fingering
G – German Fingering

○ Hole open
● Hole closed
◐ Half hole

Playing the Recorder

Using the Left Hand: Playing B, A, and G

First try this fingering without playing. Find the holes by feeling. Bring the fingers down firmly; lift them quickly.

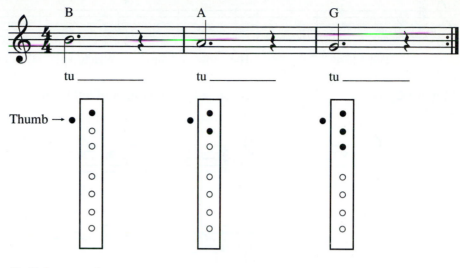

● Hole covered
○ Hole open

Now play the following preparatory exercise and songs.

HOT CROSS BUNS

Nursery Song

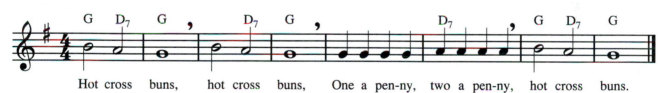

Hot cross buns, hot cross buns, One a pen-ny, two a pen-ny, hot cross buns.

FRENCH TUNE

France

FAIS DO DO

France

Fais do do, and let us go dream-ing. *Fais do do,* come dream-ing with me.

HALLOWEEN SONG

Rhoda Weber and Bob Margolis   Rhoda Weber and Bob Margolis

Hal - low - een,   Hal - low - een.   Watch out!   Don't shout!   Hal - low - een.

Playing C   Thumb and second finger of left hand. Play with clean attacks and releases.

Now play the following songs.

POLKA

Learn both parts.

DUET

TO PAREE

FRANCE

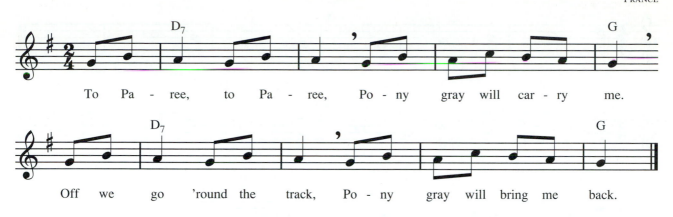

To Pa - ree, to Pa - ree, Po - ny gray will car - ry me.

Off we go 'round the track, Po - ny gray will bring me back.

CHOPSTICKS

TRADITIONAL

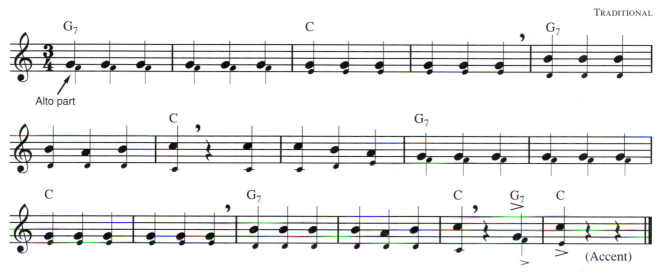

Alto part

(Accent)

Playing D
Left-hand second finger only. When playing D, the mouth and right-hand thumb and third finger support the recorder. Always lift the fingers only a short distance from the holes in order to be ready for notes requiring them.

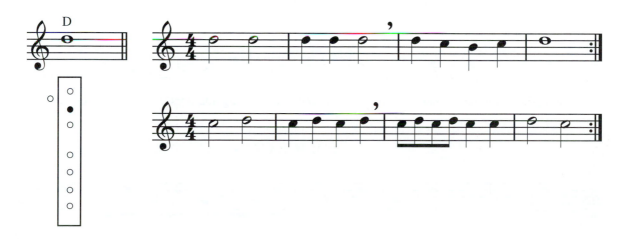

Review all fingerings for the left hand. Gradually increase speed.

Playing Tunes with the Left Hand Only

When you play the following with others, always hold the starting note until everyone has secured it.

LIGHTLY ROW

GERMANY

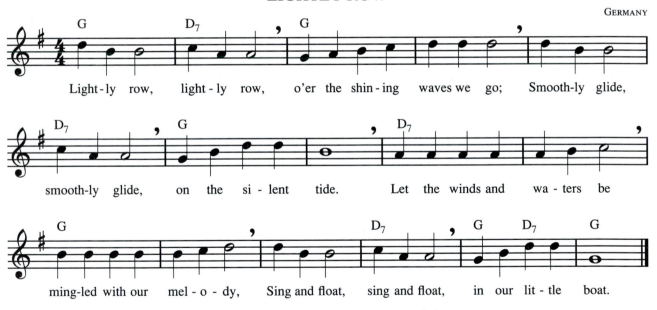

Light-ly row, light-ly row, o'er the shin-ing waves we go; Smooth-ly glide,

smooth-ly glide, on the si - lent tide. Let the winds and wa - ters be

ming-led with our mel - o - dy, Sing and float, sing and float, in our lit - tle boat.

POLICE CALL

Before playing *The Recorder Band*, practice *Police Call* several times to prepare for the difficult interval on line three indicated with an asterisk (*).

THE RECORDER BAND

R.W.W.

GERMANY

I am a mu - si - cian, I come from *(name your town)*. I

play in a re - cord - er band, the best one in the land.

I can play this tune with on - ly my left hand.

CHORALE

FROM "JESU, JOY OF MAN'S DESIRING"

J.S. BACH

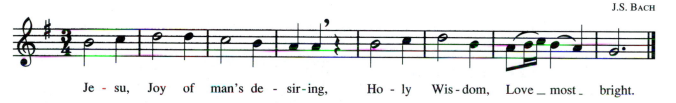

Je - su, Joy of man's de - sir - ing, Ho - ly Wis - dom, Love __ most __ bright.

Using the Right Hand: 1. Cover the holes for the left hand *firmly* as if to play G.
Playing F   2. Play F using the first, third, and fourth fingers of the right hand.

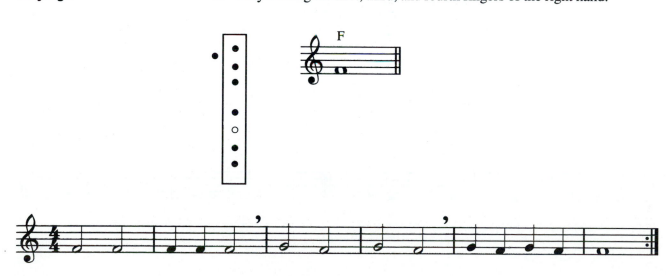

The following are for review of all fingerings thus far.

MERRILY WE ROLL ALONG

TRADITIONAL

Mer - ri - ly   we   roll   a - long,   roll   a - long,   roll   a - long.

Mer - ri - ly   we   roll   a - long   o'er   the   dark   blue   sea.

FIDDLE-DEE-DEE

ENGLAND

Fid - dle - dee - dee,   Fid - dle - dee - dee, The   fly   has mar - ried the   bum - ble - bee.

Playing E

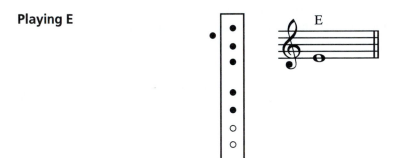

STARLIGHT

Traditional

Star - light, star - bright, First star I see to - night.

Wish I may, Wish I might Have the wish I wish to - night.

Playing D

Blow gently on all low notes.

Check fingering for low D carefully. *Cover all holes firmly.*

SNAKE DANCE

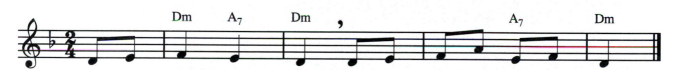

TRUMPET VOLUNTARY

Jeremiah Clarke

Playing the Recorder

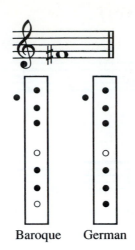

Baroque   German

Baroque

YANKEE DOODLE

UNITED STATES

Yank - ee Dood - le went to town a - rid - ing on a po — ny,

Baroque

Stuck a feath - er in his cap and called it mac - a - ro - ni.

WE WISH YOU A MERRY CHRISTMAS

ENGLISH CAROL

We wish you a mer - ry Christ - mas, We wish you a mer - ry Christ - mas,

We wish you a mer - ry Christ - mas, and a hap - py New Year!

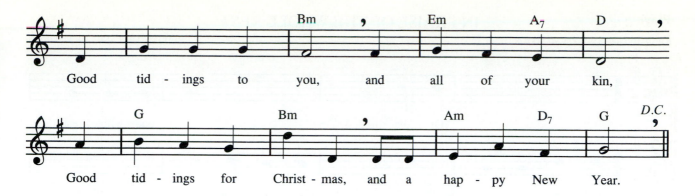

Good tid - ings to you, and all of your kin,

Good tid - ings for Christ - mas, and a hap - py New Year.

Playing Slurs

A *slur* is a curved line connecting two or more notes of different pitches. To play a slur, tongue the first note and finger the remaining notes while blowing a steady stream of air into the instrument. Remember: a *tie* connects two (or more) of the *same* notes, increasing the value of the first.

K–4, 5c
5–8, 2b, 5c

YOU CAN'T LOVE TWO

UNITED STATES

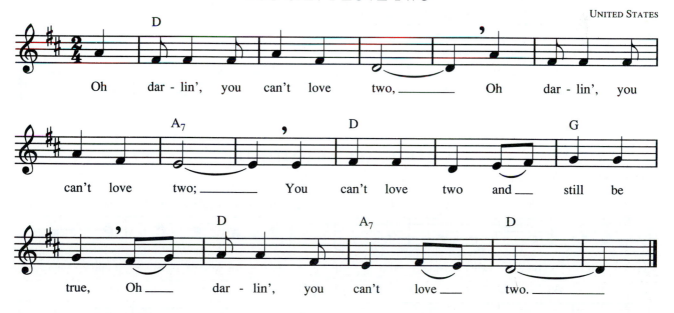

Oh dar - lin', you can't love two, _____ Oh dar - lin', you

can't love two; _____ You can't love two and __ still be

true, Oh __ dar - lin', you can't love __ two. _____

IN PRAISE OF THE WHOLE REST

RHODA WEBER AND BOB MARGOLIS

RHODA WEBER AND BOB MARGOLIS

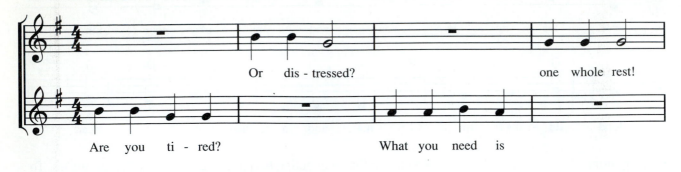

Or dis - tressed? one whole rest!

Are you ti - red? What you need is

for your trou - ble. Take a half rest, Hold it doub - le!

What a ton - ic Take a half rest, Hold it doub - le!

FANTASIE IMPROMPTU

FREDERIC CHOPIN

O COME, ALL YE FAITHFUL

TR. F. OAKLEY

J.F. WADE

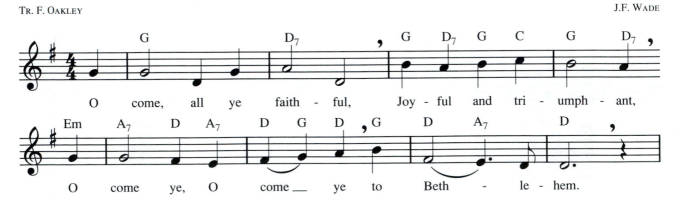

O come, all ye faith - ful, Joy - ful and tri - umph - ant,

O come ye, O come __ ye to Beth - le - hem.

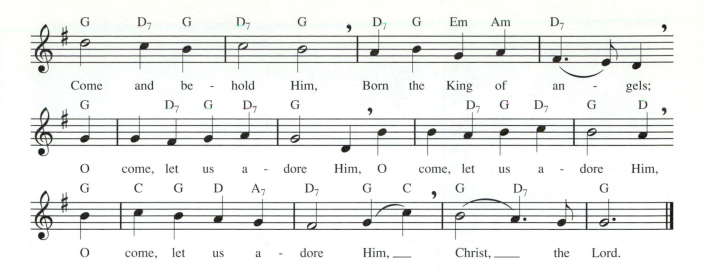

Come and be-hold Him, Born the King of an-gels;

O come, let us a-dore Him, O come, let us a-dore Him,

O come, let us a-dore Him, ___ Christ, ___ the Lord.

CHANUKAH CANDLES

Rhoda Weber and Bob Margolis

Rhoda Weber and Bob Margolis

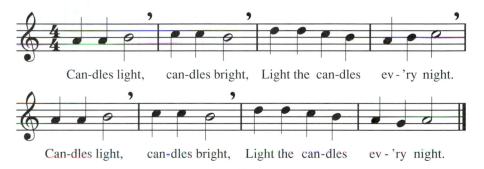

Can-dles light, can-dles bright, Light the can-dles ev-'ry night.

Can-dles light, can-dles bright, Light the can-dles ev-'ry night.

ZOODLE NOODLE ZIMMER GRUNCH

Rhoda Weber and Bob Margolis

Rhoda Weber and Bob Margolis

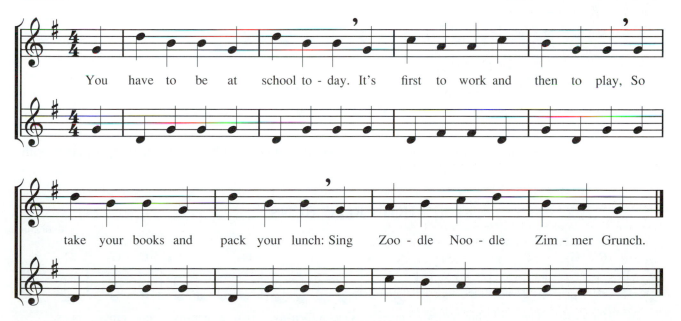

You have to be at school to-day. It's first to work and then to play, So

take your books and pack your lunch: Sing Zoo-dle Noo-dle Zim-mer Grunch.

Playing Low C

Cover the holes firmly with flat-finger position (especially the third finger).

Playing Tunes with Right Fingers

Keep all holes covered firmly with the left hand as the melody is played with the right hand.

HOT CROSS BUNS

ENGLAND

Hot cross buns, hot cross buns. One a pen-ny, two a pen-ny, hot cross buns.

CHORALE THEME

J.S. BACH

WHO'S THAT TAPPING AT THE WINDOW?

UNITED STATES

Who's that tap-ping at the win-dow? Who's that knock-ing at the door?

BARCAROLLE

OFFENBACH

Beau - teous night, O night _ of love, Smile thou _ on our en - chant - ment,

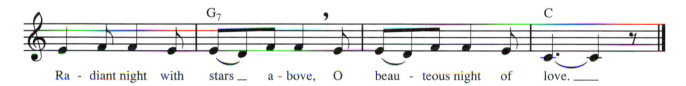

Ra - diant night with stars _ a - bove, O beau - teous night of love. ____

The teacher and advanced players can harmonize this melody by playing a third higher, i.e.,

JOY TO THE WORLD

Isaac Watts

Lowell Mason*

Joy to the world! the Lord is come; Let earth re - ceive her King;

Let ev - 'ry __ heart __ pre - pare __ Him __ room, __ And heav'n and na - ture __ sing,

and __ heav'n and na - ture __ sing, And __ heav'n, __ and heav'n __ and na - ture sing.

*This melody is frequently but questionably attributed to Handel.

Phrasing

5–8, 2b, 5c

In some compositions, the slur encompasses an entire phrase. (Read the section on phrases and sentences, beginning on page 84.) As in playing slurs that have only a few notes, maintain a continuous flow of air through the instrument until you reach the end of the slur. Try not to breathe until you reach the *breath mark* (') at the end of the first long slur.

SONG WITHOUT WORDS

PRAELUDIUM NO. 2 FOR ORGAN

Mendelssohn

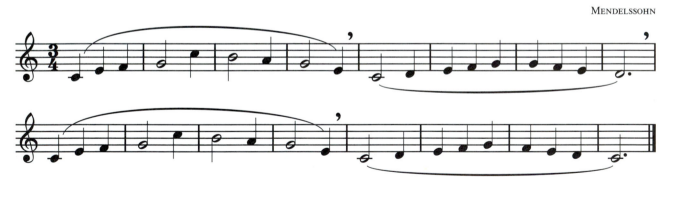

F PENTATONIC

MORNING

JAPANESE HYMN

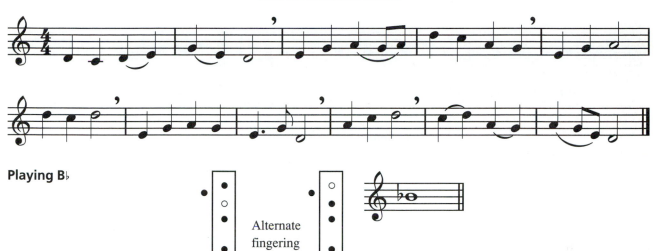

Playing B♭

Alternate fingering

THREE-CORNERED HAT

My hat, it has three cor-ners, _____ Three cor-ners has my hat, _____
Mein Hut, er hat drei Eck-en, _____ Drei Eck-en hat mein Hut, _____

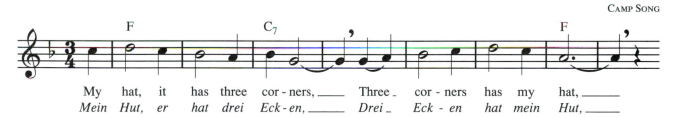

A hat with-out three cor-ners _____ Could nev-er be my hat. _____
Und hat er nicht drei Eck-en, _____ Dann ist er nicht mein Hut. _____

The accompaniments for *Oh Where, Oh Where Has My Little Dog Gone?*
(p. 224) can be played with *Three Cornered Hat* exactly as written.

EVENING SONG

Weber

Soft - ly   sighs the   breath of __ eve - ning,   Steal - ing   through the   shadow-y   grove,

While the   stars   in   heav - en __ shin - ing   Keep their   si - lent __ watch a - bove.

Also play *America* (p. 335).

MELODY

Schumann

SYMPHONIC THEME

Tchaikovsky

Also play the melody of *Symphonic Theme* as a canon by having half of the class start one measure later.

Refer to the popular canon, *Old Texas* (p. 276), for additional experience.

UPIDEE

Camp Song

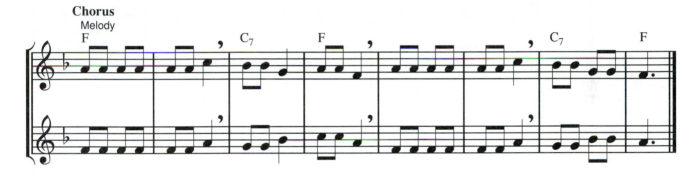

OH WHERE, OH WHERE HAS MY LITTLE DOG GONE?

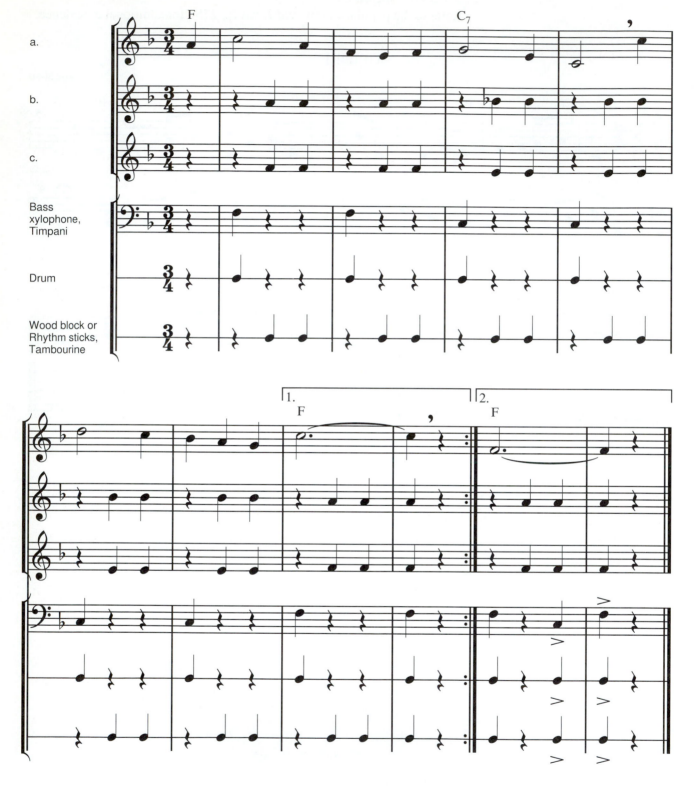

Also play *Three-Cornered Hat* (p. 221) with the same accompaniment parts.

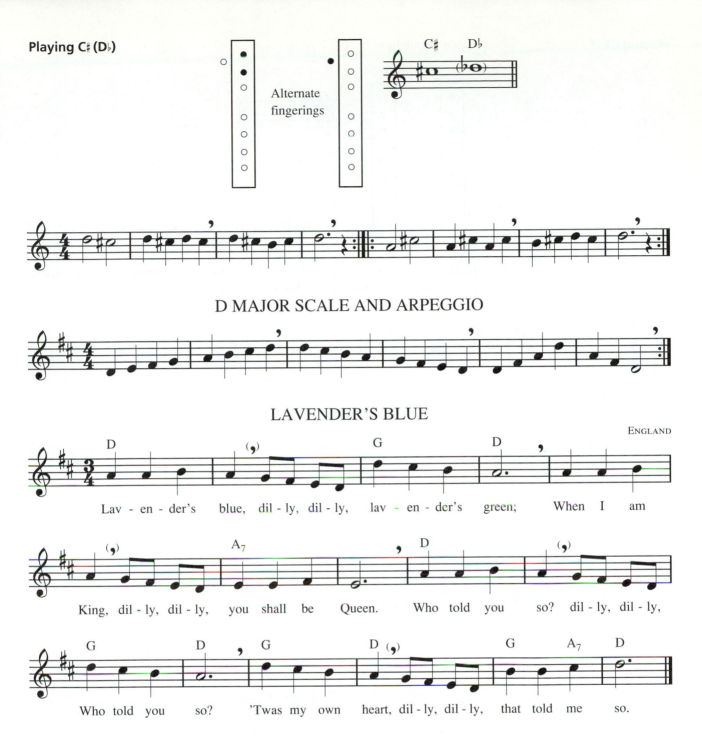

D MAJOR SCALE AND ARPEGGIO

LAVENDER'S BLUE

ENGLAND

Lav - en - der's blue, dil - ly, dil - ly, lav - en - der's green; When I am

King, dil - ly, dil - ly, you shall be Queen. Who told you so? dil - ly, dil - ly,

Who told you so? 'Twas my own heart, dil - ly, dil - ly, that told me so.

Sing and play this song with Omnichord and guitar accompaniment. For another version of this folk song, see page 157.

Open thumb hole.

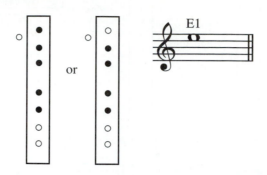

High E has two fingerings indicated E1 and E2. E1 is presented first since it is used with the first octave notes already learned.

GERMAN TUNE

THE BLACKSMITH

ARIA FROM MOZART'S OPERA *THE MARRIAGE OF FIGARO*

W.A. MOZART

Oh, the black-smith's a fine sturd-y fel-low, Hard his hands, but his heart's true and

mel-low; See him stand there, his huge bel-lows blow-ing, With his strong, brawn-y arms free and bare;

See the fire in the furn-ace a-glow-ing, Bright its spark-le, its flash, and its glare.

MELODY
DUET

ARBAN

The following *Etude* (study) is based on the G pentatonic scale.

ETUDE

Improvise and create your own melodies in duple and triple meter on the G pentatonic scale.

5–8, 3c

CINDY

UNITED STATES

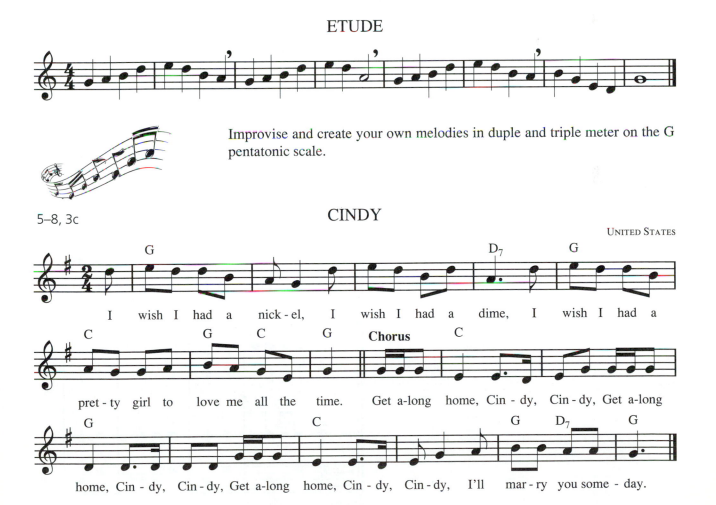

I wish I had a nick-el, I wish I had a dime, I wish I had a

pret-ty girl to love me all the time. Get a-long home, Cin-dy, Cin-dy, Get a-long

home, Cin-dy, Cin-dy, Get a-long home, Cin-dy, Cin-dy, I'll mar-ry you some-day.

Accompaniment Ostinati

Read "Rhythmic and Melodic Ostinati" (p. 194).

Melodic Ostinati

Song or Melody Bells may be used with these four ostinati:

Harmonic Ostinati

Rhythmic Ostinati

Various percussion instruments may be used for the first two ostinati below.

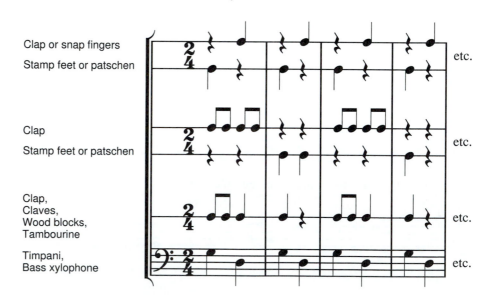

THE PAPAYA TREE

R.W.W.
FILIPINO FOLK SONG

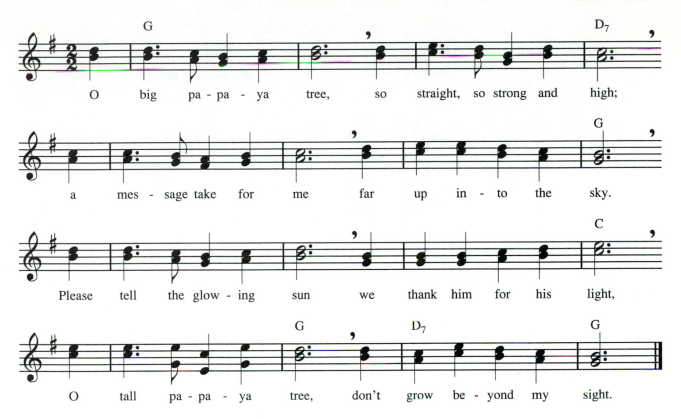

O big pa-pa-ya tree, so straight, so strong and high;

a mes-sage take for me far up in-to the sky.

Please tell the glow-ing sun we thank him for his light,

O tall pa-pa-ya tree, don't grow be-yond my sight.

Playing E2

Half-open thumb hole marked ◒ .

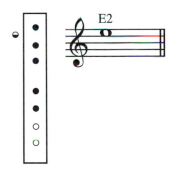

From E2 upward in the high register of the recorder, the thumb covers only half of the thumb hole.

Practice first low E and then E2 as follows:

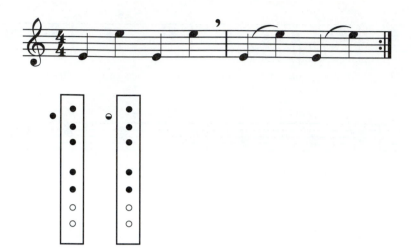

Playing High F

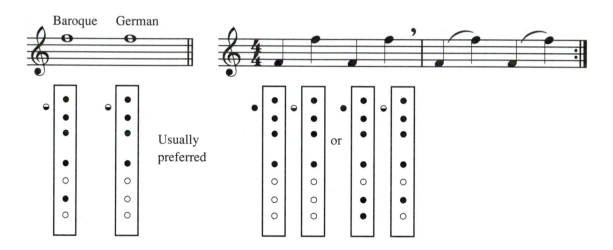

Baroque   German

Usually preferred

or

F MAJOR SCALE AND ARPEGGIO

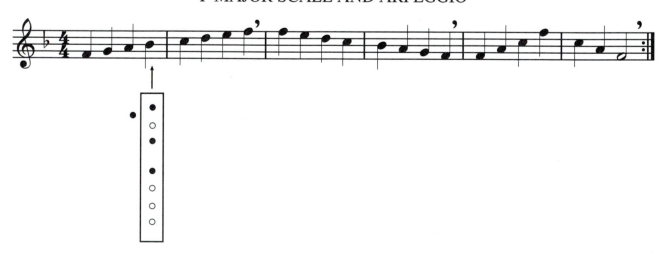

THE DESPERADO

R.W.W.

UNITED STATES

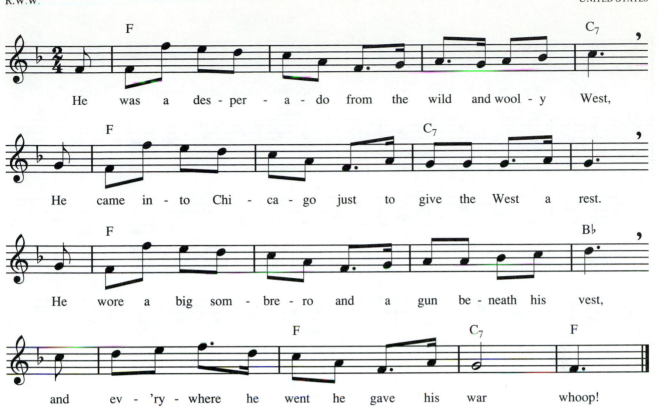

He was a des - per - a - do from the wild and wool - y West,

He came in - to Chi - ca - go just to give the West a rest.

He wore a big som - bre - ro and a gun be - neath his vest,

and ev - 'ry - where he went he gave his war whoop!

Add ostinati—accompany with Orff instruments or bells.

MARCHING SONG

R.W.W.

SILESIAN FOLK TUNE

A - step - ping brisk - ly we go to the cad - ence we all know,

A - step - ping brisk - ly we go to the cad - ence we all know,

A - step - ping brisk - ly we go to the cad - ence we all know,

the peo - ple cheer for our band when we march up to the stand.

the peo - ple cheer for our band when we march up to the stand.

the peo - ple cheer for our band when we march up to the stand.

JACOB DRINK

AMERICAN SPIRITUAL

Accompaniment Number 1 to JACOB DRINK

Accompaniment Number 2 to JACOB DRINK

Ostinato Number 1 to JACOB DRINK

Ostinato Number 2 to JACOB DRINK

JINGLE BELLS

James Pierpont (U.S. 1822–1893)

Lightly

Original: Jing - le bells, jing - le bells, jing - le all the way. Oh! what fun it
Alternate: Jing - le bells, jing - le bells, jing - le all the way. Oh! what fun it

is to ride in a one-horse o - pen sleigh, __ Jing - le bells, jing - le bells,
is to ride in an o - pen sleigh, __ Jing - le bells, jing - le bells,

jing - le all the way, Oh! what fun it is to ride in a one-horse o - pen sleigh.
jing - le all the way, Oh! what fun it is to ride in an o - pen sleigh.

Harmony Part 1 to JINGLE BELLS

Softly and lightly

Harmony Part 2 to JINGLE BELLS

Softly and lightly

CHAPTER 10

Accompanying with the Omnichord or Autoharp

K–4, 2b
5–8, 2d

For many years the Autoharp has been used in classrooms across the world to provide accompaniment for school-music singing. Its advantages have been many, but perhaps the foremost has been its playability in a very short amount of time. Students of very young ages can gain skill and experience success on the Autoharp very quickly. The wooden instrument is portable, tunable, and provides harmonic accompaniment "at the push of a button" with pick strumming.

As in so many other areas, however, technological advances have produced an instrument with many more capabilities than that of the Autoharp in the relatively new instrument called the Omnichord. A very lightweight, portable instrument, the Omnichord is made of a hard plastic shell and need not be tuned because it is electronic. In addition, it has many other features to be explored.

To many, the Autoharp is still a useful and valid instrument. Your school, church, or home may already have one or more of these instruments, so it would be helpful to learn how to operate them and to teach others how as well. The Autoharp will be discussed after the presentation of the Omnichord material.

The Omnichord

Suzuki Corp.

Description

The Omnichord ("all" chords or keys) has been developed in the last ten years as the electronic version of the Autoharp. Major, minor, and seventh chords are available on the Omnichord, making it capable of being played in all keys. It is not necessary to use a pick to strum the Omnichord. The four-octave-sounding silver strumplate *may* be used to simulate the actual strumming process. In addition the chord bars can be made to produce sound electronically (without the strumming process) by using the "chord-hold" button.

The Omnichord plays up to 84 different chords or chord combinations. Different voices, timbres, rhythms, and bass can also be added to the chord choices. The Omnichord has a built-in sound system and can be used with a power amplifier, if desired. Eight C-cell batteries can be used as a power source; however, batteries leak easily, so the use of household electric current is preferable. Headphones can be used to silence the instrument during practice.

Care

To protect the power source or batteries and to preserve the longevity of the instrument, the Omnichord should be kept in its plastic case at all times when not in use.

Holding the Omnichord

The usual method for playing the Omnichord is to hold it on the player's lap or place it on a desk or table surface so that the chord bars are on the bottom left—nearest the player's left side. Plug in the Omnichord and turn on the power switch. Set the volume in each subdivision of the instrument: memory, chord mode, rhythms, and voices. Set the sustain button according to how long you wish the chords to produce sound; you will need to experiment.

Tuning the Omnichord

No tuning is necessary.

Playing the Omnichord

Now you are ready to play the Omnichord. Four full octaves are available with this instrument. Choose the chords required with the piece of music that you want to play. Make sure that your left-hand fingers hover above those chords. Firmly press the chord(s) with the left-hand fingers (index, middle, ring) and/or thumb to get automatic sound; "chord hold" should be turned on. If the right hand is to be used to "strum" on the silver-colored electronic strumplate, then "chord hold" should be turned off and a piece of felt should become your "pick." By pressing the various chords with the left hand and simulating strumming with the right hand, various chordal and timbral effects can be played—omni, guitar, harp, banjo, strings, piano, organ, celeste, marimba, or steel drums. Ten different digital drum rhythms can play automatically with the selected chord and drum-fill. Introductions, interludes, and postludes (endings) give added dimension before, during, or after each song. Different corresponding bass lines can also be added with specific button changes.

Additional Omnichord Capabilities

Chord Memory

The Omnichord is capable of one-finger playback. After programming, the Omnichord can play back all of the chords of your chosen song(s) with the use of a button called "Chord Memory." The instruction manual discusses in more detail how to accomplish playback.

Melodic Keyboard

Three octaves of chromatic keyboard sounds can be played through another Omnichord button. Sounds include trumpet, flute, piano, organ, human voice, marimba, banjo, bass, steel drum, and harmonica.

Amplification

Play or practice in private by using headphones or plug the Omnichord into a stereo or sound system for large room amplification.

Volume

Each subdivision of the Omnichord has a button that turns to the right to produce more volume and to the left to produce less.

MIDI

A MIDI ("Musical Instrument Digital Interface") outjack lets you control other MIDI instruments, expand to other "voice" selections, and work in concert with your computer.

The Autoharp

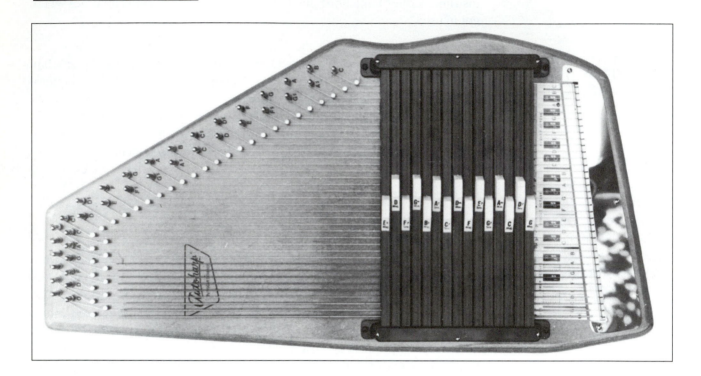

Description

Three varieties of Autoharps are available for purchase: the 12-bar, the 15-bar, and the 21-bar (called the Chromaharp). The 12-bar (or 12-chord) and 15-bar have 36 piano-type strings and a piano-related music scale on the right of the labeled chord bars. The 21-chord instrument has 43 strings. Underneath the chord bars are felts used to stop the vibration of all of the strings except those required for the chord being played. The names of the chords are indicated on each bar of the instrument, and each string is attached to a tuning pin. The 12- and 15-chord instruments are the most commonly used of the Autoharps. Autoharps have a range of nearly four octaves divided into three basic registers of low, medium, and high. The timbre of each register helps to vary rhythmic and tonal effects.

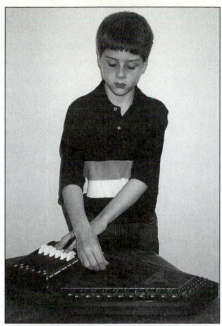

Courtesy of Brady Archambo, Ben Franklin Elementary and
Barwise Junior High, Wichita Falls, Texas.

Care

To avoid excessive maintenance, keep the Autoharp in a box or case at all times when not in use. Do not place the instrument directly under a heating or cooling vent. Store it in a place with even temperature and humidity. Sixty percent humidity is ideal. If strings or chord-bars break, they should be replaced as soon as possible.

Holding the Autoharp

The usual method for playing the Autoharp is to hold it on the player's lap or place it on a desk or table surface so that the chord bars are on the bottom right nearest the player's right side and tuning pins are on the left. Many experienced performers prefer to hold the Autoharp upright, with chord bars facing outward and with the wider end of the instrument resting on the lap.

Tuning the Autoharp

It is fortunate that the Autoharp need not be thoroughly tuned each time it is played. It is a good idea, however, to push the palms of your hands down on groups of Autoharp strings until all strings are somewhat pliable before doing a full tuning. This procedure allows the strings to be tuned without snapping or breaking them. Autoharp strings are not easily changed. With most instruments the wood portion covering where the strings are attached must be taken off before the string can be removed.

The Autoharp is tuned by placing the tuning key on the pin attached to the string to be tuned. The tuning key must be turned to the right to tighten the string

Accompanying with the Omnichord or Autoharp

(raise pitch) or to the left to loosen the string (lower pitch). Continue to pick the string aggressively while slowly turning the tuning key until the desired pitch is reached. Other strings that may vibrate can be stopped by placing felt picks between them. Tune the instrument to an in-tune piano or keyboard, chromatic pitch pipe, or any fixed-pitch instrument. Each model of Autoharp shows the corresponding piano keys under each of the strings, which helps to facilitate tuning the instrument to a keyboard.

A player with a "good ear" should be able to tune an Autoharp efficiently. To locate the out-of-tune strings, press a chord bar and run your thumb or a pick slowly across the string bed of the entire instrument. Quickly tune the out-of-tune strings and then proceed to the next chord. First tune the C-major chord, then F-major, G-major, and the remaining chords.

If the Autoharp is entirely out of tune, several procedures may be followed:

1. Start with the lowest string and proceed upward, tuning each string (to make it sharper or flatter as necessary) with an in-tune keyboard or chromatic pitch pipe.
2. Start with the bottom string and tune all of its octaves proceeding upward. Tune the next string and its octaves, etc.
3. If you are a musician with theoretical training, start on the lowest A, tune all A strings as you proceed upward, and then continue by tuning in the circle of fifths with subsequent octaves.
4. Or, tune each note of the C chord and its octaves, each note of the F chord and its octaves, each note of the G_7 chord and its octaves, etc.

Play all of the chords as a final check to locate possible strings that may still be out of tune.

Playing the Autoharp

Chord Bars

The chord bars are usually fingered with the index, middle, and ring fingers of the left hand while the right hand crosses *over* the left to strum outward or away from the body. The chord bars need to be pressed firmly to dampen and vibrate the appropriate strings. Sometimes skillful players create their own fingering patterns by jumping from one chord bar to another with just one finger.

12-Chord Autoharp

The chord bars for the 12-bar instrument are grouped together for convenient fingering of the three basic chords for each of the five keys—C, F, and G major, and A and D minor.

15-Chord Autoharp

The 15 chord bars of this instrument provide the primary chords of seven keys—those of the 12-bar (C, F, G, Am, Dm) with the addition of B♭ and D majors.

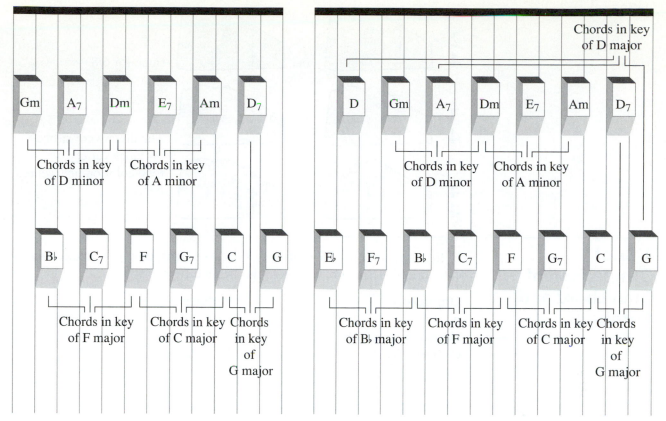

12-Bar Autoharp

15-Bar Autoharp

The 21-Chord Autoharp

This instrument provides for greater versatility in playing power. The following 21 chord bars enable the player to perform a wide variety of songs:

Major chords	$E\flat$	$B\flat$	F	C	G	D	A
Seventh chords	F_7	C_7	G_7	D_7	A_7	E_7	B_7
Minor chords, etc.	$A\flat$	$B\flat_7$	Cm	Gm	Dm	Am	Em

Strumming

Strumming needs to be somewhat aggressive so that the sound can be heard above singing and/or other instruments used with the Autoharp. It is best to use a pick to strum the strings. Use a thumb pick, a pick held with the thumb and first finger, a plastic pen cap, or a rubber door stopper to slide across the entire spectrum or selected portions of the strings. Picks made of different materials (metal, felt, plastic, etc.) can be used to achieve the desired tonal effect. Strum on the important, or strong, beats of the measure and almost always on the first beat. As the level of dexterity develops, the more experienced the performer may become in playing varied rhythmic patterns. Short strokes in the middle or upper registers can be used effectively for unaccented beats and lighter tonal effects.

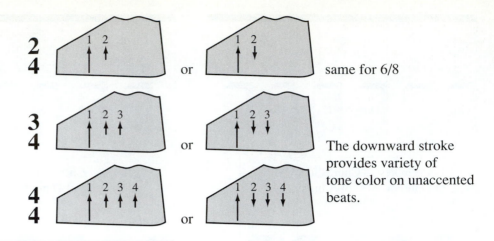

2/4 or same for 6/8

3/4 or The downward stroke provides variety of tone color on unaccented beats.

4/4 or

A Brief Comparison of Omnichord and Autoharp

Both instruments produce harmony, are easily transported, and are economically priced. There are, however, significant differences:

Omnichord	Autoharp
plastic	wooden
electronic and rhythmic "voices"	acoustic sound
can layer the "voices"	strummed tonal effect
4 pounds	12 pounds
no tuning required	must be tuned
does not have to be strummed	must be strummed
requires little or no maintenance	parts must be replaced
can record and accompany songs	

Accompanying with the Omnichord and the Autoharp

The key and the tempo of the piece(s) to be accompanied by the Omnichord or Autoharp can be readily established by providing a short introduction. An easy way is to repeat the first chord of the song three times for 3/4 time, four times for 4/4, and so on:

Introductions to Songs

Playing Introductions to Songs

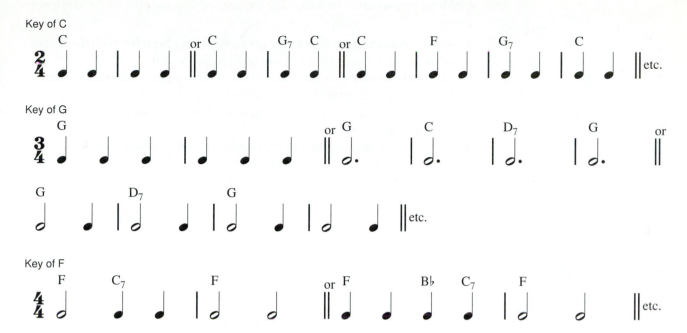

Transposing to Different Keys

It is helpful for classroom teachers to be able to transpose accompaniments for songs to lower and sometimes higher keys to fit the various vocal abilities of their singers. The following chart will serve as a guide.

Key	I	IV	V₇
C	Ceg	Fac	Gbdf
F	Fac	B♭df	Cegb♭
G	Gbd	Ceg	Df♯ac
Am	Ace	Dfa	Eg♯bd
Dm	Dfa	Gb♭d	Ac♯eg

To transpose songs for the Autoharp, refer to the chart above in making these changes:

Key of	to	Beginning note will be
D	F	1-1/2 steps higher
D	C	1 whole step lower
E	F	1/2 step higher
E	C	2 whole steps lower
A	G	1 whole step lower
Em	Dm	1 whole step lower
Em	Gm	1-1/2 steps higher

From Maurine Timmerman and Celeste Griffith, *Guitar in the Classroom*. 2d ed. Copyright © 1976 Wm. C. Brown Publishers, Dubuque, Iowa. All Rights Reserved. Reprinted by permission.

For example: Key of D (chords D G A₇) change to key of C (chords of C F G₇), or to key of F (chords F B♭ C₇).

Accompanying Songs

Most relatively new children's songbooks indicate the chord symbols over the melody line of each song, showing which chord is to be played and then when it should be changed to another chord. Chording is usually very precise and must be done accurately in the rhythm of the particular song being played. An excellent way to show chordal changes is to color code the changes with different highlighter-markers. The following are suggestions for effective accompaniments:

1. Try to coordinate accurately the pressing of the chord bar with the stroke of the strum process for a smooth and precise sound.
2. Play either loudly enough or softly enough for a good balance between singers and/or instrumentalists and Autoharp/Omnichord.
3. Be particularly aware of the rhythmic accents of the piece of music to keep the beat steady.
4. Strive to capture the mood of the music—a light flowing style for a lullaby or a firm, crisp, accented style for a march.
5. If both a bass and treble sound are desired, use the entire spectrum of the silver strum pad (Omnichord) or the string body (Autoharp) or be particularly aware when one sound is to be used more than the other.

One-Chord Accompaniments

Hold the C-chord bar down for the entire song, strumming at the marks (/).

MY GOOSE

ROUND

Why should-n't my goose sell as well as thy goose,

When I paid for my goose twice as much as you?

Two-Chord Accompaniments

This song can be strummed one full stroke per measure, two shorter strokes, or one long and two shorter strokes. Play the tune also in the key of G major, using G and D$_7$ chords.

GOING OVER THE SEA

CANADA

1. When I was one, I ate a bun, Go-ing o-ver the sea. I jumped a-board a

sail-or-man's ship And the sail-or-man said to me, "Go-ing o-ver, go-ing

Accompanying with the Omnichord or Autoharp

un - der, Stand at at - ten - tion like a sol - dier With a one, two, three."

2. When I was [a] two, I buckled my shoe, . . .

3. When I was [a] three, I banged my knee, . . .

4. When I was [a] four, I shut the door, . . .

5. When I was [a] five, I learned to dive, . . .

6. When I was [a] six, I picked up sticks, . . .

7. When I was [a] seven, I went to heaven, . . .

8. When I was [a] eight, I learned to skate, . . .

9. When I was [a] nine, I climbed a vine, . . .

10. When I was [a] ten, I caught a hen, . . .

Actions:
[a] Hold up correct number of fingers
[b] Shade eyes with hand
[c] Jump once in place
[d] Hands on hips
[e] Swoop hand up
[f] Swoop hand down
[g] Stand erect with arms at sides
[h] Salute with right hand
[i] Step in place three times

Also play and sing *Hokey Pokey* (p. 330) using G and D_7 chords. Try this tune in the key of F major, using F and C_7 chords.

Play this song with one full stroke and two short strokes on the upper strings.
Use a light, gliding stroke for harp effect.

WHEN I AM TEN YEARS OLD

NORWEGIAN FOLK SONG
COLLECTED BY JANE FARWELL

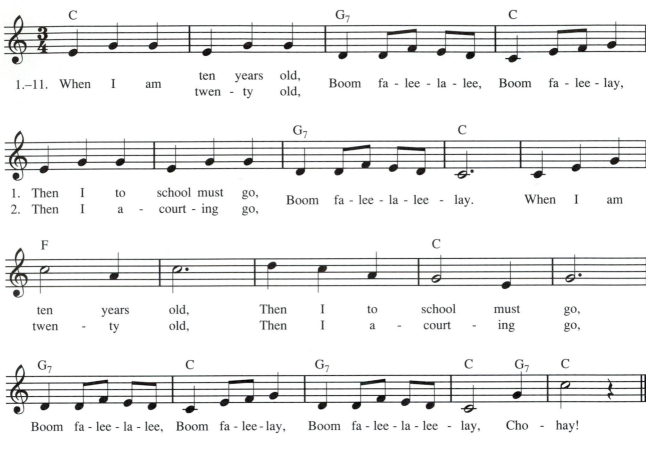

1.–11. When I am ten years old,
        twen - ty old, Boom fa - lee - la - lee, Boom fa - lee - lay,

1. Then I to school must go, Boom fa - lee - la - lee - lay. When I am
2. Then I a - court - ing go,

ten years old, Then I to school must go,
twen - ty old, Then I a - court - ing go,

Boom fa - lee - la - lee, Boom fa - lee - lay, Boom fa - lee - la - lee - lay, Cho - hay!

3. . . . thirty old, . . . I wear a band of gold, . . .   5. . . . fifty old, . . . My hair is gray with gold, . . .

4. . . . forty old, . . . Oh, how my family grows, . . .   6. . . . sixty old, . . . My hair is white as snow, . . .

OH! SUSANNA

STEPHEN C. FOSTER   STEPHEN C. FOSTER

I___ come from Al - a - bam - a with my ban - jo on my

knee, I'm_ going to Lou' - si - an - a my ___ true love for to see.

Oh! Su - san - na, Oh, don't you cry for me, For I come from Al - a - bam - a with my ban - jo on my knee.

Also play and sing *Twinkle, Twinkle, Little Star* (p. 158).

Playing in Minor Keys

Songs in minor keys are played with the chord hand moved up to the second row of chord bars. The following spiritual can be played with two firm strokes per measure, changing to four in the next-to-last bar. Play the A_7 chord at the end of the verse with a long, slow stroke to create a broken chord.

JOSHUA FIT THE BATTLE OF JERICHO

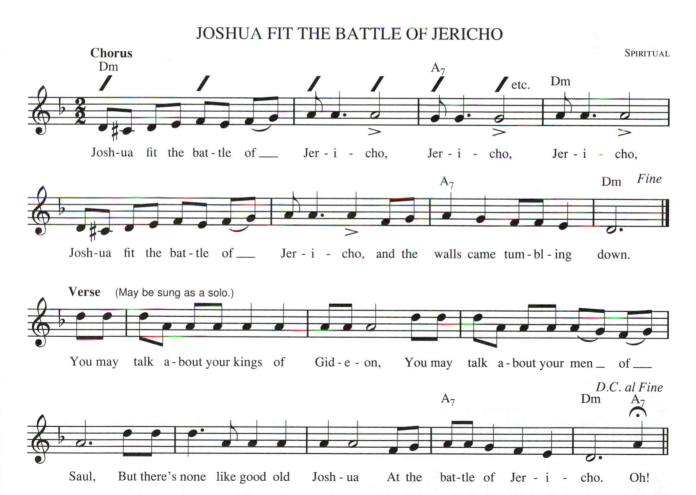

Josh-ua fit the bat-tle of ___ Jer - i - cho, Jer - i - cho, Jer - i - cho, Josh-ua fit the bat-tle of ___ Jer - i - cho, and the walls came tum-bl-ing down.

Verse (May be sung as a solo.)

You may talk a-bout your kings of Gid-e-on, You may talk a-bout your men ___ of ___ Saul, But there's none like good old Josh - ua At the bat-tle of Jer - i - cho. Oh!

Also play and sing *Shalom Chaverim* (p. 278).

Strum *Zum Gali Gali* with one easy stroke per measure.

ZUM GALI GALI

ISRAEL

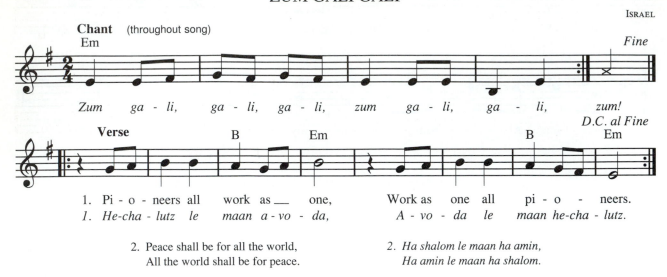

Chant (throughout song)

Zum   ga - li,   ga - li,   ga - li,   zum   ga - li,   ga - li,   zum!

Fine

D.C. al Fine

Verse

1. Pi - o - neers all   work as __ one,   Work as   one all   pi - o - neers.
1. *He-cha - lutz   le   maan a - vo - da,   A - vo - da   le   maan he-cha - lutz.*

2. Peace shall be for all the world,   2. *Ha shalom le maan ha amin,*
   All the world shall be for peace.   *Ha amin le maan ha shalom.*

Suggestion: Fade out with chant until end. On final "zum," shout it out and extend arm over head.

Playing in B♭ and D Major (15-Bar Autoharp)   When using the alternate harmony in measure 7 below, press the C₇ chord bar with the index finger. Practice it both ways. Which sounds better?

OVER THE RIVER AND THROUGH THE WOOD
THANKSGIVING SONG

LYDIA MARIE CHILDS

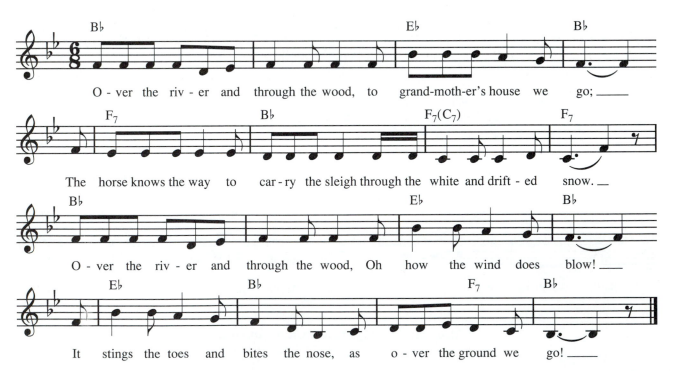

O - ver the riv - er and through the wood, to grand-moth-er's house we go; ___

The horse knows the way to car - ry the sleigh through the white and drift - ed snow. __

O - ver the riv - er and through the wood, Oh how the wind does blow! ___

It stings the toes and bites the nose, as o - ver the ground we go! ___

SHAKE MY SILLIES OUT

BERT AND BONNIE SIMPSON

RAFFI

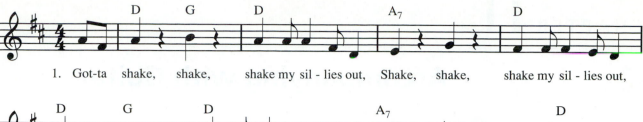

1. Got-ta shake, shake, shake my sil - lies out, Shake, shake, shake my sil - lies out,

Shake, shake, shake my sil - lies out and wig-gle my wag-gles a - way.

2. . . . clap my crazies out, . . .   4. . . . yawn my sleepies out, . . .
3. . . . jump my jiggles out, . . .   5. . . . shake my sillies out, . . .

Suggested Assignments

5–8, 3a

1. Play accompaniments to songs in state and local music series that indicate the letter names for the chords; then sing and play.
2. Practice finding and sounding the keynote, starting note, and key chord of various children's songs. **Remember to repeat the beginning chord of the song repeatedly *in rhythm* to firmly establish key and tempo.**
3. Create accompaniments for songs in texts that do not indicate the chords to be played.
4. Create two- and four-measure introductions to songs in the keys of C, F, G, D, and B♭ major and A and D minor. For some of these introductions use all three chords of the key (see p. 241).
5. Create your own rhythmic patterns for accompaniments in 2/4, 3/4, 4/4, and 6/8 time.
6. Combine bells, wind melody instruments, Omnichord, and/or Autoharp to form a classroom orchestra.
7. Transpose children's songs up or down a step. Refer to the transposition chart.

CHAPTER 11

Accompanying with Guitar

The guitar, a descendant of the ancient lute family, rapidly has become one of the most popular social instruments of this generation. Even though it is more difficult to play than the Autoharp, it now holds a prominent place as an instrument for accompanying singing in the schools. The teacher who can play the guitar has a distinct advantage in motivating children's and teenagers' singing activities. Moreover, since both melody and harmony can be played on the guitar, this versatile instrument is now recognized as a first-rate solo instrument for the concert stage. Recordings by Andrés Segovia, Julian Bream, John Williams, Oscar Ghiglia, NarcisoYepes, and many others are a colorful asset in motivation for listening lessons in the classroom.

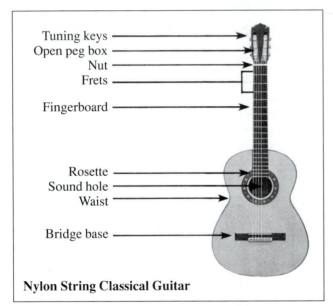

Nylon String Classical Guitar

Tuning keys
Open peg box
Nut
Frets
Fingerboard
Rosette
Sound hole
Waist
Bridge base

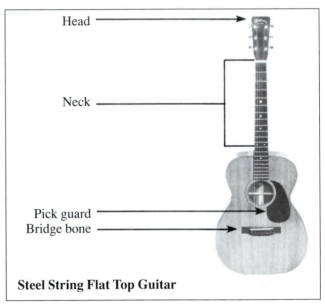

Steel String Flat Top Guitar

Head
Neck
Pick guard
Bridge bone

From Jerry Snyder's *Beginning the Guitar.* Charles Hansen Publishing Co., 1974. Used by permission.

Description of the Guitar

K–4, 6d

There are numerous models and makes of guitars manufactured today for various uses and types of playing. The two most common types of guitars, especially for classroom use, are the nylon string classical guitar and the steel string flat top guitar. Both of these may be either *acoustic* (not amplified) or *electric* (amplified). The basic difference in the two types is the tone quality; the nylon string classical guitar has a dark, mellow quality, and the steel string flat top has a bright, brassy sound. The classical guitar is recommended for beginners because the nylon strings are less taut and are therefore easier on the fingers.

Care of the Instrument

1. Keep the guitar covered at all times when it is not in use.
2. Store in a dry place with an even temperature.
3. Change the strings about every three months or whenever there are signs of wear or corrosion. If one string breaks or shows wear, all of the strings probably need changing.
4. Do not slacken strings after playing. Loose strings go out of tune faster than those kept up to pitch.
5. Do not use steel strings on guitars made for nylon strings or nylon strings on guitars made for steel strings.

Tuning the Guitar

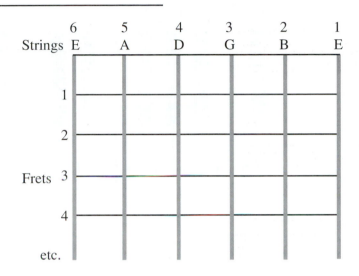

Guitar pitch pipe

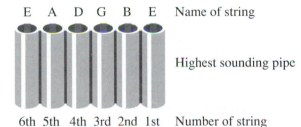

Tuning with a Pitch Pipe

A guitar pitch pipe can be purchased at most music stores. Each of the individual pipes is tuned to the correct pitch for each of the six open strings of the guitar. The strings must be tuned an octave lower than the notes of the pipe. (See diagram of notes on the piano below.)

1. Start by tuning the low E (6th) string, which is the lowest and thickest string of the guitar. Blow gently into the low E sound tube on the pitch pipe. Play the low E string of the guitar and adjust its tuning peg until the two sounds match pitch.
2. Tune each string in the same manner. Remember to match the pitch of each string to its corresponding sound on the pitch pipe. *Care should be taken on all the strings to not tune them too tightly. If you go beyond the pitch pipe's sound, you may break a string and put undue stress on the neck of the guitar.*

3. Once all the strings are tuned, recheck and re-tune each string as necessary.

Tuning with a Piano

The previous procedure may be applied in tuning the guitar with the piano. Before beginning, make sure that the piano is properly tuned. The first string, high E, is to the right of middle C on the piano. Going two octaves below that note will result in locating the low E (6th). It should be noted that the guitar sounds an octave lower than what is written on the staff. (See the diagram below).

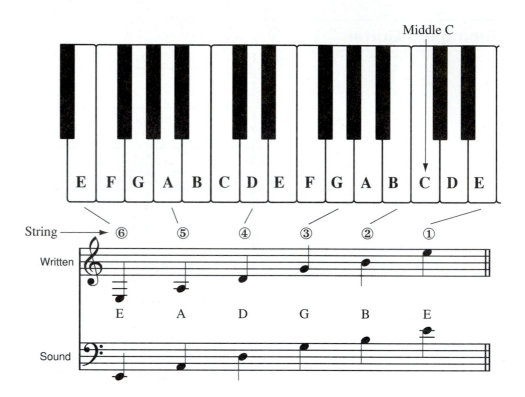

Tuning the Guitar to Itself

The guitar can be tuned to its own strings. By using a fixed pitch instrument or estimating the low E, each string may be used to tune successive strings. Once the low E is tuned properly, the following procedure will tune the remainder of the strings:

Press the fifth fret of the 6th string to produce the sound A or 5th string open.
Press the fifth fret of the 5th string to produce the sound D or 4th string open.
Press the fifth fret of the 4th string to produce the sound G or 3rd string open.
Press the fourth fret of the 3rd string to produce the sound B or 2nd string open.
Press the fifth fret of the 2nd string to produce the sound E or 1st string open.

(See diagram below.)

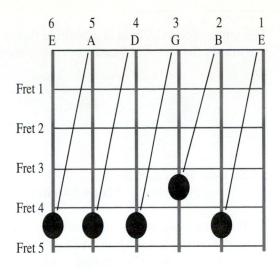

A unique way of tuning the low E is by matching its pitch to the dial tone of the telephone. Press the first fret of the 6th string. This produces the sound of F. Match that sound to the telephone's dial tone. Adjust the string until both sounds are matched. Note: The dial tone will actually sound an octave higher than the low F that is pressed, so care should be taken not to tune the string too tightly.

Tuning with an Electronic Tuner

Many professionals use electronic tuners to tune their guitars. These instruments generally have a built-in microphone that picks up the sound of the played string. A readout of the pitch is then displayed either with a needle or an LED light. These readings are used to determine whether the pitch is higher or lower than the correct pitch. The cost of an electronic tuner can range from $20 to $150, depending upon the features. For the most part, the less expensive tuners are very reliable and provide the inexperienced player with a quick and easy way of tuning the guitar.

Playing the Guitar

5–8, 6b

The guitar should be held in a position that is both comfortable to the player and allows the hands proper access to the strings.

Sitting with the Guitar

Informal Posture

1. Sit in an armless chair.
2. Elevate the right leg either with a footstool or by crossing it over the left leg.
3. Place the waist of the guitar on the raised right leg with the neck of the guitar pointing slightly upward.
4. The body of the guitar should rest against the chest.

Formal Posture (Classical Posture)

1. Sit in an armless chair.
2. Elevate the left leg with a footstool.
3. Place the waist of the guitar on the raised left leg.
4. The neck of the guitar should point upward. The head of the guitar should be about eye level.
5. The body of the guitar should rest against the chest.

In both the formal and informal postures, the right forearm should rest on the lower body of the guitar, close to the instrument's edge.

Using the Right Hand

Guitar pictures from Jerry Snyder's *Basic Instructor for Guitar*. Charles Hansen Publishing Co., 1974. Used by permission.

Right-hand Position

The guitar is plucked and strummed with the right hand using either a pick or finger-style. The latter is recommended for beginners. Finger-style uses the thumb and the first three fingers. Fingernails of the right hand may be used if they are kept smooth with a nail file and do not get too long.

The right hand should be directly over the strings just behind the sound hole. The wrist should be elevated from the body of the guitar so the fingers may extend down to the strings in a relaxed manner.

Plucking

Individual strings are plucked with each finger using a scratching motion. The motion should be generated from the first knuckle (the one closest to the palm). There should be no tension in this motion. Place a finger on a string and play through the string and into the palm of the hand.

When playing the thumb, it should remain straight through the stroke. Its motion is also initiated from the first knuckle, but its motion is more circular.

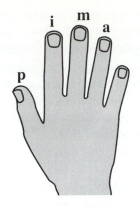

In guitar music, the thumb is designated by the small letter p, the index finger i, the middle finger m, and the ring finger a. The little finger is not used except in flamenco style so the designation for it will not be noted here.

The initials for the right hand fingers are derived from Spanish.

(p) = pulgar for thumb
(i) = indice for index finger
(m) = media for middle finger
(a) = anular for ring finger

Using the Left Hand

The strings of the guitar are depressed (fretted) with the fingers of the left hand. The fingers are numbered 1 through 4 with the index being 1 and the pinkie being 4. The nails of the left hand must be kept short so that the fingertips may be used to press the strings.

Here are some guidelines for successful left-hand technique.

1. Put the thumb behind the neck. Keep it straight and pointed toward the ceiling. *Do not let the thumb rest on top of the neck.*
2. Keep the palm of the hand from touching the bottom of the neck of the guitar.
3. Try to keep the wrist straight.
4. Curl the fingers so that the tips press the string into the fret board.
5. Press directly behind the fret bar without going over the fret bar itself.
6. Fingers should be in contact only with the string they are playing. Care should be taken not to touch any of the adjacent strings.

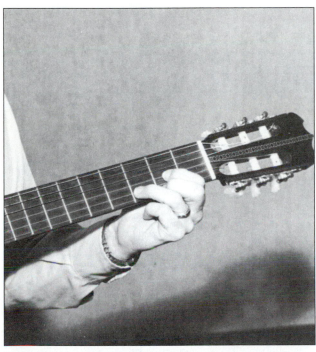

Courtesy of Jerry Rouse, Chairman, Music Department, El Toro High School, Mission Viejo, California.

Left-hand Finger Position

Strumming

With the right hand in the playing position, curl the fingers loosely into the palm. Rest the thumb lightly on the 6th string. Strum across the remainder of the strings with the back of the fingernails. One or more fingers may be used. The motion should be initiated from the first knuckle, this time in reverse from the plucking motion. Some wrist motion may be used when playing more complicated rhythms. When playing six-string chords, it will be necessary to release the thumb from the 6th string. In such cases the thumb may hang loosely in the air.

It is important to note that when playing three-, four-, or five-string chords, only the strings that make up those chords should be strummed.

Strum Notation

Standard notation makes reading strum patterns and chords very difficult. To simplify this, chord diagrams are used to show where fingers are placed to fret the chords. Chord diagrams are graphic representations of the frets and strings on the guitar. Vertical lines represent the strings while the horizontal lines represent the frets. Dots placed on the string and fret representations indicate where the fingers must be placed to produce the sound for that chord.

Tablature may also be used to show where the fingers should be placed. Tablature is a form of notation that has a line representing each string of the guitar. Numbers on the lines indicate what fret the fingers play along that corresponding string.

Rhythm may be notated with normal note values such as quarter notes or with slash marks. Quarter note rhythms are strummed with a downward motion (brush strum) as previously described. Vertical wavy lines (𝆕) alongside the regular chord notation also indicate the same kind of strumming motion.

Reading Strum Notation

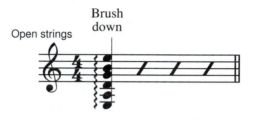

Reading Chord Frames

The position for the fingers of the left hand are as follows:

1 = index finger
2 = middle finger
3 = ring finger
4 = little finger
X = do not play
0 = open string

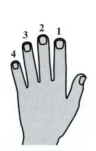

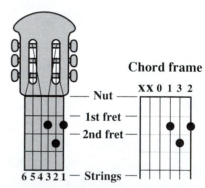

Guitar Fingerboard (D Major Chord)

D chord in tablature

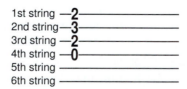

1st string —2——————
2nd string —3——————
3rd string —2——————
4th string —0——————
5th string ——————————
6th string ——————————

Note: Tablature does not tell which fingers must play the notes, only where the notes must be played. In most cases, the tablature also does not tell what the rhythm of the song should be.

Accompanying with Guitar

Arpeggio Playing

Sometimes instead of strumming, a softer accompaniment style may be used, which is called *arpeggio technique* or *broken chord style*. This involves playing each note of the chord individually with the fingers of the right hand. To try this technique, follow these directions:

1. Place the D chord in the left hand.
2. Place (plant) the thumb (p) of the right hand on the 4th string (D).
3. Plant the index (i) of the right hand on the 3rd string.
4. Plant the middle (m) of the right hand on the 2nd string.
5. Plant the ring finger (a) of the right hand on the 1st string.
6. With the thumb and fingers planted, pluck each string individually starting with the thumb and progressing up the strings until the "a" finger has played the 1st string. *Make sure the thumb strokes in a circular motion while the fingers stroke in a scratching motion.*

Playing chords in arpeggio style helps identify problems that may occur in fretting chords in the left hand.

Different time signatures will require different finger patterns, but the general rule is to always start the arpeggio with the thumb on the lowest note of the chord. Listed below are some common arpeggio patterns for different time signatures:

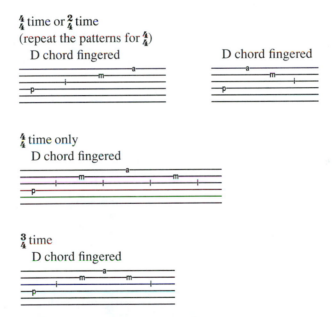

$\frac{4}{4}$ time or $\frac{2}{4}$ time
(repeat the patterns for $\frac{4}{4}$)
D chord fingered   D chord fingered

$\frac{4}{4}$ time only
D chord fingered

$\frac{3}{4}$ time
D chord fingered

Bass and Strum Style

Another accompaniment style that is popular is the bass note followed by a strum style. This technique involves plucking the bass note of the chord with the thumb and then brush strumming the rest of the chord with the fingers. Here are tablature examples of this technique:

$\frac{4}{4}$ time
D chord fingered

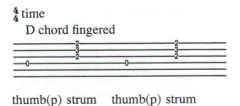

thumb(p) strum   thumb(p) strum

Accompanying with Guitar

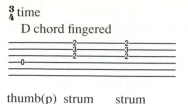

$\frac{3}{4}$ time

D chord fingered

thumb(p) strum   strum

Playing in the Key of C Major

Learn the C and G_7 chords. There is an easy way to play these two chords that involves using only the first three strings. Play them by resting your thumb on the 4th string and brush strumming your fingers across the first three strings. After doing the easy C and G_7 chords, try the basic chord fingerings shown below on the easy chord diagrams. Move your fingers smoothly from one chord to the next. Remember not to strum the strings that are marked with an "x." For practice switching chords, do the exercises that follow the diagrams.

EASY C AND G_7

Left-hand fingers

BASIC C AND G_7

MARIANNE

Caribbean

All day, all night, Mar - i - anne, Down by the

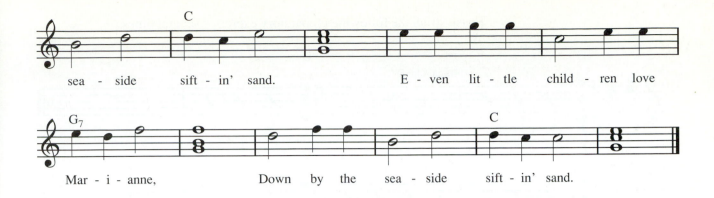

sea - side sift - in' sand.   E - ven lit - tle child - ren love

Mar - i - anne,   Down by the sea - side sift - in' sand.

ODE TO JOY

BEETHOVEN

SKIP TO MY LOU

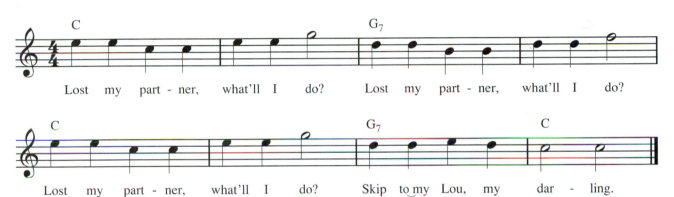

Lost my part - ner, what'll I do? Lost my part - ner, what'll I do?

Lost my part - ner, what'll I do? Skip to my Lou, my dar - ling.

Playing in the Key of G Major

Learn the chords G and D₇. These are the two most commonly used chords in the key of G major. The G chord can be played using either the basic fingering or the simplified fingering.

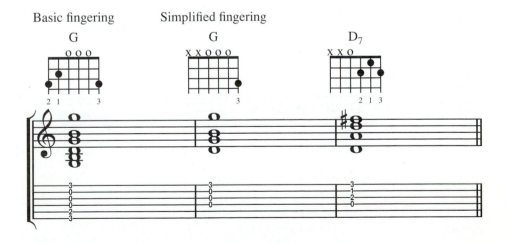

Brush strum the following preparatory exercises several times.

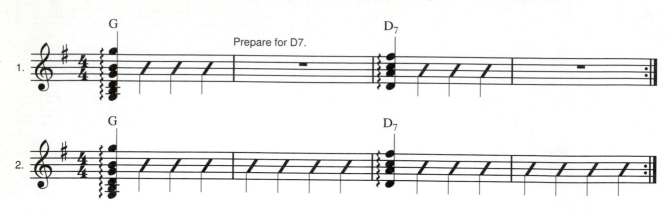

The C chord may also be used in the key of G major. Brush strum the following exercises several times. Keep the index finger down when changing from the C chord to the D₇ chord and vice versa.

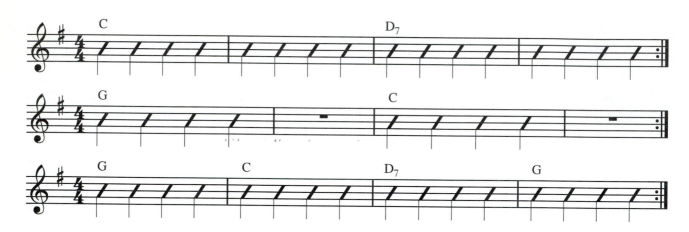

HUSH, LITTLE BABY

United States

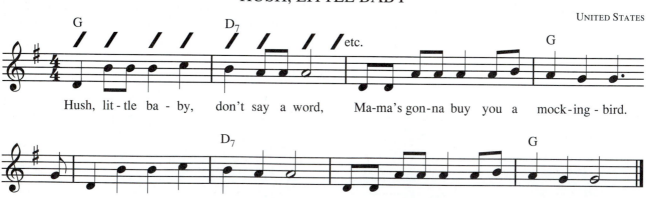

Hush, lit - tle ba - by, don't say a word, Ma-ma's gon-na buy you a mock-ing - bird.

And if that mock-ing - bird won't sing, Dad-dy's gon-na buy you a dia - mond ring.

TOM DOOLEY

Hang down your head, Tom Doo - ley, Hang down your head and cry,

Hang down your head, Tom Doo - ley, Poor boy, you're bound to die.

When changing from the G chord to the C chord, an alternative fingering may be used. Try the fingering found below in the chord diagram. This allows the second and third finger to move in parallel motion when changing from G to C.

WORRIED MAN BLUES

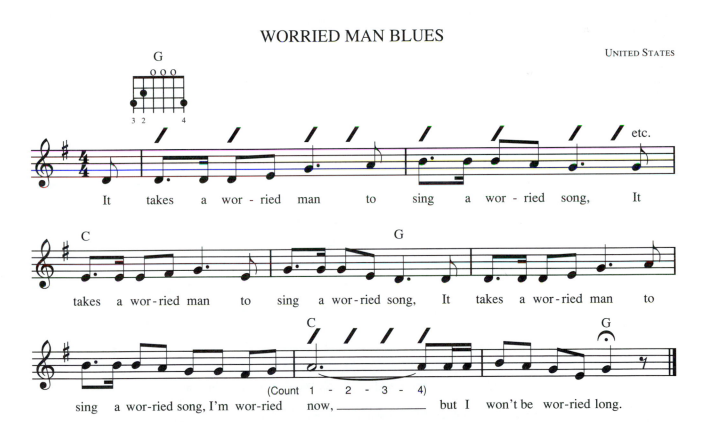

It takes a wor - ried man to sing a wor - ried song, It

takes a wor - ried man to sing a wor - ried song, It takes a wor - ried man to

sing a wor - ried song, I'm wor - ried now, _____ but I won't be wor - ried long.

(Count 1 - 2 - 3 - 4)

Playing in the Key of D Major

Chords in the key of D major include D, G, and A_7. Practice the fingerings in the following diagrams. When the fingerings are learned, practice changing from one chord to another.

COLOURS

Donovan   DONOVAN

1. Yel - low   is   the   col-our   of   my   true   love's   hair   In   the   morn-ing _____
2. Blue ___   is   the   col-our   of   the   sky   a - bove

_____ when we   rise, _____   In   the   morn - ing _____   when we   rise, _____

_____ That's the   time, _____   that's the   time _____   I   love the   best. _____

3. Green is the colour of the sparkling corn (or Douglas Fir) in the morning . . .

4. White is the colour of the new-fall'n snow in the morning . . .

5. Freedom is a word that I seldom use without thinking, *mm__* ,
   Without thinking, *mm__* , of the time,
   Of the time when we first loved.

6. *(Make up your own new verses) or repeat verse 1.*

Accompanying with Guitar

CAMPTOWN RACES

STEPHEN FOSTER

STEPHEN FOSTER

FRANKIE AND JOHNNY

UNITED STATES

Frank - ie and John - ny were lov - ers, oh, Lord - y, how they could

love. They swore to be true to each oth - er, just as true as the stars _ a -

bove, He was her man, but he done her wrong.

POLLY WOLLY DOODLE

Oh, I went down south for to see my Sal, Sing-ing Pol-ly Wol-ly Doo-dle all the day,

My Sal, she is a spunk-y gal, Sing-ing Pol-ly Wol-ly Doo-dle all the day!

Fare thee well, fare thee well, fare thee well, my fair - y fey, For I'm

goin' to Lou'-si-an-a For to see my Sus-i-an-a, Sing-ing Pol-ly Wol-ly Doo-dle all the day.

Playing in the Key of A Major

The key of A major presents new challenges. The chord requires that you place three notes down on adjacent strings in the same fret. Below are the basic fingering and some alternative fingerings for this chord.

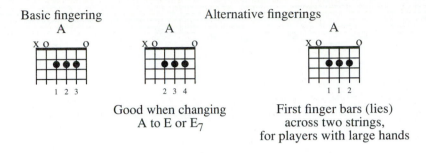

Basic fingering
A
1 2 3

Alternative fingerings

A
2 3 4
Good when changing
A to E or E₇

A
1 1 2
First finger bars (lies)
across two strings,
for players with large hands

The other chords that are found in the key of A major are D and E₇. Learn these chords and strum through the following exercises.

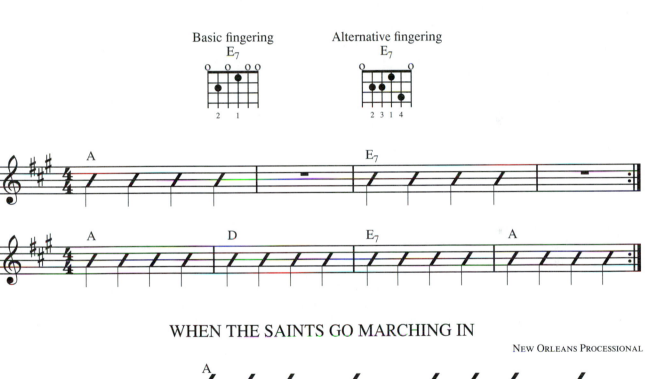

Basic fingering
E₇
2 1

Alternative fingering
E₇
2 3 1 4

WHEN THE SAINTS GO MARCHING IN

New Orleans Processional

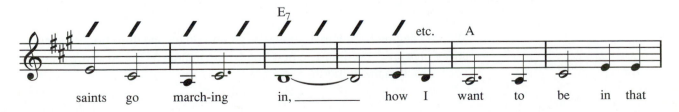

Oh, when the   saints _____   go march-ing   in, _____   oh, when the

saints   go   march-ing   in, _____   how   I   want   to   be   in   that

num - ber, _____ when the saints go march - ing in. _____

OLD SMOKY

UNITED STATES

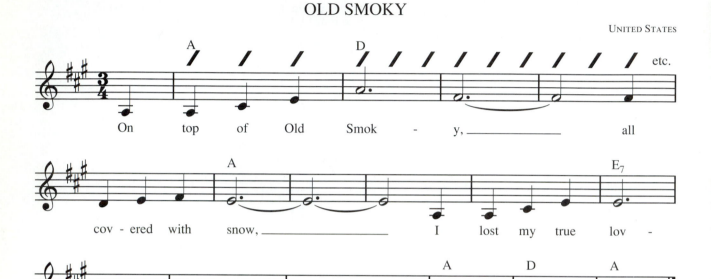

On top of Old Smok - y, _____ all

cov - ered with snow, _____ I lost my true lov -

er _____ by court - ing too slow. _____

Playing in the Key of E Major

The key of E major has the chords E, A, and B_7. The basic B_7 chord requires the use of all four left-hand fingers. Learn the chords using the fingering suggested. Practice the exercises that follow to develop skill changing from one chord to the next.

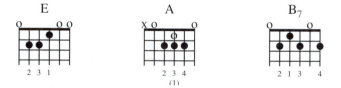

When changing from E to A, move the second finger and third finger over one string in parallel fashion. The first finger may remain on the 3d string for easy access back to the E chord.

When changing from E to B₇, leave the second finger on the 5th string.

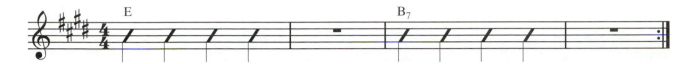

When changing from A to B₇, leave the third finger on the 3rd string.

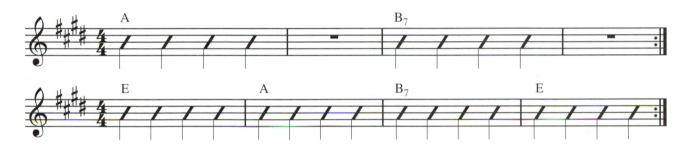

AWAY IN A MANGER

James R. Murray

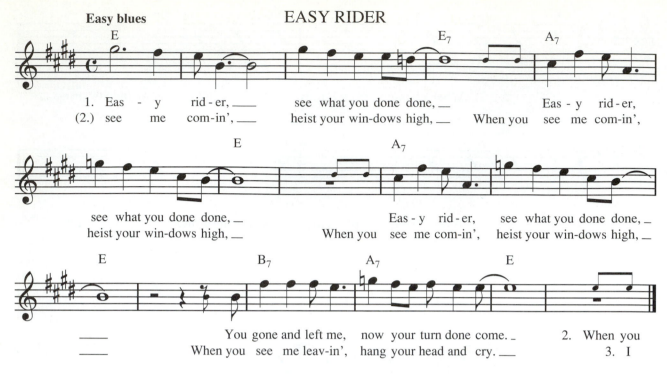

EASY RIDER

Easy blues

1. Eas - y rid - er, ____ see what you done done, __ Eas - y rid - er,
(2.) see me com-in', ____ heist your win-dows high, __ When you see me com-in',

see what you done done, __ Eas - y rid - er, see what you done done, __
heist your win-dows high, __ When you see me com-in', heist your win-dows high, __

____ You gone and left me, now your turn done come. _ 2. When you
____ When you see me leav-in', hang your head and cry. __ 3. I

3. I wish I was a catfish, swimmin' in the deep blue sea, *(3 times)*
   I'd keep those women *(fellas)* from fussin' over me.

Playing in the Key of A Minor

A number of songs are played in minor keys. The key of A minor is one of the easiest to play. The chords are Am, Dm, and E or E$_7$. The fingering for A minor is very similar to the one for E major. Play careful attention to the strings that are fingered for each note. When moving from Am to Dm, let the first and second finger move in parallel motion with the third finger making the adjustment in fret location.

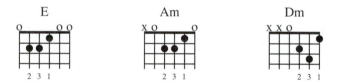

Practice the following changes:

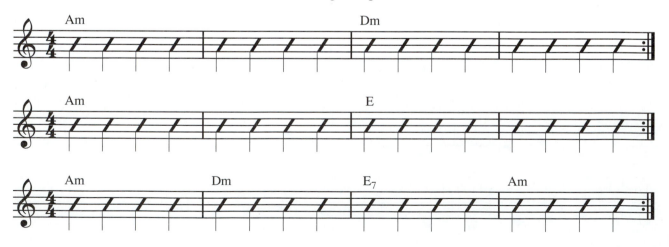

Accompanying with Guitar

JOSHUA FIT THE BATTLE OF JERICHO

Josh-ua fit the bat-tle of __ Jer - i - cho, _ Jer - i - cho, _ Jer - i - cho, _____

Josh-ua fit the bat-tle of __ Jer - i - cho, _ And the walls came tum-bling down!

HAVA NAGILA

ISRAELI FOLK DANCE

Ha - va na - gi - la, ha - va na - gi - la, ha - va na - gi - la,

vay nis - m'-cha. Ha - va na - gi - la, ha - va na - gi - la, ha - va na - gi - la,

vay nis - m'-cha. Ha-va n' ra - ne - nah, ha-va n' ra - ne - nah, ha - va n' ra - ne - nah,

vay nis - m' - cha. Ha-va n' ra - ne - nah, ha - va n' ra - ne - nah,

ha - va n' ra - ne - nah, vay nis - m'-cha. U - ru, u - ru a - chim,

u - ru a-chim b' lev-sa me-ach, u - ru a-chim b' lev-sa me-ach, u - ru a-chim b' lev-sa me-ach,

u - ru a-chim b' lev-sa me-ach, U-ru a-chim, u-ru a-chim, b' lev - sa me - ach.

Accompanying with Guitar

The chords in E minor are Em, Am, and B_7. When changing from Em to B_7, remember to keep the second finger on the 5th string. It is used as a pivot finger between the two chords.

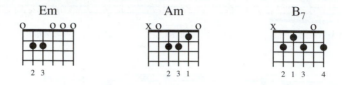

Practice the following changes:

HAIDA

ISRAEL

Hai - da - da - da, hai - da, __ hai - da, Hai - da, hai - da - da,

Hai - da, hai - da - da hai - da, Hai - da, hai - da - da.

ZUM GALI GALI

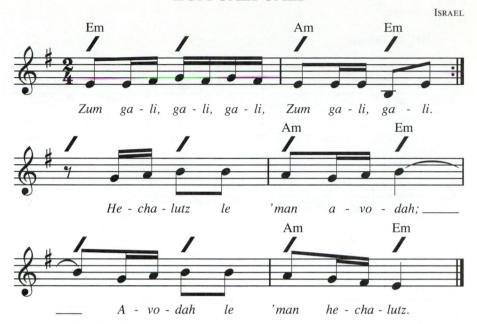

Zum ga - li, ga - li, ga - li, Zum ga - li, ga - li.

He - cha - lutz le 'man a - vo - dah; _____

_____ A - vo - dah le 'man he - cha - lutz.

Translation: "The pioneer's purpose is labor."

Bar Chords, the F Chord

Some chords require that one finger, generally the first, cover two or more strings at the same fret. These chords are referred to as *bar chords*. They are not the easiest to execute and patience is needed when trying to learn them. The most common one encountered is the F chord. It is used in the key of C major. Care should be taken when playing the F that the second and third fingers do not interfere with the sound of the 2nd and 1st strings. When the F chord is learned, try the following exercises:

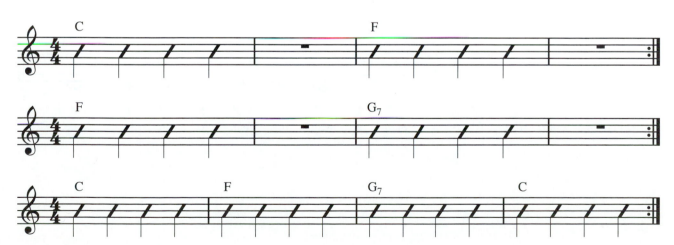

OH! SUSANNA

Stephen Foster

Stephen Foster

Bright Tempo

C ... G7

I ___ come from Al - a - bam - a with my ban - jo on my knee;

C ... G7 C

I'm ___ goin' to Lou' - si - an - a, my ___ true love for to see.

G7

It ___ rained all night the day I left, the weath - er was so dry;

C ... G7 C

The ___ sun so hot I froze to death; Su - san - na, don't you cry.

Chorus

F ... C G7

Oh! Su - san - na, Oh! don't you cry for me,

C ... G7 C

I ___ come from Al - a - bam - a with my ban - jo on my knee.

Using the Capo

At this point, the keys most commonly used for guitar have been presented. There may be times when singers may not be able to sing in those particular keys or the song is found in a key other than the ones studied. To make it easier on the player, a *capo* is used. Capos are clamps that are placed on the frets to shorten the string length and therefore raise the pitch of the guitar. This allows the player to play in more difficult keys using the basic chords. If a capo is not used, the player would have to bar the strings with the first finger and then play the chords above the barred finger. The capo allows for a quick and easy transposition of any song.

Listed below are transposition charts that will locate keys when using the capo. Clamp the capo on the fret indicated.

Using the key of C chords

Fret	Key
1	D♭
2	D
3	E♭

Using the key of A chords

Fret	Key
1	B♭
2	B
3	C

Using the key of G chords

Fret	Key
1	A♭
2	A
3	B♭

Using the key of E chords

Fret	Key
1	F
2	G♭
3	G

Using the key of D chords

Fret	Key
1	E♭
2	E
3	F

The previous charts may also be used for minor keys.

CHAPTER 12

Singing in Harmony

K–4, 1d
5–8, 1d

Learning to sing in harmony is an important phase of the elementary teacher's basic musical training. Skill in singing in harmony, or part singing, is especially useful for the teaching of fourth, fifth, and sixth grade classroom music. The introduction of songs that incorporate more than just the singing of the melody line is a process that each teacher can approach in a gradual and stepwise manner.

In this chapter various part-singing experiences are introduced in the sequence frequently found in the upper elementary school music curriculum. The following eight stages of this textbook include:

1. Chants or Ostinati
2. Call-and-Response or Echo Songs
3. Rounds or Canons
4. Partner Songs
5. Descants or Countermelodies
6. Two-part Singing
7. Bass Chanting
8. Three-part Singing

Suggestions for teaching each of these areas:

- Have the entire class learn or review a melody first. Students feel security in singing when they are confident that they know the melody line.
- Next, some or all of the class can be taught to sing the harmony part, after which the teacher can then sing or play the melody on the piano or bells. Groups can then be formed to sing the parts. The teacher can assist by singing or playing an instrument for whichever part needs support.
- If the harmony part is difficult, some of the class members can hum or sing "oo" on the melody while others are learning the harmony.
- Half of the students could play their part on the recorder while the rest of the students sing on that same part. Then the students should switch parts—the singers play and the players sing.
- While it is sometimes necessary to rehearse the harmony part alone, the learning of parts separately should be kept to a minimum.
- Always remember to secure the first pitch or pitches of the music until everyone "has them."
- As the "singing in harmony" skills progress, try to sing more *unfamiliar* songs.

Singing Chants and Ostinati

K–4, 1d

The easiest part-singing experience is that of adding one or more repeated note patterns (called chants, or ostinati) to familiar melodies. Small groups of singers may be selected, with several others playing bells, Orff instruments, and recorders.

ROW, ROW, ROW YOUR BOAT
ROUND

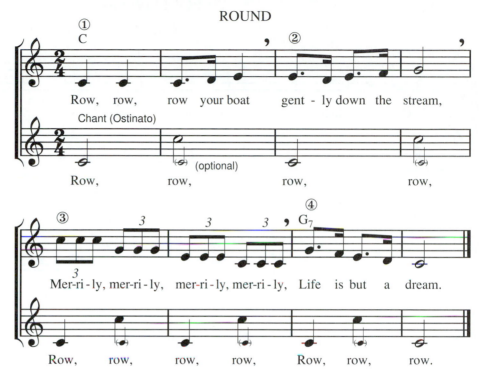

Row, row, row your boat gent-ly down the stream,

Chant (Ostinato)

Row, row, (optional) row, row,

Mer-ri-ly, mer-ri-ly, mer-ri-ly, mer-ri-ly, Life is but a dream.

Row, row, row, row, Row, row, row.

LONDON BRIDGE

ENGLAND

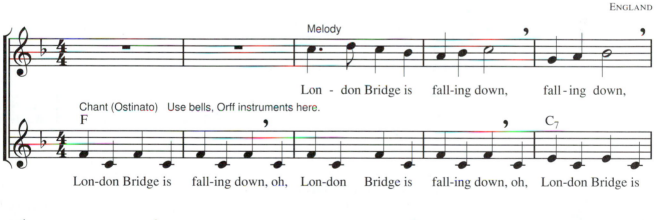

Melody

Lon - don Bridge is fall-ing down, fall-ing down,

Chant (Ostinato)   Use bells, Orff instruments here.

Lon-don Bridge is fall-ing down, oh, Lon-don Bridge is fall-ing down, oh, Lon-don Bridge is

fall-ing down, Lon - don Bridge is fall-ing down, My fair la-dy.

fall-ing down, oh, Lon-don Bridge is fall-ing down, oh, Lon-don Bridge is fall-ing down.

Singing Call-and-Response or Echo Songs

K–4, 1e

When singing these songs, sing them first with a leader, teacher, or other strong singer, then divide the class into two groups (*with strong singers in each group*). The antiphonal effect helps develop independence in singing (or playing) one's own part.

FOLLOW ON

CANON

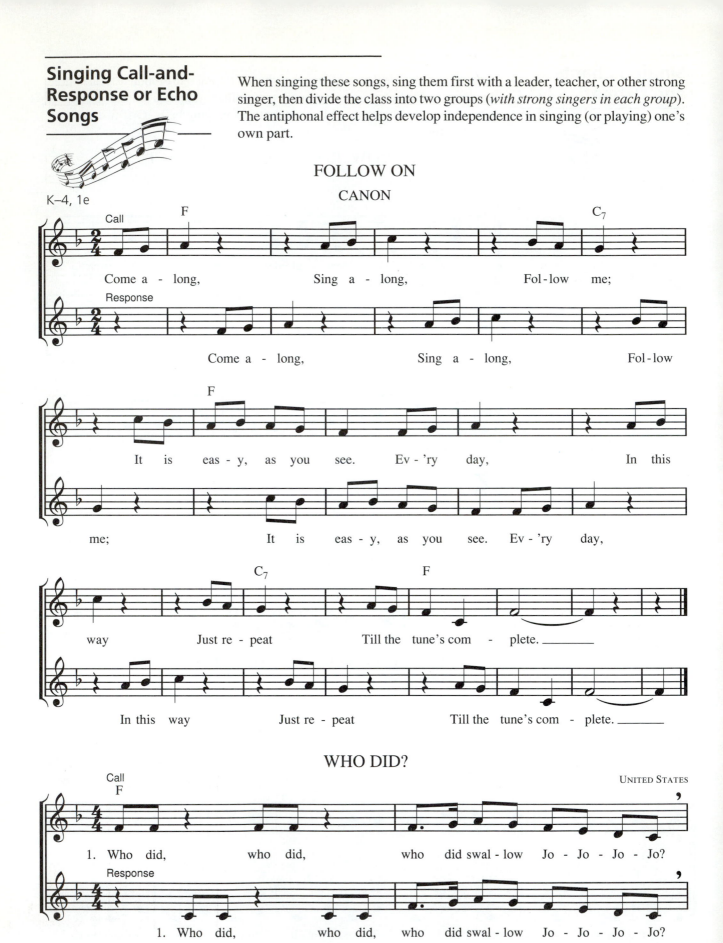

Call
Come a - long, Sing a - long, Fol-low me;
Response
Come a - long, Sing a - long, Fol-low

It is eas - y, as you see. Ev - 'ry day, In this
me; It is eas - y, as you see. Ev - 'ry day,

way Just re - peat Till the tune's com - plete. _____
In this way Just re - peat Till the tune's com - plete. _____

WHO DID?

UNITED STATES

Call
1. Who did, who did, who did swal - low Jo - Jo - Jo - Jo?
Response
1. Who did, who did, who did swal - low Jo - Jo - Jo - Jo?

Who did, who did, who did swal-low Jo - Jo - Jo - Jo?

Who did, who did, who did swal-low Jo - Jo - Jo - Jo?

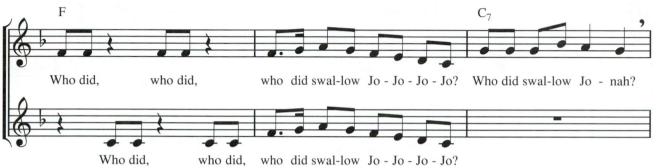

Who did, who did, who did swal-low Jo - Jo - Jo - Jo? Who did swal-low Jo - nah?

Who did, who did, who did swal-low Jo - Jo - Jo - Jo?

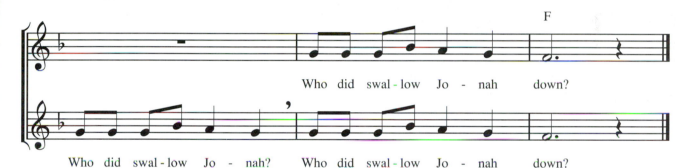

Who did swal - low Jo - nah down?

Who did swal-low Jo - nah? Who did swal-low Jo - nah down?

2.   Whale did, *(whale did,)* whale did, *(whale did,)*
  Both: Whale did swallow Jo- Jo- Jo- Jo.
         Whale did, *(whale did,)* whale did, *(whale did,)*
  Both: Whale did swallow Jo- Jo- Jo- Jo.
         Whale did, *(whale did,)* whale did, *(whale did,)*
  Both: Whale did swallow Jo- Jo- Jo- Jo.
         Whale did swallow Jonah, *(whale did swallow Jonah,)*
  Both: Whale did swallow Jonah down.

3.   Daniel, *(Daniel,)* Daniel, *(Daniel,)*
  Both: Daniel in the Li- Li- Li- Li,
         Daniel, *(Daniel,)* Daniel, *(Daniel,)*
  Both: Daniel in the Li- Li- Li- Li,
         Daniel, *(Daniel,)* Daniel, *(Daniel,)*
  Both: Daniel in the Li- Li- Li- Li,
         Daniel in the Lion's, *(Daniel in the Lion's,)*
  Both: Daniel in the Lion's Den.

Create Orff-like tonal patterns on the following pentatonic tune using the notes F, G, A, C, and D. Coconut shells or wood blocks of two different sizes can be used to create the effect of horses' hooves, for example. Play and sing:

K–4, 3b

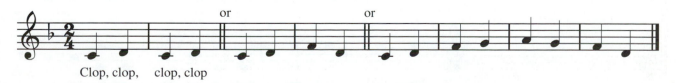

Clop, clop, clop, clop

OLD TEXAS

AMERICAN COWBOY SONG

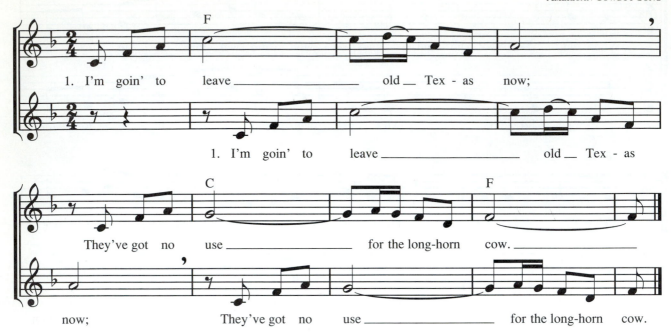

1. I'm goin' to leave ___ old __ Tex - as now;

1. I'm goin' to leave ___ old __ Tex - as

They've got no use ___ for the long-horn cow. ___

now; They've got no use ___ for the long-horn cow.

2. They've plowed and fenced my cattle range,
   And the people there are all so strange.

3. I'll take my horse, I'll take my rope,
   And hit the trail upon a lope.

4. Say *adios* to the Alamo
   And hit the trail toward Mexico.

Singing Rounds

K–4, 1d

Learn the melody well before singing a song as a round. Divide the class into sections: When group 1 reaches number 2, group 2 begins, and so forth. Repeat as many times as there are sections. In reaching the end of the melody in a round, each group goes "round" to the beginning and repeats the song. After the desired number of repetitions, each group completes the melody and drops out in the order of entry.

SCOTLAND'S BURNING

ROUND

TRADITIONAL

Scot-land's burn-ing, Scot-land's burn-ing, Look out! look out!

Fire! fire! fire! fire! Pour on wa-ter, pour on wa-ter!

After learning this two-part round, have several strong singers sing the following ostinato. Also play it on bells. Create other chants.

1. See the fire, See the fire.
2. Put it out, Put it out.

A RAM SAM SAM
ROUND

Moroccan Folk Song

A ram sam sam, a ram sam sam, Gu-li gu-li gu-li gu-li gu-li ram sam sam.

A ra-fi, a ra-fi, Gu-li gu-li gu-li gu-li gu-li ram sam sam.

I LOVE THE MOUNTAINS
ROUND

Traditional

I love the moun-tains, I love the roll-ing hills, I love the flow-ers,

I love the daf-fo-dils; I love the fire-side when all the lights are low.

This line can also be used as an ostinato.
Boom-dee-ah-da, Boom-dee-ah-da, Boom-dee-ah-da, Boom-dee-ah-da.

This 16th-century Latin hymn means "Give Us Peace."

DONA NOBIS PACEM
ROUND

LATIN HYMN

Latin: Do - na no - bis pa - cem, pa - cem. Do - na ___
Pronunciation: dɔ na nɔ bis pa chɛm pa chɛm

no - bis pa - cem. Do - na no - bis

pa - cem. Do - na no - bis pa - cem. Do - na

no - bis ___ pa - cem. Do - na no - bis pa - cem.

Shalom Chaverim can be sung in as many as eight parts. ("Shalom chaverim lehitraot" is pronounced "shall-ohm chah-vay-reem lay-hee-trah-oht.")

SHALOM CHAVERIM
ROUND

ISRAEL

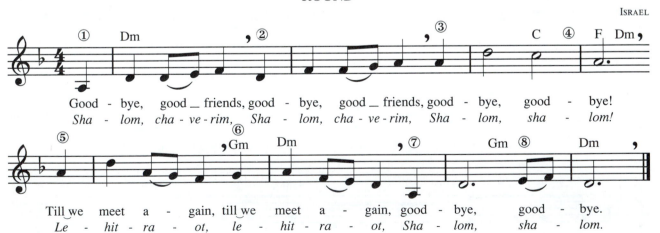

Good - bye, good ___ friends, good - bye, good ___ friends, good - bye, good - bye!
Sha - lom, cha - ve - rim, Sha - lom, cha - ve - rim, Sha - lom, sha - lom!

Till we meet a - gain, till we meet a - gain, good - bye, good - bye.
Le - hit - ra - ot, le - hit - ra - ot, Sha - lom, sha - lom.

Also sing the round *Make New Friends* on page 110. For additional rounds, see chapter 14 (p. 316).

Singing Canons

Canons in school music are sung in two parts, the second group of voices usually beginning after the first group has sung one measure. It is effective to have boys sing one part and girls the other.

Li'l Liza Jane, based on the notes of the pentatonic scale, offers numerous possibilities for Orff improvisation. Some of these improvisations are provided below.

5–8, 1d

LI'L LIZA JANE

UNITED STATES

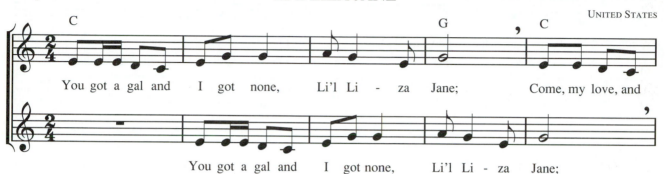

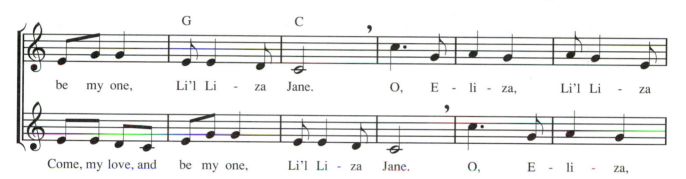

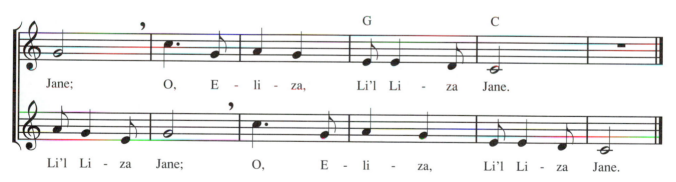

Orff Ostinati for LI'L LIZA JANE

Important: Twinkle, Twinkle, Little Star (p. 158) is especially effective when sung and played as a canon.

COME AND SING TOGETHER

CANON

Hungarian Melody

Singing in Harmony

Singing Partner Songs

K–4, 1d

Partner songs are two or more songs that can be sung together and help to establish the ability to hold one's own part while something else is being sung. They are particularly useful in fun songfests. Have the class learn each song separately before combining them.

Partner Songs "fit" together because of the following criteria:

- They have the same or compatible time signatures.
- They share the same or comparable beat patterns or pulsation.
- They include the same chord structures.
- They successfully coordinate beginnings and ends of phrases.

1. THREE BLIND MICE/2. ARE YOU SLEEPING

TRADITIONAL ROUNDS

Three blind mice, ___ three blind mice, ___ See how they
Are you sleep - ing, are you sleep - ing, Broth - er

run, ___ see how they run, ___ They all run af - ter the
John, Broth - er John? Morn - ing bells are

farm - er's wife, She cut off their tails with a carv - ing knife. Did
ring - ing, morn - ing bells are ring - ing,

ev - er you see such a sight in your life as three blind mice? ___
Ding, ding, dong, ding, ding, dong.

Next. sing and play these ostinati with these partner songs.

Ding,   ding,   dong.   Ding,   ding,   dong.   Ding,   ding,   ding,   dong.

Assign a number to each of the four rounds in the key of C: (1) *Three Blind Mice*, (2) *Are You Sleeping*, (3) *The Farmer in the Dell*, and (4) *Row, Row, Row Your Boat* (p. 273). Assign one of the numbers to each person in the class. Four songs sung simultaneously can be a rewarding and enjoyable challenge.

3. THE FARMER IN THE DELL

TRADITIONAL

The   farm - er   in   the   dell, _____   the   farm - er   in   the   dell,

Heigh - ho   the   dair - ry,   oh,   the   farm - er   in   the   dell. _____

Sing the African-American spiritual *He's Got the Whole World in His Hands*, tapping the foot on strong beats and clapping the hands on weak beats ("pattin' juba"). Create additional verses. This song can be sung effectively with *Rock-a-My Soul*, on page 284.

HE'S GOT THE WHOLE WORLD IN HIS HANDS

SPIRITUAL

He's   got   the   whole   world __   in   His   hands, _   He's   got   the

whole   world __   in   His   hands, _   He's   got   the   whole   world __

in His hands, — He's got the whole world in His hands. _____

Verse

1. He's got the lit-tle bit-ty ba-by in His hands, — He's got the
2. He's got ____ you and me, ____ broth-er, in His hands, — He's got ____
3. He's got my broth-ers and my sis-ters in His hands, — He's got my

lit-tle bit-ty ba-by in His hands, — He's got the lit-tle bit-ty ba-by
you and me, ____ broth-er, in His hands, — He's got ____ you and me, ____ broth-er,
broth-ers and my sis-ters in His hands, — He's got my broth-ers and my sis-ters

in His hands, — He's got the whole world in His hands. _____

The spiritual *Rock-a-My Soul* should be performed in the style and mood suggested for *He's Got the Whole World in His Hands*. Create simple harmony parts in bouncing rhythm, repeating only "Rock, rock, rock-a-my soul."

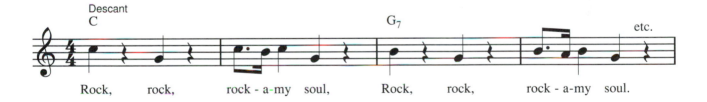

Rock, rock, rock - a-my soul, Rock, rock, rock - a-my soul.

Additional Partner Songs

The following songs also have matching chord patterns, and two or more in each group may be combined.

1. *This Old Man, Ten Little Indians, Skip to My Lou, Sandy Land, Pawpaw Patch.*
2. *Santa Lucia, Juanita, Bicycle Built for Two.*
3. *Frère Jacques, London Bridge, The Old Grey Mare.*

Frederick Beckmann's *Partner Songs* (Boston: Ginn and Company, 1958) and *More Partner Songs* (Boston: Ginn and Company, 1962) are excellent sources for partner songs.

My Home's in Montana and Home on the Range (the state song of Kansas) also coordinate very well as partner songs:

MY HOME'S IN MONTANA

AMERICAN COWBOY SONG
ADAPTED BY M. HOFFMAN

My home's in Mon - tan - a, I wear a ban - dan - na; My spurs are of

sil - ver, my po - ny is gray. When rid - ing the rang - es, my

luck nev - er chang - es; With foot in the stir - rup I gal - lop a - way.

Home on the roll - ing range, That's where I want to stay!

When rid - ing the rang - es my luck nev - er chang - es;

With foot in the stir - rup I gal - lop a - way.

HOME ON THE RANGE

AMERICAN COWBOY SONG

Oh, give me a home where the buf - fa - lo roam, Where the deer and the an - te - lope play, _____ Where sel - dom is heard a dis - cour - ag - ing word, And the skies are not cloud - y all day. _____ Home, home on the range, _____ Where the deer and the an - te - lope play, _____ Where sel - dom is heard a dis - cour - ag - ing word, And the skies are not cloud - y all day. _____

Singing with Descant

A descant (sometimes termed *obbligato*) is a relatively simplistic high-pitched part that is layered on top of the melody.

5–8, 1d

THE DEAF WOMAN'S COURTSHIP

UNITED STATES
ARR. R.W.W.

Descant (voices, melody bells, or recorder)

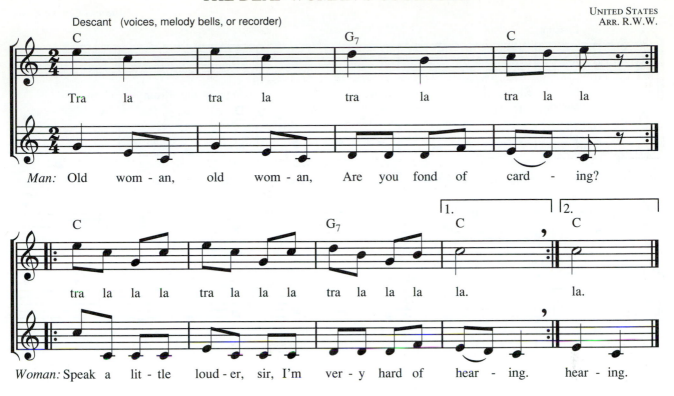

Tra la tra la tra la tra la la

Man: Old wom - an, old wom - an, Are you fond of card - ing?

tra la la la tra la la la tra la la la la. la.

Woman: Speak a lit - tle loud - er, sir, I'm ver - y hard of hear - ing. hear - ing.

Man: 2. Old woman, old woman, are you fond of knitting?
Woman: Speak a little louder, sir! I'm very hard of hearing.

Man: 3. Old woman, old woman, will you darn my stockings?
Woman: Speak a little louder, sir! I'm very hard of hearing.

Man: 4. Old woman, old woman, will you let me court you?
Woman: Speak a little louder, sir, I just begin to hear you.

Man: 5. Old woman, old woman, don't you want to marry me?
Woman: Oh! my goodness gracious me, Oh! now I think I hear you.

Chording for Resonator Bells, Tone Educator Bells, or Orff instruments.

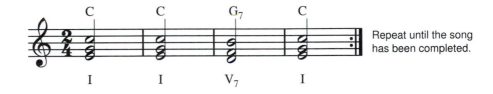

Repeat until the song has been completed.

Singing in Harmony

STREETS OF LAREDO

AMERICAN COWBOY SONG

2. "I see by your outfit that you are a cowboy,"
These words he said as I boldly walked by;
"Come listen to me and I'll tell my sad story:
I'm shot in the chest and I'm sure I will die."

3. "Now once in the saddle I used to ride handsome,
'A handsome young cowboy' is what they would say;
I'd ride into town and go down to the cardhouse,
But I'm shot in the chest and I'm dying today."

4. "Go run to the spring for a cup of cold water,
To cool down my fever," the young cowboy said.
But when I returned, his poor soul had departed,
And I wept when I saw the young cowboy was dead.

5. We'll bang the drum slowly and play the fife lowly,
We'll play the dead march as we bear him along;
We'll go to the graveyard and lay the sod o'er him;
He was a young cowboy, but he had done wrong.

A countermelody is often more challenging than a descant, but is placed above the melody as well.

ALL THE PRETTY LITTLE HORSES

AMERICAN SOUTH FOLK SONG

Singing in Two-Part Harmony

Chording in Thirds and Sixths

Singing exercises in parallel thirds and sixths help to prepare the student for successful two-part singing. Practice the following exercises slowly, using the neutral syllable "loo," *so-fa* syllables, and numbers. Listen carefully for blend and balance. Always exchange parts in both exercises and songs.

5–8, 1d

HARMONIZING

R.W.W.

Austria

Melody

We like to har-mon-ize when we're to-geth-er, Oh, we sing so joy-ful-ly where e'er we go. We raise our voic-es high, sing-ing so loud and clear. Let's sing in har-mon-y for all to hear.

(Recorder and Bells)

Singing in Harmony

DE COLORES

English Words by Alice Firgau

Mexican Folk Song

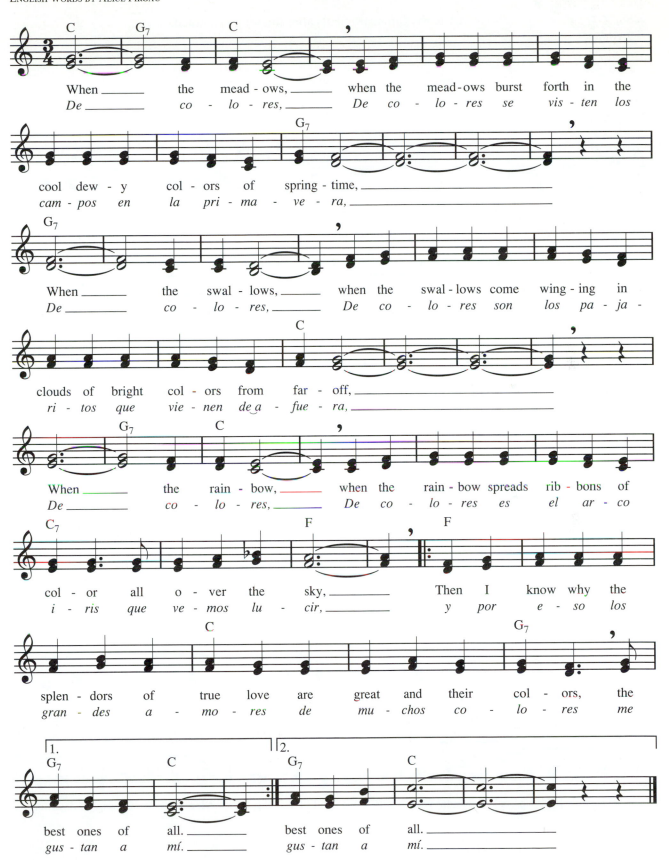

When ____ the mead - ows, ____ when the mead-ows burst forth in the
De ____ co - lo - res, ____ De co - lo - res se vis - ten los

cool dew - y col - ors of spring - time, ____
cam - pos en la pri - ma - ve - ra, ____

When ____ the swal - lows, ____ when the swal - lows come wing - ing in
De ____ co - lo - res, ____ De co - lo - res son los pa - ja -

clouds of bright col - ors from far - off, ____
ri - tos que vie - nen de a - fue - ra, ____

When ____ the rain - bow, ____ when the rain - bow spreads rib - bons of
De ____ co - lo - res, ____ De co - lo - res es el ar - co

col - or all o - ver the sky, ____ Then I know why the
i - ris que ve - mos lu - cir, ____ y por e - so los

splen - dors of true love are great and their col - ors, the
gran - des a - mo - res de mu - chos co - lo - res me

1.
best ones of all. ____
gus - tan a mí. ____

2.
best ones of all. ____
gus - tan a mí. ____

Singing in Harmony

Observe dynamics for dramatic effect (***p*** = soft, ***mf*** = moderately loud, ***f*** = loud, ***ff*** = very loud).

Add rhythm instruments after the song is learned.

K–4, 1b

NOEL

AFRICA

Sing No - el, sing No - el, No - el, No - el. _____ Sing No - el, sing No - el,

No - el, No - el. _____ Sing we all No - el, sing we all No - el,

Sing we all No - el, sing we all No - el. Sing No - el, sing No - el,

No - el, No - el. _____ Sing No - el, sing No - el, No - el, No - el. _____

OH HANUKKAH

HASIDIC FOLK SONG
ADAPTED R.W.W.

Oh Ha - nuk - kah, Oh Ha - nuk - kah, good cheer it is bring - ing. Oh

Ha - nuk - kah, we cel - e - brate with sing - ing and danc - ing. Mer - ri - ly for eight days the

Singing in Harmony

drë - dl we spin. Crisp - y lit - tle lat - kes, tast - y and thin.

tast - y and thin. And night - ly, so bright - ly the cand - les we light for Ha - nuk -

kah. Shin - ing with glor - y, re - call - ing the stor - y, the

won - ders of God long a - go. won - ders of God long a - go.

For additional songs with thirds, sing *Jacob's Ladder* (p. 184) and *Las Pollitas* (p. 317).

Singing in Bass Chanting

5–8, 3a

Many folk songs and familiar tunes can be harmonized with I, IV, and V_7 chords. An extra harmony part can be added to melodies simply by singing the *root* of the appropriate chord. Groups of students can sing *do, fa,* or *so,* or 1, 4, or 5, or a neutral syllable like "ah." Also, the words of the song can be used in the rhythm of the melody. Boys enjoy singing this added part because the notes are relatively low.

Auld Lang Syne provides an easy introduction to three-part singing. The teacher or selected students can accompany by chording on the Omnichord and piano. Add Orff effects to this pentatonic tune.

AULD LANG SYNE

Robert Burns

Scotland

do(1) _____ so(5) _____ do(1) _____
Should auld ac-quaint-ance be for-got, And nev - er brought to

fa(4) _____ do(1) _____ so(5) _____ do(1) ___ so(5) ___
mind? Should auld ac-quaint-ance be for-got, And days of auld lang

do(1) ___ do(1) _____ so(5) _____ do(1) _____ fa(4) _____
syne? For auld ___ lang ___ syne, my dear, For auld ___ lang ___ syne; We'll

do(1) _____ so(5) _____ do(1) ___ so(5) ___ do(1) _____
take a cup of kind - ness yet For auld _____ lang _____ syne.

Singing in Three-Part Harmony

5–8, 1d

Chording in Triads

One of the highlights of the elementary school music program is the singing of songs in three-part harmony. If a good foundation of readiness activities and two-part singing has been established, three-part music can be used effectively in the classroom. The procedure for learning three-part music is similar to that used in two-part music. There is usually a greater need, however, to rehearse individual parts. To establish harmonic relationships, it is advisable to have students hum (or "oo") their part while other parts are being taught. The use of the piano and bells on difficult passages may be helpful. The interchange of singers on the various parts is recommended unless a program is in preparation.

Singing triad chord progressions helps the student to develop security in three-part singing. For practicing these exercises, follow the procedures used for chording in thirds and sixths (p. 290).

hum, "Loo"
or
"La"

In singing *Koom Bah Yah* a good antiphonal effect can be created. Have a soloist sing the first part, "Someone's crying, Lord," with the chorus answering in three-part harmony on *"Koom bah yah!"*

KOOM BAH YAH
(DRAW NEARER, LORD)

AFRICA
ADAPTED R.W.W.

1. Some-one's cry - ing, Lord, *Koom bah yah!* Some-one's cry - ing, Lord, *Koom bah yah!*

Some-one's cry - ing, Lord, *Koom bah yah!* Oh, Lord, _____ *Koom bah yah!*

2. Someone's sighing, Lord, . . .

3. Someone's praying, Lord, . . .

4. Someone's singing, Lord, . . .

Singing in Harmony

Songs may fall into or incorporate more than one category. For example, *Row, Row, Row Your Boat* (p. 273) is a round that also uses an ostinato.

Rocky Top incorporates elements of two- and three-part harmony.

ROCKY TOP

Boudleaux Bryant and Felice Bryant

Boudleaux Bryant and Felice Bryant
Arranged by Patti Windes-Bridges

Singing in Harmony

Rock - y Top, you'll al - ways be home sweet home to me.

Rock - y Top, you'll al - ways be home sweet home to me.

Rock - y Top, Ten - nes - see,

Good ol' Rock - y Top, Rock - y Top, Ten - nes - see,

Rock-y Top, Ten - nes - see! _____

Rock-y Top, Ten - nes - see. Rock-y Top, Ten - nes - see. _____

Suggested Assignments

5–8, 4b

1. Have students find, identify, and sing other songs that incorporate more than one step to "Singing in Harmony."
2. Sing additional rounds and other song materials that provide readiness for part singing. These may be selected from the standard school music series and community songbooks and from the rounds and part songs found elsewhere in this book.
3. Create your own chants and descants (tenor parts) for several familiar songs.
4. Sing partner songs like these: *Three Blind Mice* with *Row, Row, Row Your Boat; There's a Long, Long Trail* with *Keep the Home Fires Burning; Old Folks at Home* with *Humoresque; Ten Little Indians* with *Skip to My Lou;* and *Goodnight Ladies* with *When the Saints Go Marching In.*
5. Create your own bass chanting (*do, fa, so*) for folk songs and familiar tunes.

6. Form a classroom orchestra of simple instruments to play along with part singing.
7. Use standard band and orchestral instruments played by members of the class or outside talent with the singing of part music. Orchestral parts for various school music series and community songbooks are readily available.

CHAPTER 13

Perceptive Listening

Sound occurs all around us in our environment. The sounds of nature, sounds around the house, mechanical sounds, animal sounds, and people sounds fill our days from beginning to end. Sound originates when an object or surface vibrates in the frequency range between approximately 20 and 20,000 *hertz* (cycles per second). If the sound waves resulting from the vibrations have a regular pattern, they are perceived as tones; otherwise, noise results. Each sound, or tone, has a distinct quality, or wave pattern, that distinguishes it from another. Other factors that affect the sound of tones are attack and decay, that is, the way tones begin and end.

The tone quality or tone color of any given sound is labeled as its *timbre*. We are able to recognize the sound of a clarinet as different from the sound of a violin because of the unique tone or timbre qualities of these musical instruments.

Music listening is a universal, lifetime activity and a significant part of every school music program. Listening to music does not involve skills in the same sense that reading and writing music and playing instruments do, but perceptive listening requires a background of knowledge and listening experiences. The concepts explored in this chapter are useful in giving music listening a point of focus and a sense of direction in both cognitive and affective domains. They can be applied by students seeking to enhance their own responses to music and by teachers guiding the listening activities of others. The objectives are to cultivate attentive listening habits, to encourage receptivity to a wide range of musical styles of various cultures and heritage, to provide essential information about some aspects of music, and to make music listening more meaningful and rewarding.

Musical Timbres

K–4, 6d

Striving to recognize the various instruments and voice types as they are heard individually and in combinations contributes to the development of perceptual skills and concentrates the listeners' attention on the music being performed.

Voices

Mature voices are classified according to sex and range, as follows:

Female	**Male**
High: Soprano	*High:* Tenor
Low: Alto (Contralto)	*Low:* Bass

Approximate ranges of singers:

The terms *soprano, alto, tenor,* and *bass* are applied not only to voices and singers but to the parts they sing in ensembles and to the corresponding parts in instrumental music. Female singers with a range lower than sopranos but not as low as altos are called *mezzo-sopranos*. Male singers with a range lower than tenors but not as low as basses are called *baritones*. These terms are usually reserved for performing artists and opera roles.

Compare and contrast the range and quality of the four basic voice types as they are heard individually in solos and collectively in choruses. The suggested selections from Handel's *Messiah*, for which many recordings are available, are appropriate for this purpose.

G. F. Handel: *Messiah* (1741)
Air: I know that my Redeemer liveth (soprano)
Air: He shall feed his flock (alto)
Air: Every valley shall be exalted (tenor)
Air: The trumpet shall sound (bass)
Chorus: Hallelujah (sopranos, altos, tenors, basses)
Chorus: For unto us a Child is born (sopranos, altos, tenors, basses)

Acoustic Instruments

Sound is produced on acoustic (nonelectronic) instruments in five different ways—by *bowing, plucking, blowing, striking,* and by means of *keyboard mechanisms*. These methods of producing sound are associated with specific instruments and types of instruments, as listed below.

Bowing/String Instruments
violin
viola
cello (violoncello)
bass (string bass, contrabass, double bass)

Plucking/String Instruments
harp
guitar
banjo
all other string instruments as a special effect

Blowing/Wind Instruments

Woodwind	*Brass*
Aperture	Valve
piccolo	trumpet
flute	cornet
Single Reed	horn (French horn)
clarinets	baritone (euphonium)
saxophones	tuba
Double Reed	sousaphone
oboe	Slide
English horn	trombone
bassoon	bass trombone
contrabassoon	

Striking/Percussion Instruments

Definite Pitch	*Indefinite Pitch*	
timpani	snare (side) drum	castanets
glockenspiel	tenor (street or field) drum	tom-tom
xylophone	bass drum	whip (slapstick)
marimba	cymbals	maracas
vibraphone (vibes)	triangle	bongos
tubular bells	tambourine	temple blocks
(chimes)	gong (tam-tam)	

Percussion instruments can also be classified by the materials from which they are constructed—skins, metals, rattles, or woods.

Keyboard Instruments

piano (acoustic, electronic)	celesta
organ (acoustic, electronic)	synthesizers
harpsichord	various electronic instruments

Some instruments fall into several areas of classification because of their use. For example, the harp may be treated as a string instrument, a percussion instrument, or a keyboard instrument in different musical compositions.

On the basis of their range and functions, basic orchestral instruments of the string, woodwind, and brass families can be equated with the four main "voice" types, as follows:

Orchestral Instruments	**Soprano**	**Alto**	**Tenor**	**Bass**
String	violin	viola	cello	bass
Woodwind	flute	oboe	clarinet	bassoon
Brass	trumpet	horn	trombone	tuba

Violin   **Viola**

String Instruments

The violin is the smallest in size, the highest in pitch, and the most brilliant in quality of the string instruments. Violins most often play the melody, but they are equally effective in a variety of supporting roles. Violas are slightly larger than violins but not as much as would be suggested by their difference in pitch, which is a fifth lower, and their quality, which is less brilliant.

Photographs courtesy of Scherl & Roth, Inc., Cleveland, Ohio.

Cello   **Double Bass**

The cello and bass are the tenor and bass members of the string family, but in orchestral music they often play the bass line together in octaves, in which case the two upper parts are assigned to the first violins and second violins, respectively, and the tenor part to the violas.

The harp is the only orchestral instrument played exclusively by plucking. It has just seven strings per octave, corresponding to the seven letter names of notes. Whether the notes are sharp, flat, or natural depends upon the position of the seven pedals, three of which can be seen in the illustration, around the base of the instrument.

Photograph courtesy of Venus Harps (W & W Instruments), Chicago, Illinois.

Harp

Woodwind Instruments

On the flute and its smaller counterpart, the piccolo, the tone is produced by a stream of air from the player's lips striking the edge of the hole in the mouthpiece. The principle can be demonstrated by blowing over the open top of a small bottle.

On the clarinets a finely shaped piece of cane, called a *reed,* attached to the underside of the mouthpiece, is the primary source of the vibrations that produce the tone.

Photographs courtesy of F. E. Olds & Sons, Lincolnwood, Illinois.

Photographs courtesy of Fox Products Corporation, South Whitley, Indiana. Joe Schnurr, photographer.

Flute   Piccolo   Clarinet   Bass Clarinet

Saxophones, which have mouthpieces and reeds similar to those on clarinets, come in several sizes. The three most common are the alto, tenor, and baritone saxophones.

Alto Saxophone   **Tenor Saxophone**   **Baritone Saxophone**

Two pieces of cane fastened together with an air passage between them form a *double reed,* the primary source of the tone-producing vibrations on oboes and English horns. The distinctive tone quality produced by the double reed on these instruments is often associated with plaintive and pastoral melodies.

Oboe   English Horn

Bassoons and contrabassoons are also double-reed instruments. The bassoon plays in the same pitch range as the cello, and they frequently share melodic lines in orchestral music. The contrabassoon range is an octave lower than the bassoon range—lower than that of any other orchestral instrument.

Fox Products Corporation, South Whitley, Indiana.
Joe Schnurr, photographer.

Bassoon Contrabassoon

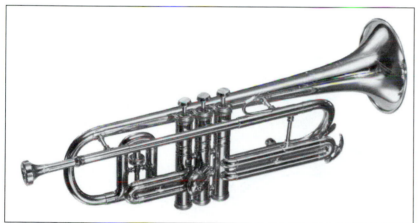

Brass Instruments

The trumpet and the cornet are similar in appearance and sound. Trumpets are ordinarily used in orchestras and jazz groups. Cornets, which have a somewhat mellower tone, are featured in bands.

Photograph courtesy of Conn Corporation, Elkhart, Indiana.

Trumpet

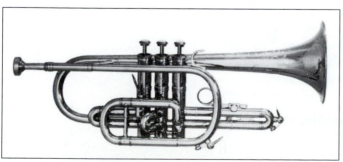

Cornet

Photograph courtesy of G. Leblanc Corporation, Kenosha, Wisconsin.

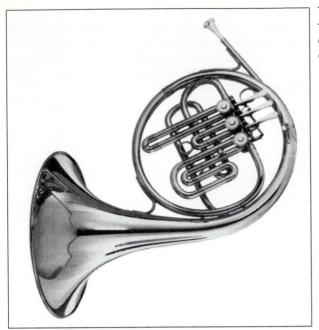

The French horn, often called simply the horn, is a versatile instrument with a surprisingly wide range. It has enough power to dominate an orchestra and enough control to blend with delicate string passages.

Photograph courtesy of Conn Corp., Elkhart, Indiana.

French Horn

The tuba provides the foundation for the brass section—and indeed, for the whole orchestra—when it plays the bass line in loud passages, which is its normal function. Sousaphones, named for John Philip Sousa, the "March King," are designed to be carried over the shoulder. They replace the tubas in marching bands.

Photographs courtesy of G. Leblanc Corporation, Kenosha, Wisconsin.

Tuba **Sousaphone**

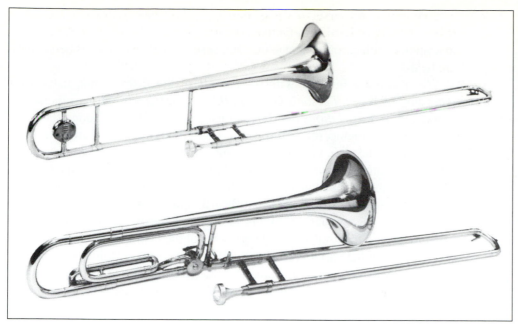

The trombone and bass trombone are the only instruments that have a slide mechanism. The position of the slide controls the pitch, as the valves do on the other brass instruments, by varying the amount of tubing the air passes through between the player's lips and the bell at the other end of the instrument.

Photographs courtesy of Conn Corp., Elkhart, Indiana.

Trombone   **Bass Trombone**

Photograph courtesy of Ludwig Drum Company, Chicago, Illinois.

Percussion Instruments

Percussion Instruments

A representative assortment of percussion instruments is shown here. The compact collection of drums and cymbals on the riser in the center is typical of the instruments, known collectively as a *drum set* or *traps,* played by the drummer in jazz and popular music, including rock. The four similarly shaped instruments on the left are the timpani. The instruments from left to right at the top of the picture are the vibraphone (vibes), tubular bells, xylophone, gong, and marimba. Also shown are drums of various types and sizes, cymbals and several smaller percussion instruments.

To familiarize yourself with the sounds of the orchestral instruments, listen to a recording of Benjamin Britten's *Young Person's Guide to the Orchestra* in a version <u>with narration</u> that names and describes the instruments before they are heard.

When you are familiar with the sounds of the instruments, listen to a recording of *Young Person's Guide to the Orchestra* without narration. The work, subtitled *Variations and Fugue on a Theme of Purcell,* consists of six versions of the theme, thirteen variations based on the theme, and a fugue— as listed in the left column of the following outline. The first and last statements of the theme are for full orchestra; each of the other four statements of the theme is for one family of instruments. As you listen to a recording, circle on the outline the name of the family of instruments heard in the themes that are not for full orchestra. In each variation (except the one for harp), two or more similar instruments are featured. Circle the name(s) of the instrument(s) most prominent in each of the variations. The fugue begins with a sprightly tune played successively by the various instruments, which are introduced in the same order as in the variations. Check your responses for the variations as the instruments enter in the fugue.

Benjamin Britten: *Young Person's Guide to the Orchestra* op. 34 (1946)

Theme A	full orchestra				
Theme B	string	woodwind	brass	percussion	
Theme C	string	woodwind	brass	percussion	
Theme D	string	woodwind	brass	percussion	
Theme E	string	woodwind	brass	percussion	
Theme F	full orchestra				
Variation A	violins	oboes	flutes	piccolo	trumpets
Variation B	clarinets	violas	horns	oboes	bassoons
Variation C	flutes	clarinets	cellos	bassoons	violins
Variation D	bassoons	oboes	violas	clarinets	trombones
Variation E	violas	cellos	violins	basses	clarinets
Variation F	cellos	violas	bassoons	violins	flutes
Variation G	bassoons	clarinets	violas	violins	cellos
Variation H	basses	violins	cellos	bassoons	clarinets
Variation I	trombones	horns	harp	xylophone	flutes
Variation J	trumpets	tuba	oboes	trombones	horns
Variation K	horns	trombones	trumpets	tuba	clarinets
Variation L	trumpets	trombones	tuba	bassoons	horns
Variation M	flutes	trombones	bassoons	percussion	oboes
Fugue					

For additional information about instruments (and voices) and experience in recognizing them, the supplementary references are useful:

- *André Previn: Guide to Music* [a set of four 50-minute cassette tapes or CDs]
- Sergei Prokofiev: *Peter and the Wolf* op. 67 (1936)
- *Discovering the Orchestra* [five videotapes available from Social Issues Resources Series (SIRS), Inc., P.O. Box 2348, Boca Raton, Florida 33427]

For information on electronic instruments, see the section of chapter 7 titled "Electronic Keyboards" (p. 163).

Classical Music Genres

K–4, 6c
5–8, 9a

The tone colors of voices and instruments are heard individually and in many varied combinations that informed listeners learn to recognize. The combinations that, by virtue of special qualifications, have become standardized constitute the common performance mediums of music. Their designations, which should be learned, are not always consistent with the literal meaning of the terms applied to them.

Solo literally means "alone," but in music the term is applied not only to works for a single instrument but to a piece, passage, or song for one predominant instrument or voice with accompaniment. The one instrument commonly played by itself is the piano, and a performance on a piano alone is a *piano solo*. A song for one voice with piano accompaniment is a *vocal solo*. An *art song*, or *lied* (plural, *lieder*), is a special type of vocal solo highly developed by nineteenth-century German composers. An instrumental solo is identified by the name of the featured instrument, such as a *violin solo*.

The term *sonata* originally meant a piece that was played, as opposed to a *cantata*, which meant a piece that was sung. *Sonata* is now applied to extended works, usually in three or four distinct parts, or *movements*, for one or two instruments, one of which is ordinarily the piano. A *piano sonata* is for piano alone. When a sonata is for two instruments, piano is implied and the other instrument is named; for example, a *violin sonata* is for violin and piano.

Ensemble or *chamber music* is a general classification for music played by a small group or ensemble with a different part for each player and with no doubling or duplication. Preeminent among the many chamber music combinations is the *string quartet*, consisting of two violins, a viola, and a cello. When a piano is added to the string quartet instrumentation, the group and the music it performs are identified as a *piano quintet*. Woodwind, brass, and percussion instruments are not as prominent in classical chamber music as string and keyboard instruments are, but contemporary composers have been attracted by the wide range of tonal colors available in the *wind quintet*, also known as a *woodwind quintet* even though it includes a brass instrument. The instrumentation of a wind quintet is flute, oboe, clarinet, horn (the brass instrument), and bassoon. The horn is also a member of *brass quintets*, usually in conjunction with two trumpets and two trombones. All of the jazz and popular music played by small combos fits the definition of chamber music. The instrumentation of such combos is as varied as the music they play. Examples of all types of chamber music, both standard and modern, abound in the recorded literature.

The larger musical organizations differ from chamber groups in that many performers are assigned to a limited number of parts. Music for choirs and choruses is most often written in four parts, one each for sopranos, altos, tenors, and basses. The sections may be divided into first and second parts, for a total of eight. Choirs may be as small as twenty or thirty singers, but festival choruses sometimes have hundreds of singers, with fifty or more for each part. The size of the group has a pronounced effect upon the tone quality. For comparison, listen to a recording of a *madrigal*, such as Thomas Morley's *My bonny lass she smileth* and a recording of a work for a large chorus, such as a choral selection from Handel's *Messiah*. Madrigals are a type of vocal chamber music originally intended for performance with one singer on each part, but they are frequently performed now by small choirs and choruses.

A *string orchestra* is a sort of instrumental counterpart of a chorus. A string orchestra includes many players, usually the full string section of a symphony orchestra, but only four different kinds of instruments and only four or five parts. The violins are divided more or less equally into first violins and second violins, accounting for two of the parts. The first violins ordinarily play the melody; the second violins are relegated to a lower, subservient part (hence the expression "playing second fiddle"). The violas play the third part. The cellos and basses may play the bass line in octaves, or they may have independent parts in a five-part texture. The instruments in a string orchestra are the same as those in a string quartet, plus basses. The difference in the sound of the two mediums is due more to the effect produced by one instrument on a part in a string quartet as opposed to the multiple instruments on each part in a string orchestra than to the addition of the basses. To compare the sound of a string orchestra with that of a string quartet, listen to a recording of a movement of a string quartet by Haydn, Mozart, or Beethoven and to the waltz from the *Serenade in C* for string orchestra by Tchaikovsky.

A string orchestra forms a nucleus to which wind and percussion instruments are added in varying numbers to make a *symphony orchestra*. The classic orchestra used by Haydn and Mozart consisted of the basic string section plus two each of the following: flutes, oboes, sometimes clarinets, bassoons, horns, trumpets, and timpani (one player). A full orchestra like the one used by Beethoven for his *Leonore Overture no. 3* has all of the instruments of the classic orchestra plus two horns (for a total of four) and three trombones. A modern large orchestra includes all of these, the specialized instruments, and several percussion players. Samuel Barber's *Symphony no. 1 in One Movement,* for example, is scored for two flutes, piccolo, two oboes, English horn, two clarinets, bass clarinet, two bassoons, contrabassoon, four horns, three trumpets, three trombones, tuba, timpani, percussion, harp, and the usual strings. The seating plan of the Philadelphia Orchestra shows how the 106 instruments of one large orchestra are arranged on the stage. An asterisk (*) by an instrument indicates the principal or first chair of each section.

Bands are instrumental ensembles comparable in size to symphony orchestras but with only three sections: woodwind, brass, and percussion. Bands are classified according to function as *marching bands* and *concert bands,* though they have many instruments and often many players in common. Marching bands are featured attractions in parades and football halftime shows. Concert bands are increasingly important as a concert medium. Band instrumentation is not uniform, but in general, bands have all of the wind instruments found in large orchestras plus cornets, saxophones, and baritones or euphoniums, which are like small tubas with the same range as trombones. There are many clarinets in various sizes and all of the specialized instruments such as piccolo, English horn, and contrabassoon. Concert bands usually have one or two string basses.

Philadelphia Orchestra Seating Plan

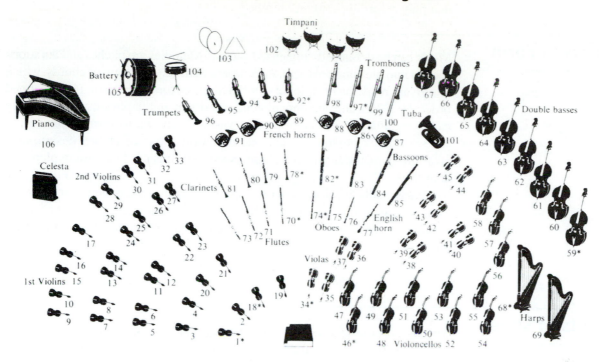

Symphonic wind ensembles are elite bands that have the same three sections and the same instruments as concert bands, but in symphonic wind ensembles the number, distribution, and uses of the instruments are significantly different. There are fewer players and much less doubling (more than one player on the same part), and the instrumentation is adjusted to the precise requirements of each work performed. The Eastman Symphonic Wind Ensemble is widely known through its recordings under the direction of its founder, Frederick Fennell, and its present conductor, Donald Hunsberger.

Eastman Wind Ensemble, Donald Hunsberger, Conductor

Photograph courtesy of Eastman School of Music, Rochester, New York.

For *pop* and *rock* music the number of players is small, as for chamber music, but in live performances the sound is amplified to a level exceeding that of a massive unamplified ensemble going full blast. A typical rock group consists of two or three electric guitars, an elaborate set of traps, usually an electronic keyboard instrument or a synthesizer, and one or more singers. Pop and rock groups can be heard at almost any hour of the day or night on radio stations that play recordings of current hits.

Concepts of Form

K–4, 6a

Music can be defined as "organized sound." Melodies are pitches and durations shaped into pleasing contours. Accompaniments are made up of chords, which in turn are made up of rational combinations of tones, occurring in a planned order. Melodies and accompaniments are organized in phrases delineated by cadences. Phrases are combined in various patterns to form sentences. A sentence may be an independent one-part form or part of a larger design, such as a binary or ternary form. These aspects of musical form are explored in chapter 4.

Conceptually, musical form results from repetition and contrast, or unity and variety. Repetitions can be immediate and note for note, or they can be varied, in another part (voice), at a different pitch level, after contrasting material, or any combination of these. The patterns and types of repetition used in a song or an instrumental composition determine its form—whether a small form or a larger formal structure.

Concepts of Style

K–4, 9a
5–8, 9a, 9c

The styles of music reflect and are the product of many interacting forces. Every musical expression is influenced by the culture, language, resources, state of development, and habitat of the people who create it and by the purpose for which it is intended. Furthermore, music develops continuously within each ethnic group and region, and over the centuries styles change dramatically. The masterpieces and major achievements of each era tend to survive and to exist side by side with current creations. The amount of viable music literature and the range of styles within our direct Western European heritage is enormous. Improved travel, communication, and recording facilities have made non-Western music increasingly accessible and awareness of its values increasingly important.

Music and Religion

Music has figured prominently in religious and ceremonial observances since the dawn of civilization. These activities are well documented in archaeological discoveries and pictorial representations, and a few isolated examples of music have been preserved from the ancient Egyptians, Sumerians and their neighbors, and Greeks. Through the centuries each religion has developed its own musical traditions. Some styles have remained virtually intact for extended periods, while others have changed with the times and have reflected concurrent secular influences. A broad spectrum of musical styles associated with religion exists today.

Music and Dance

Religious ceremonies, especially those of primitive peoples, often involve dancing. The dance influence on such music is incidental to its primary function, but there exists a large body of music in which dance influences are preeminent. This includes not only music directly associated with dancing, but also stylized dance music intended for performance in concert halls and other places of entertainment that feature passive listening. The styles of dance-inspired music are as varied as those of religion-inspired music.

Periods and Styles

Western music is divided into style periods. The dates for these periods are somewhat arbitrary, and between periods there is much overlapping of style traits.

Ancient	Before 850	Monophonic (one-part) music
Medieval	850–1400	Beginnings of polyphony (multi-part music); staff invented
Renaissance	1400–1600	Perception of vocal polyphony
Baroque	1600–1750	Ascendancy of instrumental music and homophonic (harmonic) texture
Classic	1750–1800	Reflects classic ideals of simplicity, symmetry, refinement, objectivity
Romantic	1800–1900	Emphasis on emotion and personal expression; emergence of nationalism and program music
Modern	Since 1900	Diverse styles, complex rhythms and sonorities, new methods of organization, and more recently, music by synthesizers and computers

Guided Listening

Developing and using listening skills is very important in any facet of musical activity. A teacher must have a great deal of experience in order to teach a listening lesson in the classroom. As listening skills are taught, different levels of understanding are targeted. The same piece of music might be taught for diversified reasons at various grade levels. As children develop listening abilities, they proceed from learning one or two simple concepts to a much more complicated web of musical structure.

Listening Criteria

The passive listener uses music or environmental sounds as a background to other activities. The perceptive listener sets out to purposefully develop skills in listening to music. Well-organized listening experiences in the classroom should provide students with a great deal of skill and pleasure.

The perceptive listener recognizes the importance of listening to both live performances and various media to develop acute listening skills. Recordings allow the listener to repeat the work as many times as desired. Concerts that are on television or video allow the viewer to observe performers' playing techniques. Nothing, however, can take the place of watching and hearing live performance. No matter what method is used for listening activities, the listener needs to be an active participant by concentrating on the intent of the activity, listening for specific details in the music, and responding to the questions of the lesson.

According to the *National Standards for Arts Education,* a well-rounded music program for grades K–4 should enable students to:

- Identify simple music forms when presented aurally.
- Demonstrate perceptual skills by moving, by answering questions about, and by describing aural examples of music of various styles representing diverse cultures.
- Use appropriate terminology in explaining music, music notation, music instruments and voices, and music performances.

- Identify the sounds of a variety of instruments, including many orchestra and band instruments, and instruments from various cultures as well as children's voices and male and female adult voices.
- Respond through purposeful movement to selected prominent music characteristics or to specific music events while listening to music.

Grades 5–8 should add the following listening activities to those above:

- Describe specific music events in a given aural example, using appropriate terminology.
- Analyze the uses of the elements of music in aural examples representing diverse genres and cultures.
- Demonstrate knowledge of the basic principles of meter, rhythm, tonality, intervals, chords, and harmonic progressions in their analyses of music.

Creating Interest in the Listening Lesson

As each listening lesson is being prepared, it is suggested to follow several general guidelines in order to further develop listening skills and to continue to refine them:

- Introduce the assignment with an audio and/or visual manipulative in order to call the students to active involvement in the lesson.
- Ask the students to listen for something in particular.
- Have clear objectives that allow the students to focus on specific musical ideas or concepts.
- Explain the background of the selection of music being studied.
- Keep the listening assignment short enough to sustain interest and long enough to challenge.
- Repeat the listening assignment often enough to meet the objectives without overkill.
- Guide the students through the listening process with colorful and creative visual listening guide(s), such as call chart(s)—visual presentation(s) of what is occurring in the selected musical example(s).
- Ask the students to respond by involving themselves physically and with movement in their responses.
- Talk as little as possible during the listening activity and expect the same of the students.
- Have a written listening guide for the students to follow and/or fill out during or at the end of the project.
- Have evaluation materials available that will determine whether the project's goals have been met.
- Be as enthusiastic about the music as possible.

Specific Objectives for Each Listening Lesson

K–4, 6a, 6b, 6c, 6d, 9a, 9b
5–8, 6a, 6b, 6c, 9a, 9b

With each lesson, a specific list of questions can be asked. Select from the following, according to the level of the lesson being taught:

1. Title: Is the title of the piece recognizable or previously known?
2. Composer: Is the composer recognizable or previously known?
3. Date: What is the approximate date in which the piece was composed?
4. Medium or Media: What is singing and/or playing (voice(s), instrument(s), other sounds)?
5. Timbre: How many different timbres, textures, and layers of sound are heard at the same time? Different times throughout the piece?

6. Language: If the piece is vocal or choral, what language(s) is being used?
7. Genre or Classification: Is the piece symphonic, jazz, medieval, Japanese, etc.?
8. Melody: What is the shape of the melody? Does it move up, down, both? Does it move in stepwise motion or does it involve leaps or both? Is there one melody or are more than one melody layered?
9. Meter: What is the predominant meter of the piece? Does the music contain the same meter throughout or different meters?
10. Rhythm: Is the rhythm constant, changing, smooth, jagged, etc?
11. Harmony: Is the piece major, minor, or another tonality in overall sound?
12. Form: What was the overall form or structure of this piece? Which sections were repeated? Which sections provided contrast? Can a specific form be attached to this piece of music?
13. Dynamics: Is the piece loud, soft, smooth, detached, fluctuating?
14. Expression: What was particularly unique about this piece? What specific style characteristics and/or changes in mood distinguish this piece from others?
15. Reaction: How did this piece of music help my listening skills?

Concert Etiquette

K–4, 9e

A wide array of musical events can be found in schools, communities, university towns, and especially larger cities. It is important to remember that the audience is comprised of those who desire to listen to the music and to respond to it appropriately. Proper concert etiquette is expected of teachers and students in each live (classical) musical performance:

- The concert should start on time and continue without interruption by audience members.
- Those who arrive late should not be seated until an appropriate break occurs in the music.
- Audience lighting is usually dimmed in order to separate the performers from the audience.
- Loud talking and placing feet on the backs of chairs are not permitted during a formal concert.
- Food and drink, as well as flash lighting and recording devices, are often banned from formal presentations.
- Dress varies from performance to performance, and dress codes may be required.
- Applause is not heard until the final movement of a composition that contains more than one movement, such as a symphonic orchestral piece.
- Applause is also not heard if the music on a concert program is grouped into like segments, such as a group of pieces by one composer or a group of songs in one language.
- The performers are greeted by applause when he, she, or they walk onto the stage each time.
- The concertmaster of an orchestra or the conductor of a group is greeted by applause when he or she walks onto the stage.
- Standing ovations should be reserved for truly outstanding performances.

CHAPTER **14**

Applying Your Music Skills with Songs and Instruments

K–4, 1c
5–8, 1c, 1d

The purpose of this chapter is to provide a repertory of song literature that is readily adaptable to school music programs and useful for additional practice in developing skills that have been introduced throughout this book. The following songs have been selected to increase the student's skill in unison and part singing, provide experience singing in foreign languages, and present supplementary material for playing classroom instruments.

Folk Songs Around the World

DOKTOR EISENBART

PENNSYLVANIA DUTCH FOLK SONG

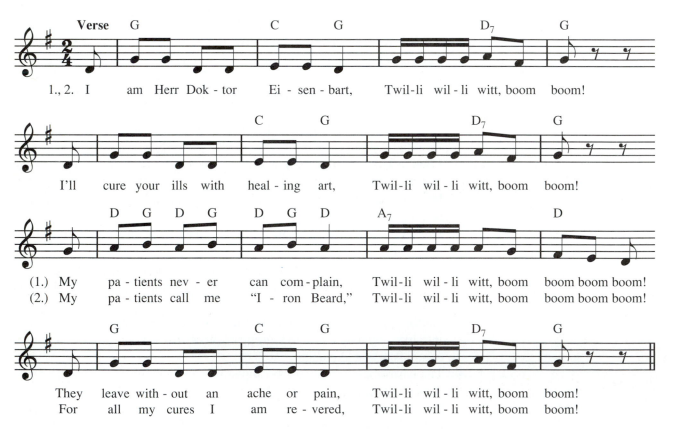

Sing to - ri - ay, sing to - ri - ay! Twil-li wil-li witt, boom boom boom boom!

Sing to - ri - ay, sing to - ri - ay! Twil-li wil-li witt, boom boom!

LAS POLLITAS

SPAIN

Pin - ti - tas de co - lo - ra - do, Son las pol - li - tas que ten - go,

Pin - ti - tas de co - lo - ra - do, Son las pol - li - tas que ten - go,

Pero es - ta - ca-pe - ton ci - ta No la ven - do, ___ no la ven - do,

Pero es - ta - ca - pe - ton ci - ta No la ven - do, ___ no la ven - do.

Chorus

No la se lle - van la pol - la Que no se la lle - va - ran, Que

si a la polla se lle - can Ca - ram - ba yo voy al - lá.

Rhythm instruments played as follows:

Also sing the Mexican folk tune (birthday song) *Las Mañanitas* (p. 119).

TINGA LAYO

WEST INDIES

Tin - ga   La - yo,   come, lit - tle donk - ey, come,   Tin - ga   La - yo,
Tin - ga   La - yo,   ay, mi bur - ri - to, ven,   Tin - ga   La - yo,

come, lit - tle donk - ey, come. My donk - ey   walk, my donk - ey   talk, my donk - ey
ay, mi bur - ri - to, ven. Bur - ri - to   sí, bur - ri - to   no, bur - ri - to

cut with a knife and fork. Tin - ga   La - yo,   come, lit - tle donk - ey, come, Tin - ga
co - me con te - ne - dor. Tin - ga   La - yo,   ay, mi bur - ri - to, ven. Tin - ga

1. La - yo,   come, lit - tle donk - ey, come. My donk - ey
La - yo,   ay, mi bur - ri - to, ven. Bur - ri - to

2. come, lit - tle donk - ey, come.
ay, mi bur - ri - to, ven.

From *Canciones Para La Juventud de America,* copyright by the Faculty of Music of the Chile University and the Association for Music Education of Chile, published by Pan American Union, Washington, D.C.

Also sing *Calypso Joe* (p. 176).

LES ANGES DANS NOS CAMPAGNES

FRENCH/ENGLISH CAROL

Recorder
Bells

1. An - gels o'er the fields were sing - ing, sing - ing — hymns from — heav'n on high,
1. Les an - ges dans nos cam - pa - gnes ont en - ton - né l'hym - ne des cieux,

And the moun - tain, — ech - oes ring - ing, ans - wered — to their — joy - ful cry:
Et l'e - cho de — nos mon - ta - gnes Re - dit ce chant mé - lo - di - eux:

Refrain

Glo - - - - - - ri - a

in ex - cel - sis De - o! Glo - - -

- ri - a in ex - cel - sis De - o!

2. Shepherds, why this celebration?
   Why this burst of heav'nly song?
   What could cause such jubilation?
   What inspired the heav'nly throng?
   Refrain

2. Bergers, pour qui cette fête!
   Quel est l'objet de tous ces chants?
   Quel vainqueur, quelle conquête
   Mérite ces cris triomphants?
   Refrain

Chords for piano:

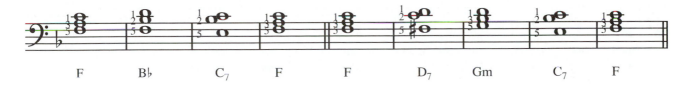

F   B♭   C₇   F   F   D₇   Gm   C₇   F

Play on the piano and sing the A pentatonic scale to help capture the oriental mood of *Cherry Blossoms*.

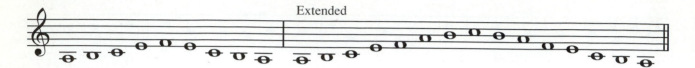

Pluck rather than strum the individual strings of the guitar or Autoharp to imitate the Japanese koto, an instrument with plucked strings and pentatonic tuning. Also use finger cymbals and triangle.

Create your own ostinati using the notes of this scale. Use Orff instruments.

Puccini used this melody in his opera *Madame Butterfly*. It was popularized in the film score of *Sayonara*.

CHERRY BLOSSOMS

SAKURA

JAPAN
ADAPTED R.W.W.

Sa - ku - ra,   Sa - ku - ra,   Cher - ry blos - soms   wave   in   the trees,
Sa - ku - ra,   Sa - ku - ra,   Ya - yo - i   no   so - ra - wa

Love - ly blos - soms   dance   in   the breeze.   Pink   and   white   the   blos - soms will fall.
Mi - wa - ta - su   ka - gi - ri   Ka - su - mi   ka   ku - mo - ka

Pet - als   send - ing   scent   to ___ all.   Sa - ku - ra,   Sa - ku - ra,
Ni - o - i   zo   i - zu - ru   I - za - ya,   I - za - ya,

Smell - ing   sweet,   Sa - ku - ra.
Mi _____   ni   yu - ka - un.

FAREWELL TO THEE

ALOHA OE

Queen Liliuokalani   Queen Liliuokalani

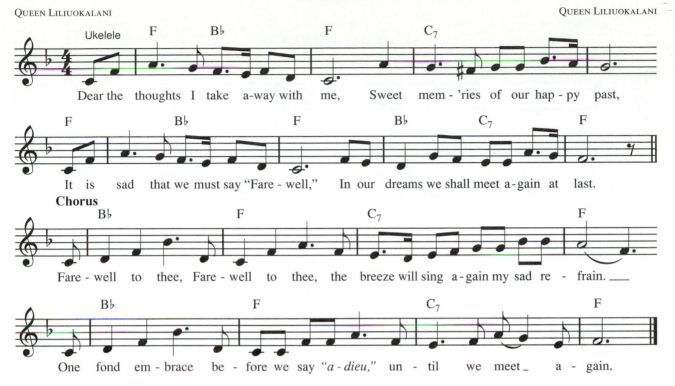

Dear the thoughts I take a-way with me, Sweet mem-'ries of our hap-py past,

It is sad that we must say "Fare - well," In our dreams we shall meet a-gain at last.

Chorus

Fare - well to thee, Fare - well to thee, the breeze will sing a-gain my sad re - frain. ___

One fond em - brace be - fore we say *"a - dieu,"* un - til we meet ___ a - gain.

O ka halia aloha kai hiki mai Ke hone ae nei i kuu manawa,
O oe no ka'u ipo aloha A loko e hana nei.
Aloha oe, aloha oe, E ke ona ona noho i ka lipo;
One fond embrace a hoi ae au, Until we meet again.

This is the harmony part for *Aloha Oe*. Sing "oo" or hum or sing the words.
Play on bells or recorder.

First sing *Hava Nagila* on the syllable "la." Then, attempt the words. Free translation: "Come, let us sing and be happy; Wake up, brothers, with a happy heart."

HAVA NAGILA

ISRAELI FOLK SONG

Also sing the popular Jewish round *Shalom Chaverim* (p. 278).

Applying Your Music Skills with Songs and Instruments

Rounds

MUSIC ALONE SHALL LIVE

GERMANY

All things shall per - ish un - der the sky; Mus - ic a - lone shall live,

Mus - ic a - lone shall live, Mus - ic a - lone shall live, Nev - er to die.

For a German language folk song sing *Du, du, liegst mir im Herzen* (p. 160).

ONE BOTTLE OF POP

ROUND

TRADITIONAL ENGLISH

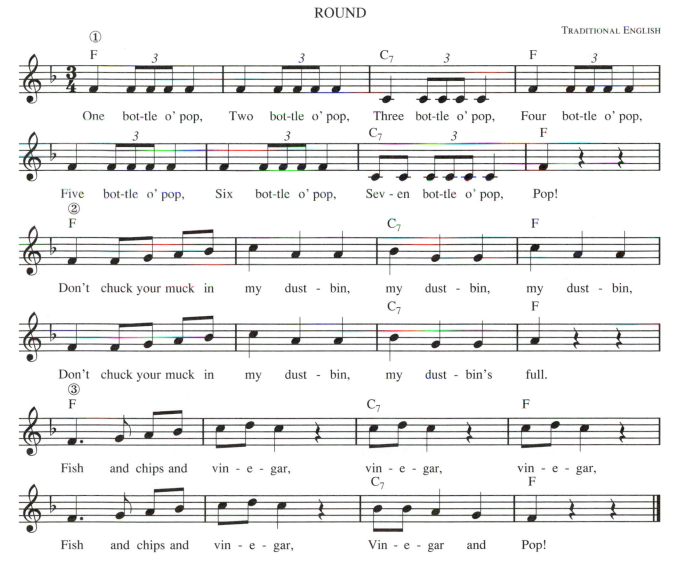

One bot-tle o' pop, Two bot-tle o' pop, Three bot-tle o' pop, Four bot-tle o' pop,

Five bot-tle o' pop, Six bot-tle o' pop, Sev - en bot-tle o' pop, Pop!

Don't chuck your muck in my dust - bin, my dust - bin, my dust - bin,

Don't chuck your muck in my dust - bin, my dust - bin's full.

Fish and chips and vin - e - gar, vin - e - gar, vin - e - gar,

Fish and chips and vin - e - gar, Vin - e - gar and Pop!

Rounds can also be spoken. Try this vegetarian round.

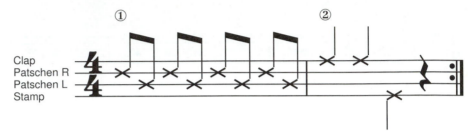

Rounds can be played using your body as a percussion instrument.

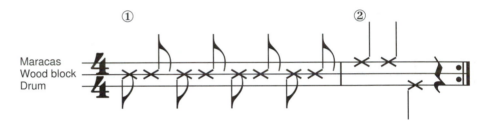

Try playing this round for percussion instruments.

Rounds can also be played on mallet instruments.

Song for Classroom Orchestra

5–8, 2c

Play and sing this rousing folk tune in three-part harmony, the first section in march time and the second with rhythmic swing. Also create your own instrumentation. With Omnichord, Autoharp, or guitar, strum the rhythms of the cymbals or drums. Include thumb-strum techniques with root bass on accents for guitar accompaniment.

UPWARD TRAIL

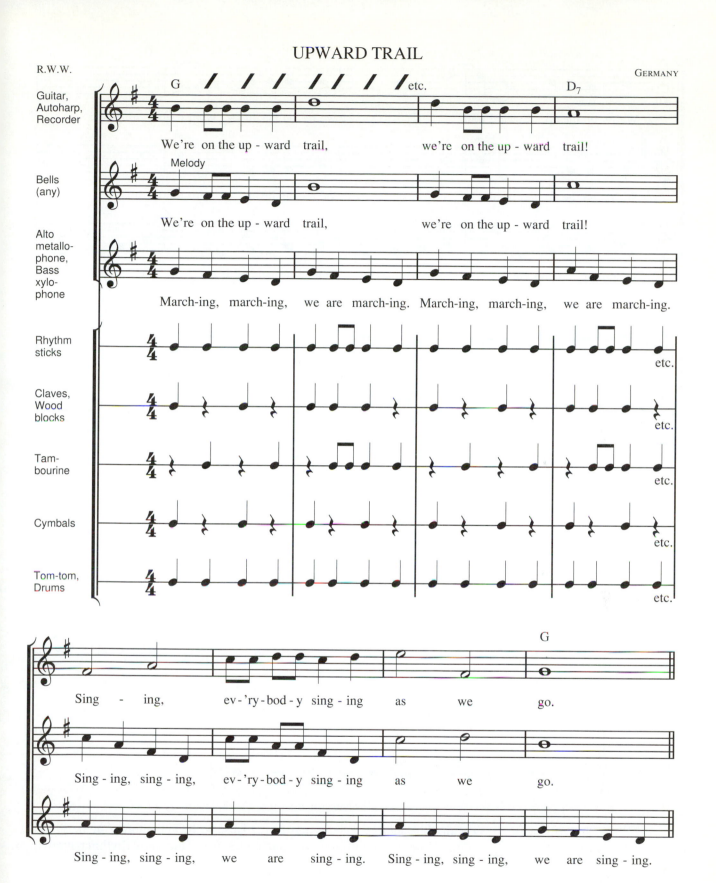

We're on the up - ward trail, ___ we're on the up - ward trail! ___

We're on the up - ward trail, ___ we're on the up - ward trail! ___

Tramp-ing, tramp-ing, we are tramp-ing. Tramp-ing, tramp-ing, we are tramp-ing.

Sing - ing, sing - ing, ev - 'ry - bod - y sing - ing, we are home - ward bound. ___

Sing - ing, sing - ing, ev - 'ry - bod - y sing - ing, we are home - ward bound. ___

Tramp-ing, tramp-ing, we are tramp-ing, we are home - ward bound. ___

The following typical jazz-rock rhythmic patterns can be used to accompany *Upward Trail* in swing time.

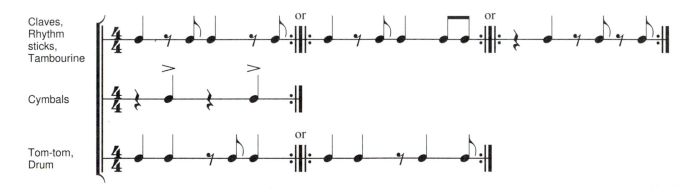

Claves, Rhythm sticks, Tambourine

Cymbals

Tom-tom, Drum

The rhythms indicated above may be used also with Omnichord, Autoharp, and guitar. Now, create introductions and codas, using the same rhythm patterns.

Action and Game Songs

K–4, 1a, 1c

The following action and game songs are included herein as resource material for *primary grade teachers*.

In 1893 when Mildred and Patty Hill wrote the song *Good Morning to All* for kindergarten children, they could not have dreamed that with a few changes in the rhythm and words it would become universally recognized as *Happy Birthday to You.*

GOOD MORNING TO ALL

Patty S. Hill   Mildred J. Hill

Copyright 1893 in Song Stories for the Kindergarten. Copyright 1921 by Clayton F. Summy Co.

I'M A LITTLE TEAPOT

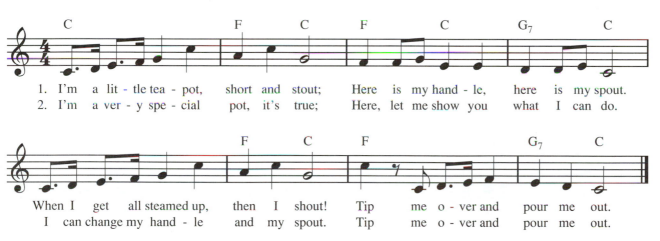

Kelman Music Corp. Publisher. Music and Lyrics by George H. Sanders and Clarence Kelly.

Act very stout. Place one hand on hip. Extend other arm, elbow and wrist bent. Nod head vigorously. Tip sideward in direction of extended arm. In second verse, reverse hand on hip and extended arm, and tip in the other direction.

The old English game song, *The Muffin Man,* has rhythm suitable for skipping and marching. It often is used as a question and answer song and offers excellent opportunity for the singers to make up verses about a variety of activities.

THE MUFFIN MAN

1. O, do you know the muf - fin man, the muf - fin man, the muf - fin man,
O, do you know the muf - fin man that lives in Dru - ry Lane?

2. Oh, yes, I know the muffin man, . . .

3. Oh, have you seen the muffin man, . . .

4. Where did you see the muffin man, . . .

For Halloween, sing these words to the tune of *The Muffin Man:*

THE PUMPKIN MAN

Oh, do you know the Pump-kin man, the Pump-kin man, the Pump-kin man,
Oh, do you know the Pump-kin man who comes on Hal - low - een?

Also sing in G minor for a more "spooky" Halloween mood.

HEAD, SHOULDERS, BABY

AFRICAN-AMERICAN GAME SONG

1. Head, shoul - ders, ba - by, one, *(clap)* two, *(clap)* three; Head,
shoul - ders, ba - by, one, *(clap)* two, *(clap)* three; Head, shoul - ders, head,
shoul - ders, head, shoul - ders, ba - by, one, *(clap)* two, *(clap)* three.

2. Shoulders, hips, baby, one, *(clap)* two, *(clap)* three; *(twice)*
Shoulders, hips, shoulders, hips,
Shoulders, hips, baby, one, *(clap)* two, *(clap)* three.

3. Hips, knees, baby, one, *(clap)* two, *(clap)* three; *(twice)*
Hips, knees, hips, knees,
Hips, knees, baby, one, *(clap)* two, *(clap)* three.

4. Knees, ankles, baby, one, *(clap)* two, *(clap)* three; *(twice)*
Knees, ankles, knees, ankles,
Knees, ankles, baby, one, *(clap)* two, *(clap)* three.

5. That's all, baby, one, *(clap)* two, *(clap)* three; *(twice)*
That's all, that's all,
That's all, baby, one, *(clap)* two, *(clap)* three.

HEAD AND SHOULDERS, BABY

AFRICAN AMERICAN STREET GAME
AS SUNG BY RENE BOYER-WHITE

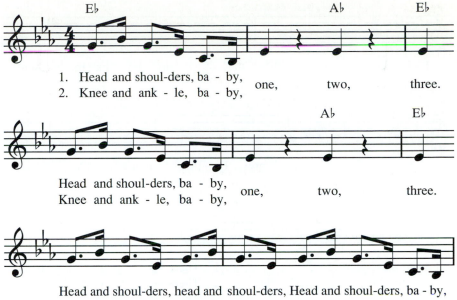

1. Head and shoul-ders, ba - by, one, two, three.
2. Knee and ank - le, ba - by,

Head and shoul-ders, ba - by, one, two, three.
Knee and ank - le, ba - by,

Head and shoul-ders, head and shoul-ders, Head and shoul-ders, ba - by,
Knee and ank - le, knee and ank - le, Knee and ank - le, ba - by,

one, two, three.

3. Milk the cow, . . .

4. Throw the ball, . . .

The stunt song *Bingo* serves as an *effective icebreaker for students of all ages,* especially those who are shy about singing. Sing it six times. The first time, sing it as written. The second time, omit the letter *B* in the spelling of *B-I-N-G-O* and clap instead. The third time, omit *B* and *I* and clap. Continue until the entire word has been clapped in rhythm.

BINGO

There was a farm-er had a dog, and Bin-go was his name - o. B - I -

N - G - O, B - I - N - G - O, B - I - N - G - O, and Bin-go was his name - o.

MY FATHER'S HOUSE

TRADITIONAL ACTION SONG

1.–3. Won't you come with me to my Fa - ther's house, To my Fa - ther's house, to my Fa - ther's house? Oh, won't you come with me to my Fa - ther's house?

1. There is peace, peace, peace.
2. There is joy, joy, joy.
3. There is love, love, love.

HOKEY POKEY

ACTION SONG

In jazz style

1. You put your right foot in, ___ You take your right foot out, ___ You put your right foot in ___ And shake it all a-bout, And then you do the hok - ey pok - ey And you turn your-self a - bout, And that's what it's all a - bout. *Hey!*

2. . . . left foot . . .
3. . . . right arm . . .
4. . . . left arm . . .
5. . . . head . . .
6. . . . whole self . . .

Applying Your Music Skills with Songs and Instruments

THE BUS SONG

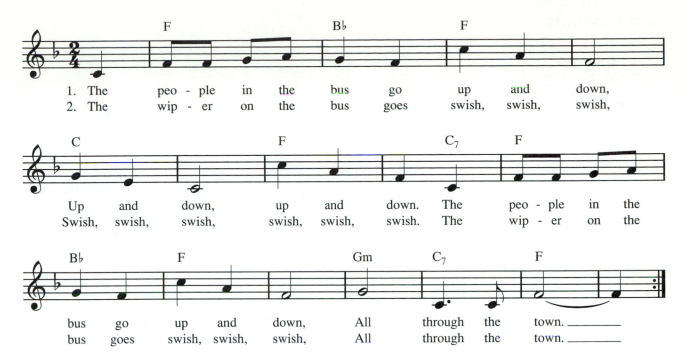

1. The peo - ple in the bus go up and down,
2. The wip - er on the bus goes swish, swish, swish,

Up and down, up and down. The peo - ple in the
Swish, swish, swish, swish, swish, swish. The wip - er on the

bus go up and down, All through the town. _____
bus goes swish, swish, swish, All through the town. _____

3. The money in the bus goes clink, clink, clink, . . .

4. The wheels on the bus go 'round and around, . . .

For additional verses have children suggest other things that happen on the bus.

THIS OLD MAN

ENGLISH SINGING GAME

1. This old man, he played one, He played nick - nack on my thumb, With a

(Roll hands)

nick - nack pad - dy whack, give the dog a bone! This old man came roll - ing home.

2. This old man, he played two,
   He played nick-nack on my shoe; *(tap shoe)*. . .

3. . . . three . . . knee; *(tap knee)* . . .

4. . . . four . . . door; *(tap forehead)* . . .

5. . . . five . . . hive; *(shoo bees away)* . . .

6. . . . six . . . sticks; *(tap two fingers)* . . .

7. . . . seven . . . up in heaven; *(flying motion)* . . .

8. . . . eight . . . pate; *(tap top of head)* . . .

9. . . . nine . . . spine; *(tap spine)* . . .

10. This old man, he played ten,
    He played nick-nack once again;
    With a nick-nack, paddy whack, give the dog a bone,
    Now we'll all go rolling home.

5–8, 1d

THE WATER IS WIDE

ENGLISH FOLK SONG

Countermelody

1. The wa-ter is wide, _____ I can't get
2. There is a _____ ship _____ sailing on the
3. Oh, love is _____ hand - some and love is

Melody

F

1. The wa-ter is wide, _____ I can-not get o'er,
2. There is a _____ ship _____ sail-ing on the sea;
3. Oh, love is _____ handsome _____ and _ love is fine,

o'er, And I've no _____ wings, _____ no wings to
sea; She's load - ed _____ deep _____ as deep can
fine, And love is _____ charm - ing when it is

And nei - ther have _____ I wings to _____ fly,
She's load - ed deep _____ as deep can _ be,
And love is charm - ing when it is true,

fly. Oh go and _ get _____ a lit - tle _ boat,
be, But not so _ deep as in love I _ am;
true, As it grows _ old - er, it grows _ cold

Oh, go and get _____ me some lit - tle boat
But not so deep _____ as in love I _____ am;
As it grows old - er it grows _ cold

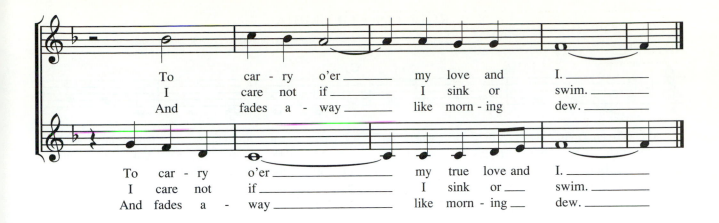

To car-ry o'er _____ my love and I. _____
I care not if _____ I sink or swim. _____
And fades a-way _____ like morn-ing dew. _____

To car-ry o'er _____ my true love and I. _____
I care not if _____ I sink or _ swim. _____
And fades a-way _____ like morn-ing _ dew. _____

AMAZING GRACE

JOHN NEWTON

EARLY AMERICAN MELODY WITH COUNTERMELODY

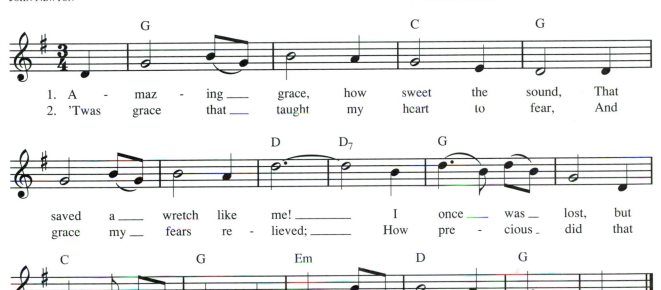

1. A - maz - ing _____ grace, how sweet the sound, That
2. 'Twas grace that _____ taught my heart to fear, And

saved a _____ wretch like me! _____ I once _____ was _ lost, but
grace my _ fears re - lieved; _____ How pre - cious _ did that

now _____ am _ found, Was blind, but _ now I see. _____
grace _____ ap - pear The hour I _____ first be - lieved! _____

3. Through many dangers, toils, and snares
   I have already come;
   'Tis grace has brought me safe thus far.

4. The Lord has promised good to me;
   His word my hope secures;
   He will my shield and portion be

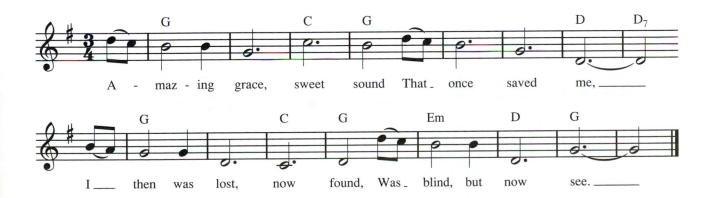

A - maz - ing grace, sweet sound That _ once saved me, _____

I _ then was lost, now found, Was _ blind, but now see. _____

ROLL ON, COLUMBIA

WOODY GUTHRIE

BASED ON "GOODNIGHT, IRENE" BY HUDDIE LEDBETTER AND JOHN A. LOMAX

1. Green Doug-las fir where the wa-ters cut through, Down her wild
2. Oth-er big rivers add __ pow-er to you, Yak-i-ma,
3. At Bon-ne-ville now there are __ ships in the locks, The wa-ter has
4. And on up the river is the Grand Cou-lee Dam, The big-gest thing

mount-ains and can-yons she flew, Ca-na-di-an North-west to the
Snake, and the Klick-i-tat, too. Sand-y, Wil-lam-ette, and the
ris-en and cov-ered the rocks. Ship-loads a-plen-ty are __
built by the hand of a man, To run the great fac-t'ries and __

o-cean so blue,
Hood Riv-er, too,   Roll on, Co-lum-bia, roll on. _____
soon past the docks,
wa-ter the land,

Descant

Roll on, __ Co-lum-bia, roll on. Roll on, __ Co-lum-bia, roll on. Your

Melody

pow-er is turn-ing our dark-ness to dawn, Roll on, Co-lum-bia, roll on. _____

Applying Your Music Skills with Songs and Instruments

Patriotic Songs

K–4, 9c
5–8, 9c

Traditional (and new) patriotic songs that are sung regularly in classrooms and school assembly programs throughout the United States should be a part of the basic song repertory of all teachers. Four-part harmonizations of these songs are included for students and teachers who play the piano. The more experienced singers in college classes may be taught to sing the parts.

When only the melody is played or sung, the simplified chording can be used for Omnichord, Autoharp, piano, or Resonator Bells.

AMERICA

S.F. Smith

Henry Carey

1. My coun - try, 'tis of thee, Sweet land of lib - er - ty,
Of thee I sing; Land where my fa - thers died! Land of the
Pil - grims' pride! From ev - 'ry ___ mount - ain-side Let ___ free - dom ring!

2. My native country, thee,
Land of the noble free,
Thy name I love.
I love thy rocks and rills,
Thy woods and templed hills;
My heart with rapture thrills
Like that above.

3. Our fathers' God, to Thee,
Author of liberty,
To Thee we sing.
Long may our land be bright
With freedom's holy light;
Protect us by Thy might,
Great God, our King.

Applying Your Music Skills with Songs and Instruments

THE STAR-SPANGLED BANNER

Francis Scott Key

John Stafford Smith

1. O ___ say! can you see, by the dawn's ear - ly light, What so

proud - ly we hailed at the twi - light's last gleam-ing? Whose broad stripes and bright

stars, through the per - il - ous fight, O'er the ram - parts we watched, were so

gal - lant - ly stream-ing! And the rock - ets' red glare, the bombs burst - ing in

Applying Your Music Skills with Songs and Instruments

air, Gave proof through the night that our flag was still there.

Chorus

O say, does that — Star - Spang - led Ban - ner — yet — wave —

O'er the land ——— of the free and the home of the brave?

2. On the shore, dimly seen through the mists of the deep,
   Where the foe's haughty host in dread silence reposes,
   What is that which the breeze, o'er the towering steep,
   As it fitfully blows, half conceals, half discloses?
   Now it catches the gleam of the morning's first beam;
   In full glory reflected now shines on the stream;
   'Tis the Star-Spangled Banner, oh, long may it wave
   O'er the land of the free and the home of the brave!

3. O, thus be it ever when free men shall stand
   Between their loved homes and the war's desolation!
   Blest with vict'ry and peace, may the heav'n-rescued land
   Praise the Pow'r that hath made and preserved us a nation!
   Then conquer we must, when our cause it is just,
   And this be our motto: "In God is our trust!"
   And the Star-Spangled Banner in triumph shall wave
   O'er the land of the free and the home of the brave!

FIFTY NIFTY UNITED STATES

Ray Charles

Ray Charles

Applying Your Music Skills with Songs and Instruments

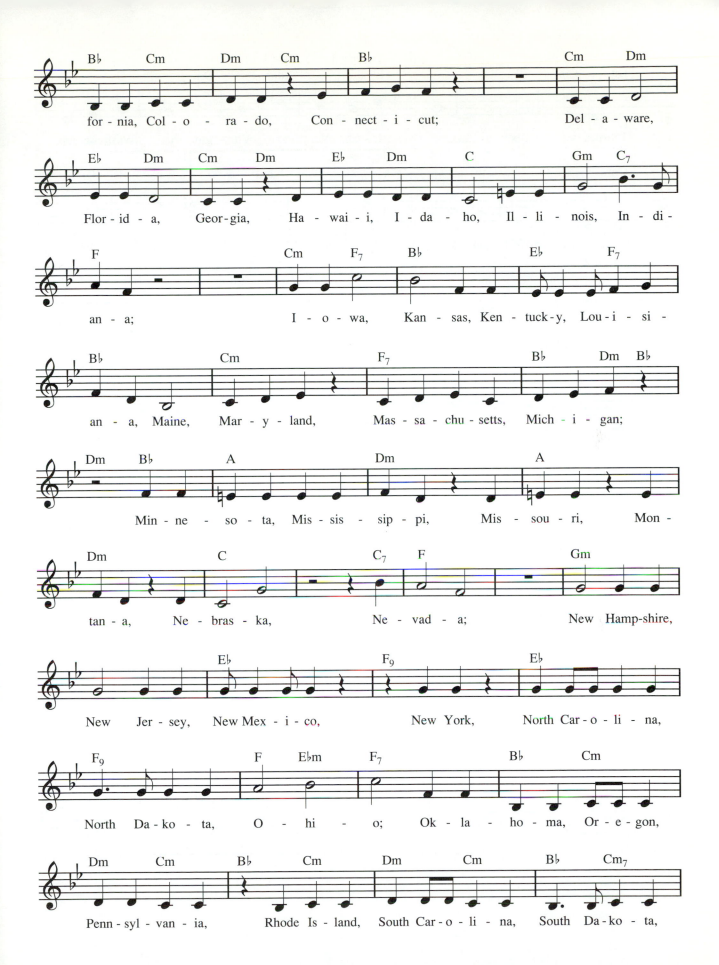

Applying Your Music Skills with Songs and Instruments

Appendix 1
Performance Directions

Certain signs and terms, largely Italian, are used to convey directions to performers.

Tempo Indications

The *tempo* is the pace of music. It is often specified by one of the following Italian terms, which are arranged in order from the slowest to the fastest.

Extremely slow   Largo (broad, large)

Lento (slow)

Adagio (leisurely)

Andante (going along, flowing)

Moderate   Moderato (moderate)

Allegretto (cheerful, lively)

Allegro (brisk, rapid, lively)

Vivace (quick, lively)

Extremely fast   Presto (very fast)

A *metronome* is a mechanical device used to establish and maintain tempos in music. A metronome mark is another way of indicating tempo. A metronome mark consists of a note symbol representing the beat and a number showing the number of beats per minute. Thus:

♩ = 72 means a tempo of 72 quarter-note beats per minute.

𝅗𝅥 = 84 means a tempo of 84 half-note beats per minute.

Gradual slowing of the tempo is indicated by *ritardando* (abbreviated *rit.* or *ritard.*). Gradual acceleration is indicated by the Italian word *accelerando* (abbreviated *accel.*). A return to the preceding tempo after *ritardando* or *accelerando* is indicated by *a tempo*.

Dynamic Marks

Italian words, or more often their abbreviations, are used to indicate degrees of loudness and softness.

Word	Abbreviation	Meaning
pianissimo	*pp*	very soft
piano	*p*	soft
mezzo piano	*mp*	moderately soft
mezzo forte	*mf*	moderately loud
forte	*f*	loud
fortissimo	*ff*	very loud
crescendo	*cresc.*	gradually louder
decrescendo	*decresc.*	gradually softer
diminuendo	*dim., dimin.*	gradually softer

Spreading lines are often used in place of *crescendo* (*cresc.*) and contracting lines in place of *decrescendo* (*decresc.*), as shown below.

crescendo
(gradually louder)

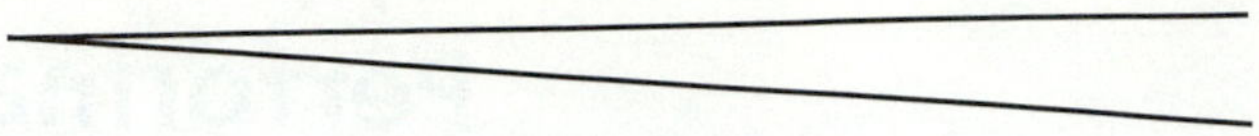

decrescendo
(gradually softer)

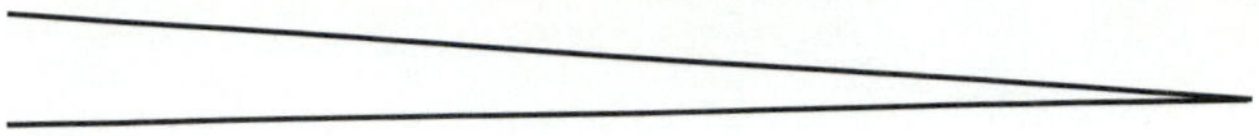

Several pocket dictionaries that give translations and definitions of musical terms are available in book stores and music stores.

Appendix 2
Guitar Fingering Chart

This appendix presents the principal chords for the keys used in this book. Some keys may not be practical for beginners of the guitar.

Note: R stands for the root or base note of the chord.

Key of C Major

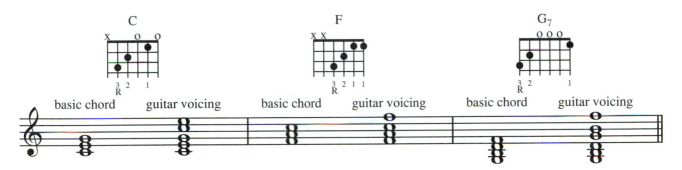

Key of G Major

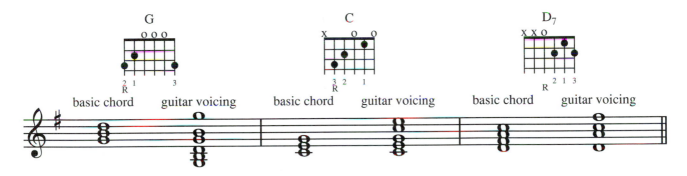

Key of D Major

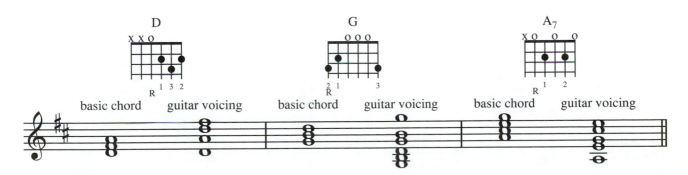

Key of A Major

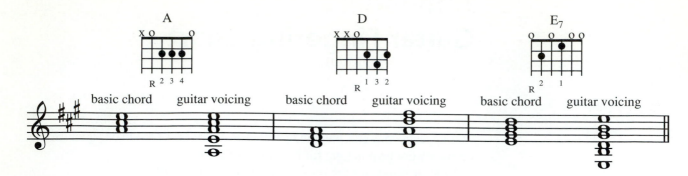

Key of E Major

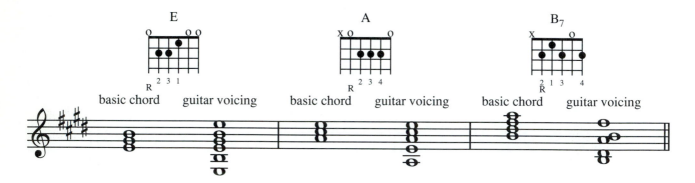

Key of B Major

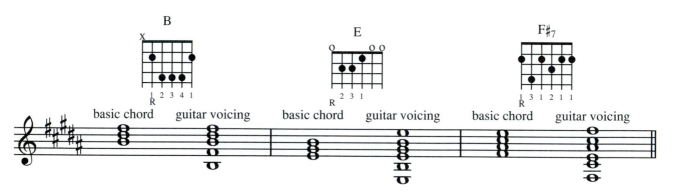

Key of F♯ Major

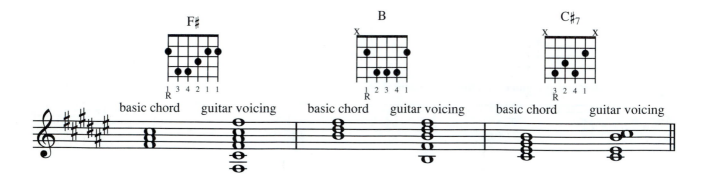

Key of F Major

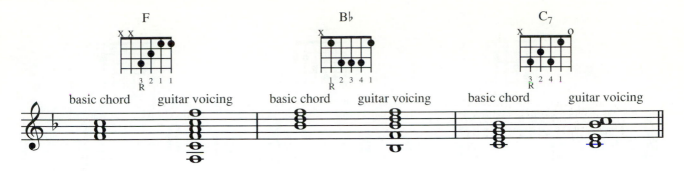

Key of B♭ Major

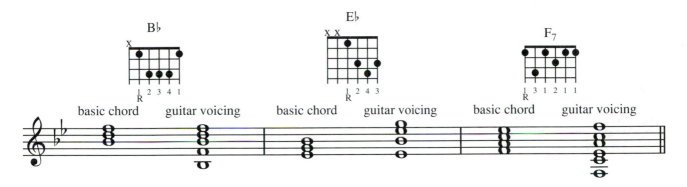

Key of E♭ Major

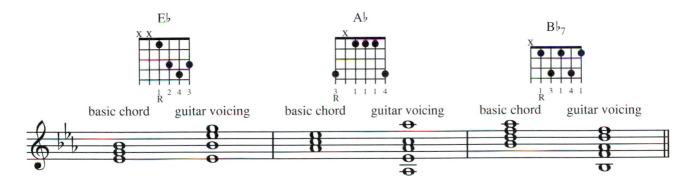

Key of A♭ Major

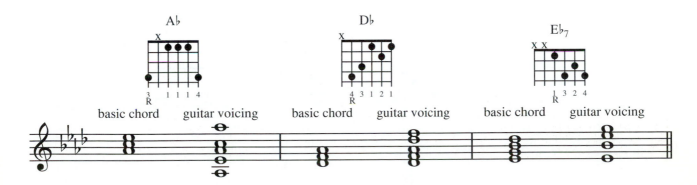

Key of D♭ Major

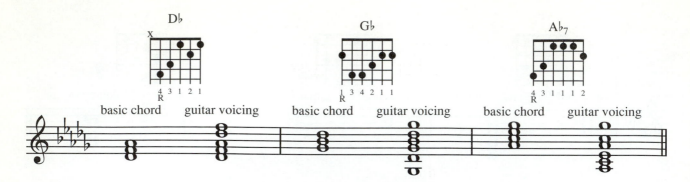

For the minor keys, the notation will not be presented.

Key of A Minor

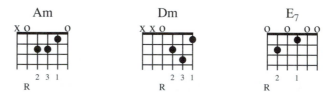

Key of D Minor

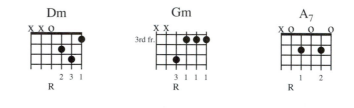

Key of G Minor

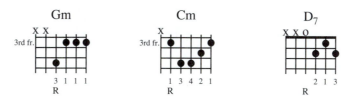

Key of C Minor

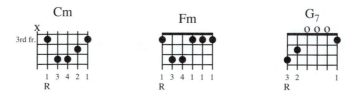

Key of F Minor

Fm
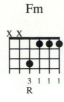

B♭m

C₇

Key of B♭ Minor

B♭m

E♭m
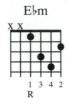

F₇

Key of E♭ Minor

E♭m
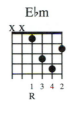

A♭m

B♭₇

Key of A♭ Minor

A♭m
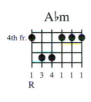

D♭m

E♭₇

Key of C♯ Minor

C♯m
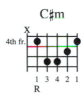

F♯m

G♯₇

Key of F♯ Minor

F♯m

Bm
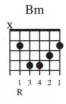

C♯₇
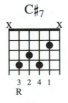

Key of B Minor

Bm

Em

F#7

Key of E Minor

Em

Am

B7

Appendix 2 Guitar Fingering Chart

Appendix 3
Piano Chord Chart

*The same fingerings apply to each exercise.

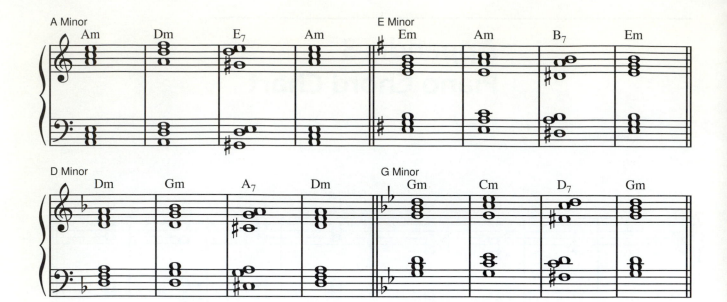

Appendix 3 Piano Chord Chart

Credits

Lone Star Trail, American cowboy song, from *The Music Connection, Grade 2* by Jane Beethoven, et al. Copyright © 1995 by Silver Burdett Ginn, Inc. Reprinted by permission of Addison-Wesley Educational Publishers, Inc. All Rights Reserved.

Mail Myself to You, words and music by Woody Guthrie. Copyright © 1962 (Renewed), 1963 (Renewed) by TRO - Ludlow Music, Inc. Used by Permission. All Rights Reserved.

Make New Friends, round, from *The Music Connection, Grade 4* by Jane Beethoven, et al. Copyright © 1995 by Silver Burdett Ginn, Inc. Reprinted by permission of Addison-Wesley Educational Publishers, Inc. All Rights Reserved.

Marianne, traditional, from *Contemporary Class Guitar, Book 1* by Will Schmid. Copyright © Hal Leonard Corporation. Reprinted by Permission. All Rights Reserved.

Mickey Mouse March, words and music by Jimmie Dodd. Copyright © 1955 by Walt Disney Music Company. Reprinted by Permission. All Rights Reserved.

Minka, Russian folk song, collected by Louise Garnett, from *New Music Horizons, Book 5,* copyright © 1946 by Silver Burdett and Company. Reprinted by permission of Addison-Wesley Educational Publishers, Inc. All Rights Reserved.

Monster Frankenstein, traditional melody "Oh, My Darling, Clementine," Orff arrangement and words by Mary Lou Frierdich, as reprinted in Keeping Up with Orff Schulwerk in the Classroom. Copyright © 1976 by Keeping Up with Music Education, Muncie, IN. Reprinted by permission. All rights reserved.

My Boat, Hawaiian folk song, collected and adapted by Ermine and Elsa Cross from *Songs Children Like.* Copyright © 1954, 1958, page 42. Reprinted by permission of the Association for Childhood Education International, 17904 Georgia Ave., Olney, MD 20832. All Rights Reserved.

My Father's House, from *The Music Connection, Grade 2* by Jane Beethoven, et al. Copyright © 1995 by Silver Burdett Ginn, Inc. Reprinted by permission of Addison-Wesley Educational Publishers, Inc. All Rights Reserved.

My Home's in Montana, American folk song, from *The Music Connection, Grade 5* by Jane Beethoven, et al. Copyright © 1995 by Silver Burdett Ginn, Inc. Reprinted by permission of Addison-Wesley Educational Publishers, Inc. All Rights Reserved.

Ode to Joy, by Ludwig van Beethoven, from *Contemporary Class Guitar, Book 1* by Will Schmid. Copyright © Hal Leonard Corporation. Reprinted by Permission. All Rights Reserved.

Oh, My Darling, Clementine, American folk song, from *Share the Music, Grade 5* by Marilyn Davidson, et al. Copyright © 2000 by The McGraw-Hill Companies. Reprinted by permission. All Rights Reserved.

Oh! Susanna, by Stephen C. Foster, from *Mel Bay Guitar Class Method, Book 1.* Arrangement © 1972 by Mel Bay Publications, Inc. Used by Permission. All Rights Reserved.

Old Dan Tucker, American folk song, from *The Music Connection, Grade 2* by Jane Beethoven, et al. Copyright © 1995 by Silver Burdett Ginn, Inc. Reprinted by permis-

sion of Addison-Wesley Educational Publishers, Inc. All Rights Reserved.

One Bottle of Pop, traditional English round, from *Share the Music, Grade 3* by Marilyn Davidson, et al. Copyright © 2000 by The McGraw-Hill Companies. Reprinted by permission. All Rights Reserved.

Polly Wolly Doodle, American folk song, from *Contemporary Class Guitar, Book 2* by Will Schmid. Copyright © Hal Leonard Corporation. Reprinted by Permission. All Rights Reserved.

The Pumpkin Man, traditional melody "The Muffin Man," words by Grant Newman. Copyright © by Brown & Benchmark. Reprinted by permission of The McGraw-Hill Companies. All Rights Reserved.

Rocky Top, by Boudleaux Bryant and Felice Bryant. Copyright © House of Bryant. Reprinted by permission of Hal Leonard Corporation. All Rights Reserved.

Roll On, Columbia, words by Woody Guthrie, music based on "Goodnight Irene" by H. Ledbetter & J. A. Lomax. Copyright © by TRO-Ludlow Music, Inc. Used by Permission. All Rights Reserved.

Round In a Circle, by Margaret Campbell-Holman. Copyright © by Margaret Campbelle-Holman. Reprinted by permission of Jematé Publishing, a division of Creative Links, LLC, 1318 Seventh Ave. N., Nashville, TN 37208. All Rights Reserved.

Sarasponda, Dutch spinning song, from *Share the Music, Grade 4* by Marilyn Davidson, et al. Copyright © 2000 by The McGraw-Hill Companies. Reprinted by permission. All Rights Reserved.

Save the Planet, by Gene Grier and Lowell Everson, from *Ziggy's Save the Earth Activity Book.* Copyright © by Heritage Press. Reprinted by permission of The Lorenz Corporation. All Rights Reserved.

Shake My Sillies Out, Words by Raffi, B & B Simpson. Music by Raffi. Copyright © 1977 Homeland Publishing (CAPAC), a division of Troubadour Records Ltd. Used by Permission. All Rights Reserved.

Sieben Steps, German folk song, from *Share the Music, Grade 2* by Marilyn Davidson, et al. Copyright © 2000 by The McGraw-Hill Companies. Reprinted by permission. All Rights Reserved.

Simple Gifts, traditional Shaker song, from *Share the Music, Grade 4* by Marilyn Davidson, et al. Copyright © 2000 by The McGraw-Hill Companies. Reprinted by permission. All Rights Reserved.

Skinnamarink, American Tin Pan Alley song from *Share the Music, Grade 2* by Marilyn Davidson, et al. Copyright © 2000 by The McGraw-Hill Companies. Reprinted by permission. All Rights Reserved.

Skip to My Lou, American folk song, from *Contemporary Class Guitar, Book 1* by Will Schmid. Copyright © Hal Leonard Corporation. Reprinted by Permission. All Rights Reserved.

Soprano Recorder Finger Placement and Fingering Chart System from *Do It! Play recorder* by James O. Froseth. Copyright © GIA Publications, Inc., Chicago, IL. Reprinted by Permission. All Rights Reserved.

The Streets of Laredo, American cowboy song, from *The Music Connection, Grade 5* by Jane Beethoven, et al. Copyright © 1995 by Silver Burdett Ginn, Inc. Reprinted

by permission of Addison-Wesley Educational Publishers, Inc. All Rights Reserved.

This Land Is Your Land, words and music by Woody Guthrie. Copyright © 1956 (Renewed), 1958 (Renewed), 1970 (Renewed) by TRO - Ludlow Music, Inc., New York, NY. Used by Permission. All Rights Reserved.

The Turtle Dove, traditional English, arr. Van A. Christy, from *Foundations in Singing, 4th Ed.* Copyright © 1979 by Wm. C. Brown Publishers. Reprinted by permission of The McGraw-Hill Companies. All Rights Reserved.

Two, Four, Six, Eight, English nursery rhyme, music by Marilyn Davidson, from *Share the Music, Grade 1* by Marilyn Davidson, et al. Copyright © 2000 by The McGraw-Hill Companies. Reprinted by permission. All Rights Reserved.

The Wabash Cannonball, American folk song, from *The Music Connection, Grade 5* by Jane Beethoven, et al. Copyright © 1995 by Silver Burdett Ginn, Inc. Reprinted by permission of Addison-Wesley Educational Publishers, Inc. All Rights Reserved.

The Water is Wide, folk song from England, from *The Music Connection, Grade 6* by Jane Beethoven, et al. Copyright © 1995 by Silver Burdett Ginn, Inc. Reprinted by permission of Addison-Wesley Educational Publishers, Inc. All Rights Reserved.

When I Am 10 Years Old, Norwegian folk song, collected by Jane Farwell, from *This Is Music, Grade 5.* Copyright © by Allyn & Bacon, a division of Silver Burdett Ginn, Inc. Reprinted by permission of Pearson Educational Publishing. All Rights Reserved.

When the Saints Go Marching In, traditional American, from *Share the Music, Grade 5* by Marilyn Davidson, et al. Copyright © 2000 by The McGraw-Hill Companies. Reprinted by permission. All Rights Reserved.

Who Built the Ark, African-American spiritual, from *Share the Music, Grade 1* by Marilyn Davidson, et al. Copyright © 2000 by The McGraw-Hill Companies. Reprinted by permission. All Rights Reserved.

Yankee Doodle, traditional melody, words by Dr. Richard Shuckburgh, from *Share the Music, Grade 1* by Marilyn Davidson, et al. Copyright © 2000 by The McGraw-Hill Companies. Reprinted by permission. All Rights Reserved.

Yankee Doodle, traditional melody, words by Dr. Richard Shuckburgh, from *Share the Music, Grade K* by Marilyn Davidson, et al. Copyright © 2000 by The McGraw-Hill Companies. Reprinted by permission. All Rights Reserved.

Zoodle Noodle Zimmer Grunch, by Rhoda Weber and Bob Margolis, from *Soprano Recorder Book for Children* by Rhoda B. Weber. Additional music by Bob Margolis and Rhoda B. Weber. Copyright © 1984 by Manhattan Beach Music, http://www.manhattanbeachmusic.com, 1595 E. 46 St., Brooklyn, NY 11234. Reprinted by Permission. All Rights Reserved.

Zum Gali, Gali, from *Wee Sing around the World* by Pamela Conn Beall and Susan Hagen Nipp. Copyright © 1994 by Pamela Conn Beall and Susan Hagen Nipp. Reprinted by permission of Price, Stern & Sloan, Inc., a division of Penguin Putnam Inc. All Rights Reserved.

Glossary and Index of Terms

omnichord, 234; orchestral, 301; Orff approach, 190; percussion, 166, 301, 307; string, 300, 302; woodwind, 303

Interval, the difference in pitch between two tones, 49; harmonic, 77; melodic, 77; perfect, 78; quality, 77

Interval chart, 80

Introduction, a preliminary phrase or section

Jingle sticks (clogs), 167

Keyboard instruments, 134, 301

Keynote, scale degree 1 (*do*), for which the key is named, 56, 60

Key signatures, 55; major, 56, 60; minor, 70

Kodály approach, 9, 27, 30, 48, 49

Largo, a broad, very slow tempo, 341

Larynx, the vocal organ, 100

Leading tone, the seventh degree of the scale and the chord built on it, 82

Ledger lines, 46

Legato, a smooth, connected manner of performance, 100

Leger lines, 46

Lento, a slow tempo, 341

Lied (pl., lieder), an art song, 309

Line notation, 44, 180

Madrigal, 309

Major keys, 55; signatures, 60

Maracas, 167

Mass, the solemn service of the Roman Catholic liturgy

Measure, a metric unit in music, 6, 89

Mediant, the third degree of the scale and the chord built on it, 82

Melodic interval, two notes written or sounded in succession, 77

Melodic minor, 67

Metallophones, 191

Meter signature. See *Time signature*

Metronome, a mechanical device used to establish and maintain tempos, 341

Metronome mark, a precise way of indicating a tempo, 341

Mezzo forte (mf), moderately loud, 341

Mezzo piano (mp), moderately soft, 341

Mezzo-soprano, 300

Middle C, 61, 134

Minor keys, 64; harmonic, 66; melodic, 67; natural, 64; parallel, 65; relative, 64; signatures, 70

Mixolydian mode, 71

Modal scales, 71

Moderato, a moderate tempo, 341

Modes, 71

Motive, the smallest identifiable unit of music

Movement, a distinct and separate part of a large work such as a symphony or suite, 309

Natural, the symbol that cancels the effect of a sharp or a flat, 51

Notes, symbols used to show rhythm and

pitch of musical sounds, 5; names, 47; values, 27, 30, 33

Obbligato, a harmony part added above the melody, 286

Oboe, 304

Octave, span of notes including one note through the next with the same name, 48

Omnichord, 234

One-part form, 87

Oompah, bass notes alternating with chords in an accompaniment pattern

Orchestra, 310; seating plan, 311; string, 310; symphony, 310

Orff approach, 186; instruments, 190; sources, 201

Ostinato (pl., ostinati), a persistently repeated tonal pattern, 194

Parallel keys, major and minor keys with the same keynote, 65

Partner songs, 281

Patschen, patting thighs in rhythm, 188

Pentatonic, a five-tone scale, 52, 192

Percussion instruments, 166, 301, 307

Performance directions, 341

Period. See Sentence

Periods and styles, 312

Phrase, an incomplete musical idea, 84

Phrasing, the articulation of phrases in performance, 220

Pianissimo (pp), very soft, 341

Piano chord chart, 349

Pianoforte, the complete name of the keyboard instrument commonly known as the piano

Piano keyboard, in the endleaf pocket

Piano quintet, 309

Piano (p), soft, 341

Piccolo, 303

Plucking, 252

Pop music, 311

Presto, a very fast tempo, 341

Primary chords, 82

Progression, going from one chord to another, 83

Quarter notes, 5

Quartet, a chamber ensemble consisting of four performers, 309

Quintet, a chamber ensemble consisting of five performers, 309; brass, 309; piano, 309; wind, 309

Range, the compass of a voice or instrument, 299, 300

Recorder, 202; fingering chart, 204

Reed, 303; double, 304

Relative keys, a major and a minor key with the same key signature, 64

Repeat sign, double bar and two dots that indicates to repeat a passage, 11

Repertoire, a collection of music ready or available for performance

Rests, the symbols for silence, 26

Rhythm sticks, 166

Rhythm, the temporal aspect of music, 5; duple, 7; triple, 7

Ritardando (ritard, rit.), slowing the tempo gradually, 341

Rock, 311

Root, of chord, 81, 293

Rounds, 276

Sand blocks, 167

Saxophones, 304

Scale builder, in endleaf pocket

Scales, series of consecutive notes arranged in ascending or descending order, 48; chromatic, 52; major, 48, 55; minor, 64; pentatonic, 52, 192

Semitone, a half step, 49

Sentence, a complete musical idea, 84

Sharp, the symbol that raises the pitch a semitone, 51

Sixteenth notes, 32

Slur, a curved line indicating that notes are to be performed smoothly as a group, 215

Sol-fa. See *Solfège*

Solfège, a method of sight singing in which notes are associated with syllables, 48

Solo, a piece or prominent part for one instrument or voice, 309

Sonata, 309

Song form, 87

Soprano voice, 299

Sousaphone, 306

Staccato, detached, separated, 100

Staff, 45

Stem, the vertical line connected to a note head, 8

String bass, 302

String instruments, 300, 302

String orchestra, 310

Strumming, 239, 253

Styles of music, 312

Subdominant, the fourth degree of the scale and the chord built on it, 82

Submediant, the sixth degree of the scale and the chord built on it, 82

Subphrase, a structural unit smaller than a phrase, 87

Subtonic, the seventh degree of the scale and the chord built on it, 82

Suite, previously a group of stylized dance movements in the same key; now the term is applied to a variety of multimovement compositions

Supertonic, the second degree of the scale and the chord built on it, 82

Syllables, euphonious sounds used in solfège: pitch, 48; rhythm, 9, 27, 30, 33

Symphonic wind ensemble, 311

Symphony orchestra, 310

Syncopation, weak beats that are accented, 39

Synthesizers, 163

Tambourine, 167

Tempo, the pace of the beat, 24; terms, 341

Tenor voice, 299

Ternary form, 89

Theme, a melodic idea in a composition
Tie, 19
Timbale, 192
Timbre, tone quality or tone color of given
  sound, 299
Time signature (meter signature), 7; 2/2, 21;
  2/4, 7; 3/4, 14; 3/8, 23; 4/4, 16; 6/8, 23
Timpani, 307
Tone, a musical sound, 5; singing, 98
Tone blocks, 166
Tone color (quality), 299
Tonic, the first degree of the scale and the
  chord built on it, 82
Transition, a passage between two thematic
  elements in a form: rhythm, 30
Transpose, to write or perform in a higher or
  lower key, 100, 241, 271

Traps, 307
Treble clef, 46
Triads, three-tone chords, 81, 294; primary,
  82
Triangle, 168
Triple rhythm, three beats, 7
Triplet, three notes of equal value within
  beat, 38
Trombones, 307
Trumpet, 305
Tuba, 306
Two-part form, 87

Unaccented beat, beat that is not stressed, 6
Upbeat, unaccented beat that comes before
  first beat, 7, 27

Viola, 302
Violin, 302
Violoncello, the complete name for the cello,
  302
Vivace, a quick, lively tempo, 341
Voices: classifications, 299; range, 299, 300;
  registers, 94
Vowels, 100

Waltz, 6, 295
Whole notes, 17
Whole step (tone), 49
Wind instruments, 301
Woodwind instruments, 303

Xylophones, 190

Classified Song Index

Recreational Songs: Action, Game, Stunt, and Camp

Acitrón, 124
Barnyard Song, 53
Bingo, 329
Bow, Belinda, 85
Bus Song, 331
Chopsticks, 209
Cotton-Eyed Joe, 125
Good Morning to All, 327
Head, Shoulders, Baby, F, 328
Head and Shoulders, Baby, 329
Hokey Pokey, 330
If You're Happy, 124
I'm a Little Teapot, 327
London Bridge, 273
Long-Legged Sailor, rhythm, 41
March Time, C, 138
Meet Me at the Garden Gate, rhythm, 32
Merrily We Roll Along, 151, 212
Muffin Man, 328
My Father's House, 330
Polly, Put the Kettle On, 196
Pumpkin Man, 72
Scale Song, 50
This Old Man, 331
Three-Cornered Hat, 221
Upidee, 223

Rounds and Canons

Are You Sleeping, 17, 56, 281
Come and Sing Together, 280
Dona Nobis Pacem, 278
Farmer in the Dell, 282
Follow On, 274
I Love the Mountains, 277
Li'l Liza Jane, 279
Make New Friends, 110
Music Alone Shall Live, 323
My Goose, 242
Old Texas, 276
One Bottle of Pop, 323
A Ram Sam Sam, 105, 277
Row, Row, Row Your Boat, 38, 273
Scotland's Burning, 276
Shalom Chaverim, 278
Three Blind Mice, 24, 281
Water Is Wide, 332
White Coral Bells, 183

Songs of Other Lands

Acitrón, Spain, 124
A-Hunting We Will Go, England, 162
All through the Night, Wales, 20
Aloha Oe, Hawaii, 321
Are You Sleeping, France, 17, 56, 281
Ash Grove, Wales, 90
Auf Widersehen, Germany, 153
Auld Lang Syne, Scotland, 294
Barbara Allen, Scotland, 85
Big Ben Clock, England, 182
Calypso Joe, Caribbean, 176
Charlie Is My Darling, England, 67
Cherry Blossoms, Japan, 320
Come and Sing Together, Hungary, 280
Cuckoo, Germany, 152

Dame, Get Up, England, 66
Dance, Hungary, 156
De Colores, Mexico, 291
Don Gato, Mexico, 120
Down in Mexico, Mexico, 174
Du, Du Liegst Mir im Herzen, Germany, 160
Fais Do Do, France, 207
Farewell to Thee, Hawaii, 321
Fiddle-Dee-Dee, England, 212
Folk Tune, Russia, 154
French Tune, France, 207
German Folk Tune, Germany, 149
German Tune, Germany, 226
Give Me Your Hand, France, 110
God Rest You Merry, Gentlemen, England, 86
Going Over the Sea, Canada, 242
Haida, Israel, 268
Harmonizing, Austria, 290
Hava Nagila, Israel, 267, 322
Hot Cross Buns, England, 8, 10, 144, 181, 207, 218
Japanese Hymn, 221
Johnny Has Gone for a Soldier, Ireland, 64
Koom Bah Yah, Africa, 295
Ladies of Chiapas (Chiapanecas), Mexico, 118
La Raspa, Mexico, 175
Las Mañanitas, Mexico, 119
Las Pollitas, Spain, 317
Lavender's Blue, England, 15, 157, 225
Les Anges dans nos Campagnes, France/England, 319
Lightly Row, Germany, 144, 210
London Bridge, England, 273
Marching Song, Silesia, 232
Marianne, Caribbean, 256
Merry Bells, Wales, 181
Michael, Row the Boat Ashore, Georgia Islands, 113
Muffin Man, England, 328
Music Alone Shall Live, Germany, 323
Noel, Africa, 292
Norwegian Dance, Norway, 162
Oh Hanukah, Hasidic folk song, 292
One Bottle of Pop, England, 323
Papaya Tree, Philippines, 229
To Paree, France, 209
A Ram Sam Sam, Morocco, 105, 277
Recorder Band, Germany, 211
Sakura, Japan, 320
Sarasponda, Netherlands, 106
Seven Steps, Germany, 121
Shalom Chaverim, Israel, 278
Singing on the Playground, Germany, 147
Sleep, My Baby, Sweden, 155
Under the Spreading Chestnut Tree, England, 45, 46, 47
Steeple Bells, France, 182
This Old Man, England, 331
Three-Cornered Hat, Germany, 221
Tinga Layo, West Indies, 318
Twinkle, Twinkle, Little Star, France, 158
Two, Four, Six, Eight, England, 103
Upward Trail, Germany, 325
Water is Wide, England, 332

We Wish You a Merry Christmas, England, 214
When I Am Ten Years Old, Norway, 244
White Coral Bells, England, 183
Zum Gali Gali, Israel, 246, 269

Spirituals and Hymns

Away in a Manger, 265
Chatter with the Angels, 114
Do, Lord, 115
Dona Nobis Pacem, 278
He's Got the Whole World in His Hands, 282
Jacob Drink, 232
Jacob's Ladder, 22, 184
Joshua Fit the Battle of Jericho, 245, 267
Joyful, Joyful, We Adore Thee, 63
Koom Bah Yah, 295
Michael, Row the Boat Ashore, 113
Noel, 292
O Come, All Ye Faithful, 216
Rock-A-My Soul, 284
Shortnin' Bread, 40
Simple Gifts, 91, 106
Sweet and Low, 40
When the Saints Go Marching In, 148, 263
Who Built the Ark?, 114

U.S. Folk Songs

All the Pretty Little Horses, 68, 289
Animal Fair, 105
Barnyard Song, 53
Bow, Belinda, 85
Cindy, 227
Cotton-Eyed Joe, 125
Deaf Woman's Courtship, 287
Desperado, 231
Doktor Eisenbart, 316
Frankie and Johnny, 262
Go Tell Aunt Rhodie, 147
Hush, Little Baby, 258
Jim Along, Josie, 122
Johnny Has Gone for a Soldier, Ireland, 64
Li'l Liza Jane, 279
Oh, My Darling, Clementine, 58
Old Dan Tucker, 116
Old Joe Clark, 71
Old Smoky, 264
Old Texas, 276
Playground Tune, C, 150
Police Call, C, 210
Polly Wolly Doodle, 262
Rockabye, Baby, 24, 80
Skinnamarink, B-flat, 60
Skip to My Lou, 257
Snake Dance, F, 213
Sourwood Mountain, 197
Sweet Betsy from Pike, 59
Tom Dooley, 39, 259
Valentine Song, 181
Wabash Cannon Ball, 129
When the Saints Go Marching In, 148, 263
Who Did?, 274
Who's That Tapping at the Window?, 219
Woodchuck, 18, 141
Yankee Doodle, 122, 123, 172, 214
You Can't Love Two, 215

Alphabetical Song Index

Melody
   C, 227
   F, 222
Merrily We Roll Along
   C, 151
   F, 212
Merry Bells, rhythm, 181
Michael, Row the Boat Ashore, C, 113
Mickey Mouse March, F, 13
Monster Frankenstein, F minor, 73, 200
Morning, F pentatonic, 221
Muffin Man, G, 328
Music Alone Shall Live, F, 323
My Father's House, F, 330
My Goose, C, 242
My Home's in Montana, D, 285

Noel, C, 292
Norwegian Dance, C, 162

O Come, All Ye Faithful, G, 216
Ode to Joy, C, 257
Oh, Dear! What Can the Matter Be? F, 13
Oh, My Darling, Clementine, F, 58
Oh Hanukah, D minor, 292
Oh! Susanna
   C, 270
   F, 12, 244
Oh Where, Oh Where Has My Little Dog
   Gone?
   F, 224
   rhythm, 28
Old Dan Tucker, F, 116
Old Joe Clark, D, 71
Old Smoky, A, 264
Old Texas, F, 276
One Bottle of Pop, F, 323
Over There, B-flat, 12
Over the River and Through the Wood, B-
   flat, 246

Papaya Tree, G, 229
Playground Tune, C, 150
Police Call, C, 210
Polka, C, 208
Polly, Put the Kettle On, C, 196
Polly Wolly Doodle, D, 262
Pumpkin Man, F minor, 72

Rain, Rain, C, 195
Recorder Band, G, 211
Ring, Ring the Banjo, C, 185
Ring around a rosy, rhythm, 187
Rockabye, Baby
   C, 80
   rhythm, 24
Rock-A-My Soul, C, 284
Rocky Top, A, 296
Roll On, Columbia, F, 334
'Round in a Circle, rhythm, 173
Row, Row, Row Your Boat
   C, 273
   rhythm, 38

Sarasponda, C, 106
Save the Planet, C, 127
Scale Song, C, 50
Scotland's Burning, F, 276
Seven Steps, F, 121
Shake My Sillies Out, D, 247
Shortnin' Bread, rhythm, 40
Silent Night, C, 163
Simple Gifts, F, 91, 106
Singing on the Playground, F, 147
Skinnamarink, B-flat, 60
Skip to My Lou, C, 257
Sleep, My Baby, E minor, 155
Snake Dance, F, 213
Some Folks Do! C, 152
Song Without Words, C, 220
Sourwood Mountain, F, 197
Starlight, C, 213
Star-Spangled Banner, A-flat, 336
Steeple Bells, C, 182
Streets of Laredo, D, 288
Sweet and Low, rhythm, 40
Sweet Betsy from Pike, D, 59
Symphonic Theme, B-flat, 222

Theme from the Surprise Symphony, C, 148
This Land Is Your Land, G, 113
This Old Man, C, 331
Three Blind Mice
   C, 281
   rhythm, 24
Three-Cornered Hat, F, 221
Tinga Layo, C, 318

Tom Dooley
   G, 259
   rhythm, 39
To Paree, G, 209
Trumpet Voluntary, G, 213
Twinkle, Twinkle, Little Star, C, 158
Two, Four, Six, Eight, D, 103

Under the Spreading Chestnut Tree
   C, 46, 47
   line notation, 45
Upidee, F, 223
Upward Trail, G, 325

Valentine Song, C, 181

Wabash Cannon Ball, G, 129
Water Is Wide, F, 332
We Wish You a Merry Christmas, G, 214
When I Am Ten Years Old, C, 244
When Johnny Comes Marching Home
   Again, G minor, 69
When the Saints Go Marching In
   A, 263
   F, 148
White Coral Bells, C, 183
Who Built the Ark? G, 114
Who Did? F, 274
Who's That Tapping at the Window? C, 219
Woodchuck
   C, 141
   rhythm, 18
Worried Man Blues, G, 259

Yankee Doodle
   G, 122, 123, 214
   rhythm, 172
Yankee Doodle Dandy, F, 112
You Can't Love Two, D, 215

Zoodle Noodle Zimmer Grunch, G, 217
Zum Gali Gali, E minor, 246, 269

CD to Accompany Music Skills for Classroom Teachers

1. Oh, My Darling, Clementine
2. Johnny Has Gone for a Soldier
3. All the Pretty Little Horses
4. Monster Frankenstein
5. God Rest You, Merry Gentlemen
6. The Big Corral
7. Hello Song
8. Two, Four, Six, Eight
9. Mail Myself to You
10. Lone Star Trail
11. Sarasponda
12. Who Built the Ark?
13. Hello to All the Children of the World
14. I Can't Spell Hippopotamus
15. The Animal Band
16. Lightly Row
17. Dance
18. Twinkle, Twinkle Little Star
19. Ebeneeer Sneezer
20. Jacob's Ladder
21. C Major scale up and down
22. Lightly Row
23. We Wish You a Merry Christmas
24. Three-Cornered Hat
25. Marianne
26. Worried Man Blues
27. My Home's in Montana
28. Home on the Range
29. De Colores
30. Auld Lang Syne
31. Les Anges dans nos Campagnes
32. Amazing Grace

Vocals: Allison Foss

Accompaniment: Christopher Freitag

Engineered by Marv Nonn

Produced by Nadia Bidwell